The
PHILOSOPHY
of
CIVILIZATION

D1278873

The
PHILOSOPHY
of
CIVILIZATION

ALBERT
SCHWEITZER

Translated by C. T. Campion

PART I—The Decay and the
Restoration of Civilization

PART II—Civilization and Ethics

PROMETHEUS BOOKS
Buffalo, New York

First published in English by The Macmillan Company, New York, 1949 and reprinted in 1980 by University Presses of Florida

Published 1987 by Prometheus Books
700 East Amherst Street
Buffalo, New York 14215

Copyright © 1987 by Rhena Schweitzer Miller
All Rights Reserved

Published in cooperation with
The Albert Schweitzer Fellowship
866 United Nations Plaza
New York, New York 10017

Cover photo courtesy of The Albert Schweitzer Fellowship.

Library of Congress Cataloging-in-Publication Data

Schweitzer, Albert, 1875-1965.
    The philosophy of civilization.

    Translation of: Kulturphilosophie.
    Reprint. Originally published: Tallahasse:
University Presses of Florida, 1980.
    "Published in cooperation with the
Albert Schweitzer Fellowship"—T.p. verso.
    Includes index.
    Contents: The decay and the restoration of
civilization—Civilization and ethics.
    1. Civilization—Philosophy. I. Title.
[CB19.S42313 1987]   901   87-2576
ISBN 0-87975-403-6 (pbk.)

Printed in the United States of America

CONTENTS

PART I
THE DECAY AND THE RESTORATION OF CIVILIZATION

PART II
CIVILIZATION AND ETHICS

[v]

Part I

�֍

THE DECAY AND THE RESTORATION

OF CIVILIZATION

TO

Annie Fischer

IN DEEPEST GRATITUDE

AUTHOR'S PREFACE TO THE FIRST

ENGLISH EDITION

"THE DECAY AND THE RESTORATION OF CIVILIZATION" IS THE FIRST part of a complete philosophy of civilization with which I have been occupied since the year 1900.

The second part, entitled "Civilization and Ethics," will appear immediately. The third is called "The World-View * of Reverence for Life." The fourth has to do with the civilized State.

That over which I have toiled since 1900 has been finally ripened in the stillness of the primeval forest of Equatorial Africa. There, during the years 1914–17, the clear and definite lines of this philosophy of civilization have been developed.

The first part, "The Decay and the Restoration of Civilization," is a kind of introduction to the philosophy of civilization. It states the problem of civilization.

Entering on the question as to what is the real essential nature of civilization, I come to the pronouncement that this is ultimately ethical. I know that in thus stating the problem as a moral one I shall surprise and even disgust the spirit of our times, which is accustomed to move amidst æsthetic, historical and material considerations. I imagine, however, that I am myself enough of an artist and also of an historian to be able to comprehend the æsthetic and historical elements in civilization, and that, as a modern physician and surgeon, I am sufficiently modern to appreciate the glamour of the technical and material attainments of our age.

Notwithstanding this, I have come to the conviction that the æsthetic and the historical elements, and the magnificent extension of our material knowledge and power, do not themselves

---

* *Weltanschauung.* See Translator's note on p. xvii.

form the essence of civilization, but that this depends on the mental disposition of the individuals and nations who exist in the world. All other things are merely accompanying circumstances of civilization, which have nothing to do with its real essence.

Creative, artistic, intellectual, and material attainments can only show their full and true effects when the continued existence and development of civilization have been secured by founding civilization itself on a mental disposition which is truly ethical. It is only in his struggle to become ethical that man comes to possess real value as a personality; it is only under the influence of ethical convictions that the various relations of human society are formed in such a way that individuals and people can develop in an ideal manner. If the ethical foundation is lacking, then civilization collapses, even when in other directions creative and intellectual forces of the strongest nature are at work.

This moral conception of civilization, which makes me almost a stranger amidst the intellectual life of my time, I express clearly and unhesitatingly, in order to arouse amongst my contemporaries reflection as to what civilization really is. We shall not succeed in re-establishing our civilization on an enduring basis until we rid ourselves completely of the superficial concept of civilization which now holds us in thrall, and give ourselves up again to the ethical view which obtained in the eighteenth century.

The second point which I desire should obtain currency is that of the connection between civilization and our theory of the universe. At the present time no regard is paid to this connection. In fact, the period in which we are living altogether misses the significance of having a theory of the universe. It is the common conviction nowadays, of educated and uneducated alike, that humanity will progress quite satisfactorily without any theory of the universe at all.

The real fact is that all human progress depends on progress in its theory of the universe, whilst, conversely, decadence is conditioned by a similar decadence in this theory. Our loss of real civilization is due to our lack of a theory of the universe.

Only as we again succeed in attaining a strong and worthy

theory of the universe, and find in it strong and worthy convictions, shall we again become capable of producing a new civilization. It is this apparently abstract and paradoxical truth of which I proclaim myself the champion.

Civilization, put quite simply, consists in our giving ourselves, as human beings, to the effort to attain the perfecting of the human race and the actualization of progress of every sort in the circumstances of humanity and of the objective world. This mental attitude, however, involves a double predisposition: firstly, we must be prepared to act affirmatively toward the world and life; secondly, we must become ethical.

Only when we are able to attribute a real meaning to the world and to life shall we be able also to give ourselves to such action as will produce results of real value. As long as we look on our existence in the world as meaningless, there is no point whatever in desiring to effect anything in the world. We become workers for that universal spiritual and material progress which we call civilization only in so far as we affirm that the world and life possess some sort of meaning, or, which is the same thing, only in so far as we think optimistically.

Civilization originates when men become inspired by a strong and clear determination to attain progress, and consecrate themselves, as a result of this determination, to the service of life and of the world. It is only in ethics that we can find the driving force for such action, transcending, as it does, the limits of our own existence.

Nothing of real value in the world is ever accomplished without enthusiasm and self-sacrifice.

But it is impossible to convince men of the truth of world- and life-affirmation and of the real value of ethics by mere declamation. The affirmative and ethical mentality which characterizes these beliefs must orginate in man himself as the result of an inner spiritual relation to the world. Only then will they accompany him as strong, clear, and constant convictions, and condition his every thought and action.

To put it in another way: World- and life-affirmation must be the products of thought about the world and life. Only as the majority of individuals attain to this result of thought and continue under its influence will a true and enduring civilization make progress in the world. Should the mental disposition toward world- and life-affirmation and toward ethics begin to wane, or become dim and obscured, we shall be incapable of working for true civilization, nay, more, we shall be unable even to form a correct concept of what such civilization ought to be.

And this is the fate which has befallen us. We are bereft of any theory of the universe. Therefore, instead of being inspired by a profound and powerful spirit of affirmation of the world and of life, we allow ourselves, both as individuals and as nations, to be driven hither and thither by a type of such affirmation which is both confused and superficial. Instead of adopting a determined ethical attitude, we exist in an atmosphere of mere ethical phrases or declare ourselves ethical sceptics.

How is it that we have got into this state of lacking a theory of the universe? It is because hitherto the world- and life-affirming and ethical theory of the universe had no convincing and permanent foundation in thought. We thought again and again that we had found such a basis for it; but it lost power again and again without our being aware that it was doing so, until, finally, we have been obliged, for more than a generation past, to resign ourselves more and more to a complete lack of any world-theory at all.

Thus, in this introductory part of my work, I proclaim two truths and conclude with a great note of interrogation. The truths are the following: The basic ethical character of civilization, and the connection between civilization and our theories of the universe. The question with which I conclude is this: Is it at all possible to find a real and permanent foundation in thought for a theory of the universe which shall be both ethical and affirmative of the world and of life?

The future of civilization depends on our overcoming the meaninglessness and hopelessness which characterize the thoughts and convictions of men to-day, and reaching a state of fresh hope and fresh determination. We shall be capable of this, however, only when the majority of individuals discover for themselves both an ethic and a profound and steadfast attitude of world- and life-affirmation, in a theory of the universe at once convincing and based on reflection.

Without such a general spiritual experience there is no possibility of holding our world back from the ruin and disintegration toward which it is being hastened. It is our duty then to rouse ourselves to fresh reflection about the world and life.

In "Civilization and Ethics," the second part of this philosophy of civilization, I describe the road along which thought has led me to world- and life-affirmation and to ethics. The root-idea of my theory of the universe is that my relation to my own being and to the objective world is determined by reverence for life. This reverence for life is given as an element of my will-to-live, and becomes clearly conscious of itself as I reflect about my life and about the world. In the mental attitude of reverence for life which should characterize my contact with all forms of life, both ethics and world- and life-affirmation are involved. It is not any kind of insight into the essential nature of the world which determines my relation to my own existence and to the existence which I encounter in the world, but rather only and solely my own will-to-live which has developed the power of reflection about itself and the world.

The theory of the universe characterized by reverence for life is a type of mysticism arrived at by self-consistent thought when persisted in to its ultimate conclusion. Surrendering himself to the guidance of this mysticism, man finds a meaning for his life in that he strives to accomplish his own spiritual and ethical self-fulfilment, and, simultaneously and in the same act, helps forward all the processes of spiritual and material progress which have to be actualized in the world.

I do not know how many, or how few, will allow themselves to be persuaded to travel with me on the road indicated above. What I desire above all things—and this is the crux of the whole affair—is that we should all recognize fully that our present entire lack of any theory of the universe is the ultimate source of all the catastrophes and misery of our times, and that we should work together for a theory of the universe and of life, in order that thus we may arrive at a mental disposition which shall make us really and truly civilized men.

It was a great joy to me to be afforded the opportunity of putting forward, in the *Dale Lectures,* delivered in Oxford, the views on which this philosophy of civilization is based.

I would tender my deepest thanks to my friends, Mr. C. T. Campion, M.A., now of Grahamstown, South Africa, and Dr. J. P. Naish, of Oxford. Mr. Campion is the translator of this first part of the "Philosophy of Civilization." Dr. Naish has seen the book through the press and translated this preface.

Strasbourg, Alsace
February, 1923

ALBERT SCHWEITZER

TRANSLATOR'S NOTE

The compound word *Weltanschauung* may be translated "theory of the universe," "world-theory," "world-conception," or "world-view." The first is misleading as suggesting, wrongly, a scientific explanation of the universe; the second and third as suggesting, less ambitiously but still wrongly, an explanation of how and why our human world is what it is. The last indicates a sufficiently wide knowledge of our corner of the universe to allow all factors to be taken into consideration which bear on the question at issue.

There may be passages in which it is desirable to vary the translation, and others in which it is possible to give the meaning in more elegant English, for good English style does not take kindly to such compound words. But this latter consideration can only be a secondary one in the translation of a philosophical work, the first object of which must be to ensure that the author's meaning is reproduced as clearly as possible.

1932. *C. T. C.*

Chapter 1

HOW PHILOSOPHY IS RESPONSIBLE FOR THE

COLLAPSE OF CIVILIZATION

*Our self-deception as to the real conditions of
our civilization.*

*The collapse of the world-view on which our
ideals were based.*

The superficial character of modern philosophizing.

WE ARE LIVING TO-DAY UNDER THE SIGN OF THE COLLAPSE OF
civilization. The situation has not been produced by the war;
the latter is only a manifestation of it. The spiritual atmosphere
has solidified into actual facts, which again react on it with
disastrous results in every respect. This interaction of material
and spiritual has assumed a most unhealthy character. Just below a mighty cataract we are driving along in a current full of
formidable eddies, and it will need the most gigantic efforts to
rescue the vessel of our fate from the dangerous side channel
into which we have allowed it to drift, and bring it back into the
main stream, if, indeed, we can hope to do so at all.

We have drifted out of the stream of civilization because
there was amongst us no real reflection upon what civilization
is. It is true that at the end of the last century and the beginning
of this there appeared a number of works on civilization with
the most varied titles; but, as though in obedience to some se-

[1]

cret order, they made no attempt to settle and make clear the conditions of our intellectual life, but devoted themselves exclusively to its origin and history. They gave us a relief map of civilization marked with roads which men had observed or invented, and which led us over hill and dale through the fields of history from the Renaissance to the twentieth century. It was a triumph for the historical sense of the authors. The crowds whom these works instructed were filled with satisfied contentment when they understood that their civilization was the organic product of so many centuries of the working of spiritual and social forces, but no one worked out and described the content of our spiritual life. No one tested its value from the point of view of the nobility of its ideas, and its ability to produce real progress.

Thus we crossed the threshold of the twentieth century with an unshakable conceit of ourselves, and whatever was written at that time about our civilization only confirmed us in our ingenuous belief in its high value. Anyone who expressed doubt was regarded with astonishment. Many, indeed, who were on the road to error, stopped and returned to the main road again because they were afraid of the path which led off to the side. Others continued along the main road, but in silence; the understanding and insight which were at work in them only condemned them to isolation.

It is clear now to everyone that the suicide of civilization is in progress. What yet remains of it is no longer safe. It is still standing, indeed, because it was not exposed to the destructive pressure which overwhelmed the rest, but, like the rest, it is built upon rubble, and the next landslide will very likely carry it away.

But what was it that preceded and led up to this loss of power in the innate forces of civilization?

The age of the Illuminati and of rationalism had put forward ethical ideals, based on reason, concerning the development of the individual to true manhood, his position in society, the material and spiritual problems which arose out of society, the relations of the different nations to each other, and their issue in a humanity which should be united in the pursuit of the highest moral and spiritual objects. These ideals had begun, both in philosophy and in general thought, to get into contact with reality and to alter the general environment. In the course of three or four generations there had been such progress made, both in the ideas underlying civilization and in their material embodiment, that the age of true civilization seemed to have dawned upon the world and to be assured of an uninterrupted development.

But about the middle of the nineteenth century this mutual understanding and co-operation between ethical ideals and reality began to break down, and in the course of the next few decades it disappeared more and more completely. Without resistance, without complaint, civilization abdicated. Its ideas lagged behind, as though they were too exhausted to keep pace with it. How did this come about?

* * *

The decisive element in the production of this result was philosophy's renunciation of her duty.

In the eighteenth century and the early part of the nineteenth it was philosophy which led and guided thought in general. She had busied herself with the questions which presented themselves to mankind at each successive period, and had kept the thought of civilized man actively reflecting upon them. Philosophy at that time included within herself an elementary philosophizing about man, society, race, humanity and civilization, which produced in a perfectly natural way a living popular philosophy that controlled the general thought, and maintained the enthusiasm for civilization.

But that ethical, and at the same time optimistic, view of things in which the Illuminati and rationalism had laid the foundations of this healthy popular philosophy, was unable in the long run to meet the criticism levelled at it by pure thought. Its naïve dogmatism raised more and more prejudice against it. Kant tried to provide the tottering building with new foundations, undertaking to alter the rationalistic view of things in accordance with the demands of a deeper theory of knowledge, without, however, making any change in its essential spiritual elements. Goethe, Schiller and other intellectual heroes of the age, showed, by means of criticism both kindly and malicious, that rationalism was rather popular philosophy than real philosophy, but they were not in a position to put into the place of what they destroyed anything new which could give the same effective support to the ideas about civilization which were current in the general thought of the time.

Fichte, Hegel, and other philosophers, who, for all their criticism of rationalism, paid homage to its ethical ideals, attempted to establish a similar ethical and optimistic view of things by speculative methods, that is by logical and metaphysical discussion of pure being and its development into a universe. For three or four decades they succeeded in deceiving themselves and others with this supposedly creative and inspiring illusion, and in doing violence to reality in the interests of their theory of the universe. But at last the natural sciences, which all this time had been growing stronger and stronger, rose up against them, and, with a plebeian enthusiasm for the truth of reality, reduced to ruins the magnificent creations of their imagination.

Since that time the ethical ideas on which civilization rests have been wandering about the world, poverty-stricken and homeless. No theory of the universe has been advanced which can give them a solid foundation; in fact, not one has made its appearance which can claim for itself solidity and inner consistency. The age of philosophic dogmatism had come definitely to an end, and after tnat nothing was recognized as truth except the science which described reality. Complete theories of the universe no longer appeared as fixed stars; they were regarded as resting on hypothesis, and ranked no higher than comets.

The same weapon which struck down the dogmatism of knowledge about the universe struck down also the dogmatic enunciation of spiritual ideas. The early simple rationalism, the critical rationalism of Kant, and the speculative rationalism of the great philosophers of the nineteenth century had all alike done violence to reality in two ways. They had given a position above that of the facts of science to the views which they had arrived at by pure thought, and they had also preached a series of ethical ideals which were meant to replace by new ones the various existing relations in the ideas and the material environment of mankind. When the first of these two forms of violence was proved to be a mistaken one, it became questionable whether the second could still be allowed the justification which it had hitherto enjoyed. The doctrinaire methods of thought which made the existing world nothing but material for the production of a purely theoretical sketch of a better future were replaced by sympathetic attempts to understand the historical origin of existing things for which Hegel's philosophy had prepared the way.

With a general mentality of this description, a real combination of ethical ideals with reality was no longer possible; there was not the freedom from prejudice which that required, and so there came a weakening of the convictions which were the driving power of civilization. So, too, an end was put to that justifiable violence to human convictions and circumstances without which the reforming work of civilization can make no advance, because it was bound up with that other unjustifiable violence to reality. That is the tragic element in the psychological development of our spiritual life during the latter half of the nineteenth century.

Rationalism, then, had been dismissed; but with it went also the optimistic convictions as to the moral meaning of the universe and of humanity, of society and of man, to which it had given birth, though the conviction still exerted so much influence that no attention was paid to the catastrophe which had really begun.

*   *   *

Philosophy did not realize that the power of the ideas about civilization which had been entrusted to it was becoming a doubtful quantity. At the end of one of the most brilliant works on the history of philosophy which appeared at the close of the nineteenth century philosophy is defined as the process "by which there comes to completion, step by step, and with ever clearer and surer consciousness, that conviction about the value of civilization the universal validity of which it is the object of philosophy itself to affirm." But the author has forgotten the essential point, viz., that there was a time when philosophy did not merely convince itself of the value of civilization, but also let its convictions go forth as fruitful ideas destined to influence the general thought, while from the middle of the nineteenth century onwards these convictions had become more and more of the nature of hoarded and unproductive capital.

Once philosophy had been an active worker producing universal convictions about civilization. Now, after the collapse in the middle of the nineteenth century, this same philosophy had become a mere drawer of dividends, concentrating her activities far from the world on what she had managed to save. She had become a mere science, which sifted the results of the historical and natural sciences, and collected from them material for a future theory of the universe, carrying on with this object in view a learned activity in all branches of knowledge. At the same time she became more and more absorbed in the study of her own past. Philosophy came to mean practically the history of philosophy. The creative spirit had left her. She became more and more a philosophy which contained no real thought. She reflected, indeed, on the results achieved by the individual sciences, but she lost the power of elemental thought.

She looked back with condescending pity on the rationalism which she had outstripped. She prided herself on having got beyond the ideas of Kant, on having been shown by Hegel the inner meaning of history, and on being at work to-day in close sympathy with the natural sciences. But for all that she was poorer than the poorest rationalism, because she now carried on in imagination only, and not in reality, the recognized work of philosophy, which the latter had practised so zealously. Rationalism, for all its simplicity, had been a working philosophy, but philosophy herself had now become, for all her insight, merely a pedantic philosophy of degenerates. She still played, indeed, some sort of *rôle* in schools and universities, but she had no longer any message for the great world.

In spite of all her learning, she had become a stranger to the world, and the problems of life which occupied men and the whole thought of the age had no part in her activities. Her way lay apart from the general spiritual life, and just as she derived no stimulus from the latter, so she gave none back. Refusing to concern herself with elemental problems, she contained no elemental philosophy which could become a philosophy of the people.

From this impotence came the aversion to all generally intelligible philosophizing which is so characteristic of her. Popular philosophy was for her merely a review, prepared for the use of the crowd, simplified, and therefore rendered inferior, of the results given by the individual sciences which she had herself sifted and put together in view of a future theory of the universe. She was wholly unconscious of several things, viz., that there is a popular philosophy which arises out of such a review; that it is just the province of philosophy to deal with the elemental, inward questions about which individuals and the crowd are thinking, or ought to be thinking, to apply to them more comprehensive and more thorough methods of thought, and then restore them to general currency; and, finally, that the value of any philosophy is in the last resort to be measured by its capacity, or incapacity, to transform itself into a living philosophy of the people.

Whatever is deep is also simple, and can be reproduced as such, if only its relation to the whole of reality is preserved. It is then something abstract, which secures for itself a many-sided life as soon as it comes into contact with facts.

Whatever of inquiring thought there was among the general public was therefore compelled to languish, because our philosophy refused either to acknowledge or to help it. It found in front of it a deep chasm which it could not cross.

Of gold coinage, minted in the past, philosophy had abundance; hypotheses about a soon to be developed theoretical theory of the universe filled her vaults like unminted bullion; but food with which to appease the spiritual hunger of the present she did not possess. Deceived by her own riches, she had neglected to plant any ground with nourishing crops, and therefore, ignoring the hunger of the age, she left the latter to its fate.

That pure thought never managed to construct a theory of the universe of an optimistic, ethical character, and to build up on that for a foundation the ideals which go to produce civilization, was not the fault of philosophy; it was a fact which became evident as thought developed. But philosophy was guilty of a wrong to our age in that it did not admit the fact, but remained wrapped up in its illusion, as though this were really a help to the progress of civilization.

The ultimate vocation of philosophy is to be the guide and guardian of the general reason, and it was her duty, in the circumstances of the time, to confess to our world that ethical ideals were no longer supported by any general theory of the universe, but were, till further notice, left to themselves, and must make their way in the world by their own innate power. She ought to have shown us that we have to fight on behalf of the ideals on which our civilization rests. She ought to have tried to give these ideals an independent existence by virtue of their own inner value and inner truth, and so to keep them alive and active without any extraneous help from a corresponding theory of the universe. No effort should have been spared to direct the attention of the cultured and the uncultured alike to the problem of the ideals of civilization.

But philosophy philosophized about everything except civilization. She went on working undeviatingly at the establishment of a theoretical view of the universe, as though by means of it everything could be restored, and did not reflect that this theory, even if it were completed, would be constructed only out of history and science, and would accordingly be unoptimistic and unethical, and would remain for ever an "impotent theory of the universe," which could never call forth the energies needed for the establishment and maintenance of the ideals of civilization.

So little did philosophy philosophize about civilization that she did not even notice that she herself and the age along with her were losing more and more of it. In the hour of peril the watchman who ought to have kept us awake was himself asleep, and the result was that we put up no fight at all on behalf of our civilization.

Chapter 2

HINDRANCES TO CIVILIZATION

IN OUR ECONOMIC AND SPIRITUAL LIFE

The unfree economic position of the modern man.

His overwork and incapacity for self-collectedness.

The undeveloped condition of the modern man and his lack of humanity.

The lack of spiritual independence in the man of to-day.

EVEN IF THE ABDICATION OF THOUGHT HAS BEEN, AS WE HAVE SEEN, the decisive factor in the collapse of our civilization, there are yet a number of other causes which combine with it to hinder our progress in this regard. They are to be found in the field of spiritual as well as in that of economic activity, and depend, above all, on the interaction between the two, an interaction which is unsatisfactory and continually becoming more so.

The capacity of the modern man for progress in civilization is diminished because the circumstances in which he finds himself placed injure him psychically and stunt his personality.

The development of civilization comes about—to put it quite generally—by individual men thinking out ideals which aim at the progress of the whole, and then so fitting them to the realities of life that they assume the shape in which they can influence most effectively the circumstances of the time. A man's ability to be a pioneer of progress, that is, to understand what civilization is and to work for it, depends, therefore, on his being a thinker and on his being free. He must be the former if he is to be capable of comprehending his ideals and putting them into shape. He must be free in order to be in a position to launch his ideals out into the general life. The more completely his activities are taken up in any way by the struggle for existence, the more strongly will the impulse to improve his own condition find expression in the ideals of his thought. Ideals of self-interest then get mixed up with and spoil his ideals of civilization.

Material and spiritual freedom are closely bound up with one another. Civilization presupposes free men, for only by free men can it be thought out and brought to realization.

But among mankind to-day both freedom and the capacity for thought have been sadly diminished.

If society had so developed that a continually widening circle of the population could enjoy a modest, but well-assured, condition of comfort, civilization would have been much more helped than it has been by all the material conquests which are lauded in its name. These do, indeed, make mankind as a whole less dependent upon nature, but at the same time they diminish the number of free and independent lives. The artisan who was his own master becomes the factory hand through the compulsion of machinery. Because in the complicated business world of to-day only undertakings with abundant capital behind them can maintain their existence, the place of the small, independent dealer is being taken more and more completely by the employee. Even the classes which still possess a larger or smaller amount of property or maintain a more or less independent activity get drawn more and more completely into the struggle for existence because of the insecurity of present conditions under the economic system of to-day.

The lack of freedom which results is made worse still because the factory system creates continually growing agglomerations of people who are thereby compulsorily separated from the soil which feeds them, from their own homes and from nature. Hence comes serious psychical injury. There is only too much truth in the paradoxical saying that abnormal life begins with the loss of one's own field and dwelling-place.

Civilization is, it is true, furthered to a certain extent by the self-regarding ideals produced by the groups of people who unite and co-operate in defence of their similarly threatened interests in so far as they seek to obtain an improvement in their material, and thereby also in their spiritual, environment. But these ideals are a danger to the idea of civilization as such, because the form which they assume is either not at all, or very imperfectly, determined by the really universal interests of the community. The consideration of civilization as such is held back by the competition between the various self-regarding ideals which go under its name.

To the want of freedom we have to add the evil of overstrain. For two or three generations numbers of individuals have been living as workers merely, not as human beings. Whatever can be said in a general way about the moral and spiritual significance of labour has no bearing on what they have to do. An excessive amount of labour is the rule to-day in every circle of society, with the result that the labourer's spiritual element cannot possibly thrive. This overwork hits him indirectly even in his childhood, for his parents, caught in the inexorable toils of work, cannot devote themselves to his up-bringing as they should. Thus his development is robbed of something which can never be made good, and later in life, when he himself is the slave of over-long hours, he feels more and more the need of external distractions. To spend the time left to him for leisure in self-cultivation, or in serious intercourse with his fellows or with books, requires a mental collectedness and a self-control which he finds very difficult. Complete idleness, forgetfulness, and diversion from his usual activities are a physical necessity. He does not want to think, and seeks not self-improvement, but entertainment, that kind of entertainment, moreover, which makes least demand upon his spiritual faculties.

The mentality of this mass of individuals, spiritually relaxed and incapable of self-collectedness, reacts upon all those institutions which ought to serve the cause of culture, and therewith of civilization. The theater takes a second place behind the pleasure resort or the picture show, and the instructive book behind the diverting one. An ever increasing proportion of periodicals and newspapers have to accommodate themselves to the necessity of putting their matter before their readers in the shape which lets it be assimilated most easily. A comparison of the average newspapers of to-day with those of fifty or sixty years ago shows how thoroughly such publications have had to change their methods in this respect.

When once the spirit of superficiality has penetrated into the institutions which ought to sustain the spiritual life, these exercise on their part a reflex influence on the society which they have brought to this condition, and force on all alike this state of mental vacuity.

How completely this want of thinking power has become a second nature in men to-day is shown by the kind of sociability which it produces. When two of them meet for a conversation each is careful to see that their talk does not go beyond generalities or develop into a real exchange of ideas. No one has anything of his own to give out, and everyone is haunted by a sort of terror lest anything original should be demanded from him.

The spirit produced in such a society of never-concentrated minds is rising among us as an ever growing force, and it results in a lowered conception of what man should be. In ourselves, as in others, we look for nothing but vigour in productive work, and resign ourselves to the abandonment of any higher ideal.

When we consider this want of freedom and of mental concentration, we see that the conditions of life for the inhabitants of our big cities are as unfavourable as they could be. Naturally, then, those inhabitants are in most danger on their spiritual side. It is doubtful whether big cities have ever been foci of civilization in the sense that in them there has arisen the ideal of a man well and truly developed as a spiritual personality; to-day, at any rate, the condition of things is such that true civilization needs to be rescued from the spirit that issues from them and their inhabitants.

*   *   *

But, besides the hindrance caused to civilization by the modern man's lack of freedom and of the power of mental concentration, there is a further hindrance caused by his imperfect development. The enormous increase of human knowledge and power, in specialized thoroughness as well as in extent, necessarily leads to individual activities being limited more and more to well-defined departments. Human labour is organized and co-ordinated so that specialization may enable individuals to make the highest and most effective possible contribution. The results obtained are amazing, but the spiritual significance of the work for the worker suffers. There is no call upon the whole man, only upon some of his faculties, and this has a reflex effect upon his nature as a whole. The faculties which build up personality and are called out by comprehensive and varied tasks are ousted by the less comprehensive ones, which from this point of view are, in the general sense of the word, less spiritual. The artisan of to-day does not understand his trade as a whole in the way in which his predecessor did. He no longer learns, like the latter, to work the wood or the metal through all the stages of manufacture; many of these stages have already been carried out by men and machines before the material comes into his hands. Consequently his reflectiveness, his imagination, and his skill are no longer called out by ever varying difficulties in the work, and his creative and artistic powers are atrophied. In place of the normal self-consciousness which is promoted by work into the doing of which he must put his whole power of thought and his whole personality, there comes a self-satisfaction which is content with a fragmentary ability which, it may be admitted, is perfect, and this self-satisfaction is persuaded by its perfection in mastering details to overlook its imperfection in dealing with the whole.

In all professions, most clearly perhaps in the pursuit of science, we can recognize the spiritual danger with which specialization threatens not only individuals, but the spiritual life of the community. It is already noticeable, too, that education is carried on now by teachers who have not a wide enough outlook to make their scholars understand the interconnection of the individual sciences, and to be able to give them a mental horizon as wide as it should be.

Then, as if specialization and the organization of work, where it is unavoidable, were not already injurious enough to the soul of the modern man, it is pursued and built up where it could be dispensed with. In administration, in education, and in every kind of calling the natural sphere of activity is narrowed as far as possible by rules and superintendence. How much less free in many countries is the elementary school teacher of to-day compared with what he was once! How lifeless and impersonal has his teaching become as a result of all these limitations!

Thus through our methods of work we have suffered loss spiritually and as individuals just in proportion as the material output of our collective activity has increased. Here, too, is an illustration of that tragic law which says that every gain brings with it, somehow or other, a corresponding loss.

* * *

But man to-day is in danger not only through his lack of freedom, of the power of mental concentration, and of the opportunity for all-round development: he is in danger of losing his humanity.

The normal attitude of man to man is made very difficult for us. Owing to the hurry in which we live, to the increased facilities for intercourse, and to the necessity for living and working with many others in an overcrowded locality, we meet each other continually, and in the most varied relations, as strangers. Our circumstances do not allow us to deal with each other as man to man, for the limitations placed upon the activities of the natural man are so general and so unbroken that we get accustomed to them, and no longer feel our mechanical, impersonal intercourse to be something that is unnatural. We no longer feel uncomfortable that in such a number of situations we can no longer be men among men, and at last we give up trying to be so, even when it would be possible and proper.

In this respect, too, the soul of the townsman is influenced most unfavourably by his circumstances, and that influence, in its turn, works most unfavourably on the mentality of society.

Thus we tend to forget our relationship with our fellows, and are on the path towards inhumanity. Wherever there is lost the consciousness that every man is an object of concern for us just because he is man, civilization and morals are shaken, and the advance to fully developed inhumanity is only a question of time.

As a matter of fact, the most utterly inhuman thoughts have been current among us for two generations past in all the ugly

clearness of language and with the authority of logical principles. There has been created a social mentality which discour-
ages humanity in individuals. The courtesy produced by natural
feeling disappears, and in its place comes a behaviour which
shows entire indifference, even though it is decked out more or
less thoroughly in a code of manners. The standoffishness and
want of sympathy which are shown so clearly in every way to
strangers are no longer felt as being really rudeness, but pass
for the behaviour of the man of the world. Our society has also
ceased to allow to all men, as such, a human value and a human
dignity; many sections of the human race have become merely
raw material and property in human form. We have talked for
decades with ever increasing light-mindedness about war and
conquest, as if these were merely operations on a chess-board;
how was this possible save as the result of a tone of mind which
no longer pictured to itself the fate of individuals, but thought
of them only as figures or objects belonging to the material
world? When the war broke out the inhumanity within us had
a free course. And what an amount of insulting stuff, some de-
cently veiled, some openly coarse, about the coloured races, has
made its appearance during the last decades, and passed for
truth and reason, in our colonial literature and our parliaments,
and so become an element in general public opinion! Twenty
years ago there was a discussion in one of our Continental parliaments about some deported Negroes who had been allowed to
die of hunger and disease; and there was no protest or comment
when, in a statement from the tribune, it was said that they
"had been lost" (*"eingegangen"* or *"crévé"*), as though it were
a question of cattle!

In the education and the school books of to-day the duty of
humanity is relegated to an obscure corner, as though it were
no longer true that it is the first thing necessary in the training
of personality, and as if it were not a matter of great importance
to maintain it as a strong influence in our human race against
the influence of outer circumstances. It has not been so always.
There was a time when it was a ruling influence not only in
schools, but in literature, even down to the book of adventures.
Defoe's hero, Robinson Crusoe, is continually reflecting on the
subject of humane conduct, and he feels himself so responsible

for loyalty to this duty that when defending himself he is continually thinking how he can sacrifice the smallest number of human lives; he is so faithful, indeed, to this duty of humanity, that the story of his adventures acquires thereby quite a peculiar character. Is there among works of this kind to-day a single one in which we shall find anything like it?

*　　*　　*

Another hindrance to civilization to-day is the over-organization of our public life.

While it is certain that a properly ordered environment is the condition and, at the same time, the result of civilization, it is also undeniable that, after a certain point has been reached, external organization is developed at the expense of spiritual life. Personality and ideas are then subordinated to institutions, when it is really these which ought to influence the latter and keep them inwardly alive.

If a comprehensive organization is established in any department of social life, the results are at first magnificent, but after a time they fall off. It is the already existing resources which are realized at the start, but later on the destructive influence of such organization on what is living and original is clearly seen in its natural results, and the more consistently the organization is enlarged, the more strongly its effect is felt in the repression of creative and spiritual activity. There are modern States which cannot recover either economically or spiritually from the effects of over-centralization of government dating from a very early period of their history.

The conversion of a wood into a park and its maintenance as such may be a step toward carrying out several different objects, but it is all over then with the rich vegetation which would assure its future condition in nature's own way.

Political, religious and economic associations aim to-day at forming themselves in such a way as will combine the greatest possible inner cohesion with the highest possible degree of external activity. Constitution, discipline, and everything that belongs to administration are brought to a perfection hitherto unknown. They attain their object, but just in proportion as they do so these centres of activity cease to work as living organizations, and come more and more to resemble perfected machines. Their inner life loses in richness and variety because the personalities of which they are composed must needs become impoverished.

Our whole spiritual life nowadays has its course within organizations. From childhood up the man of to-day has his mind so full of the thought of discipline that he loses the sense of his own individuality and can only see himself as thinking in the spirit of some group or other of his fellows. A thorough discussion between one idea and another or between one man and another, such as constituted the greatness of the eighteenth century, is never met with now. But at that time fear of public opinion was a thing unknown. All ideas had then to justify themselves to the individual reason. To-day it is the rule—and no one questions it—always to take into account the views which prevail in organized society. The individual starts by taking it for granted that both for himself and his neighbours there are certain views already established which they cannot hope to alter, views which are determined by nationality, creed, political party, social position, and other elements in one's surroundings. These views are protected by a kind of taboo, and are not only kept sacred from criticism, but are not a legitimate subject of conversation. This kind of intercourse, in which we mutually abjure our natural quality as thinking beings, is euphemistically described as respect for other people's convictions, as if there could be any convictions at all where there is no thought.

The modern man is lost in the mass in a way which is without precedent in history, and this is perhaps the most characteristic trait in him. His diminished concern about his own nature makes him as it is susceptible, to an extent that is almost pathological, to the views which society and its organs of expression have put, ready made, into circulation. Since, over and above this, society, with its well-constructed organization, has become a power of as yet unknown strength in the spiritual life, man's want of independence in the face of it has become so serious that he is almost ceasing to claim a spiritual existence of his own. He is like a rubber ball which has lost its elasticity, and preserves indefinitely every impression that is made upon it. He is under the thumb of the mass, and he draws from it the opinions on which he lives, whether the question at issue is national or political or one of his own belief or unbelief.

Yet this abnormal subjection to external influences does not strike him as being a weakness. He looks upon it as an achievement, and in his unlimited spiritual devotion to the interests of the community he thinks he is preserving the greatness of the modern man. He intentionally exaggerates our natural social instincts into something fantastically great.

It is just because we thus renounce the indefeasible rights of the individual that our race can neither produce new ideas nor make current ones serviceable for new objects; its only experience is that prevailing ideas obtain more and more authority, take on a more and more one-sided development, and live on till they have produced their last and most dangerous consequences.

Thus we have entered on a new mediæval period. The general determination of society has put freedom of thought out of fashion, because the majority renounce the privilege of thinking as free personalities, and let themselves be guided in everything by those who belong to the various groups and cliques.

Spiritual freedom, then, we shall recover only when the majority of individuals become once more spiritually independent and self-reliant, and discover their natural and proper relation to those organizations in which their souls have been entangled. But liberation from the Middle Ages of to-day will be a much more difficult process than that which freed the peoples of Europe from the first Middle Ages. The struggle then was against external authority established in the course of history. To-day the task is to get the mass of individuals to work themselves out of the condition of spiritual weakness and dependence to which they have brought themselves. Could there be a harder task?

Moreover, no one as yet clearly perceives what a condition of spiritual poverty is ours to-day. Every year the spread of opinions which have no thought behind them is carried further by the masses, and the methods of this process have been so perfected, and have met with such a ready welcome, that our confidence in being able to raise to the dignity of public opinion the silliest of statements, wherever it seems expedient to get them currently accepted, has no need to justify itself before acting.

During the war the control of thought was made complete. Propaganda definitely took the place of truth.

With independence of thought thrown overboard, we have, as was inevitable, lost our faith in truth. Our spiritual life is disorganized, for the over-organization of our external environment leads to the organization of our absence of thought.

Not only in the intellectual sphere, but in the moral also, the relation between the individual and the community has been upset. With the surrender of his own personal opinion the modern man surrenders also his personal moral judgment. In order that he may find good what the mass declares to be such, whether in word or deed, and may condemn what it declares to be bad, he suppresses the scruples which stir in him. He does not allow them to find utterance either with others or with himself. There are no stumbling-blocks which his feeling of unity with the herd does not enable him to surmount, and thus he loses his judgment in that of the mass, and his own morality in theirs.

Above all, he is thus made capable of excusing everything that is meaningless, cruel, unjust, or bad in the behaviour of his nation. Unconsciously to themselves, the majority of the members of our barbarian civilized States give less and less time to reflection as moral personalities, so that they may not be continually coming into inner conflict with their fellows as a body, and continually having to get over things which they feel to be wrong.

Public opinion helps them by popularizing the idea that the actions of the community are not to be judged so much by the standards of morality as by those of expediency. But they suffer injury to their souls. If we find among men of to-day only too few whose human and moral sensibility is still undamaged, the chief reason is that the majority have offered up their personal morality on the altar of their country, instead of remaining at variance with the mass and acting as a force which impels the latter along the road to perfection.

Not only between the economic and the spiritual, then, but also between the mass of men and individuals, there has developed a condition of unfavourable action and reaction. In the days of rationalism and serious philosophy the individual got help and support from society through the general confidence in the victory of the rational and moral, which society never failed to acknowledge as something which explained and justified itself. Individuals were then carried along by the mass; we are stifled by it. The bankruptcy of the civilized State, which becomes more manifest every decade, is ruining the man of to-day. The demoralization of the individual by the mass is in full swing.

The man of to-day pursues his dark journey in a time of darkness, as one who has no freedom, no mental collectedness, no all-round development, as one who loses himself in an atmosphere of inhumanity, who surrenders his spiritual independence and his moral judgment to the organized society in which he lives, and who finds himself in every direction up against hindrances to the temper of true civilization. Of the dangerous position in which he is placed philosophy has no understanding, and therefore makes no attempt to help him. She does not even urge him to reflection on what is happening to himself.

The terrible truth that with the progress of history and the economic development of the world it is becoming not easier, but harder, to develop true civilization, has never found utterance.

Chapter 3

CIVILIZATION ESSENTIALLY ETHICAL

IN CHARACTER

What is civilization?

Origin of the unethical conception of civilization.

Our sense of reality. Our historical sense. Nationalism as a product of these.

National civilization. Our misleading trust in facts and organization.

The true sense for reality.

WHAT IS CIVILIZATION? This question ought to have been pressing itself on the attention of all men who consider themselves civilized, but it is remarkable that in the world's literature generally one hardly finds that it has been put at all until to-day, and still more rarely is any answer given. It was supposed that there was no need for a definition of civilization, since we already possessed the thing itself. If the question was ever touched upon, it was considered to be sufficiently settled with references to history and the present day. But now, when events are bringing us inexorably to the consciousness that we live in a dangerous medley of civilization and barbarism, we must, whether we wish to or not, try to determine the nature of true civilization.

For a quite general definition we may say that civilization is progress, material and spiritual progress, on the part of individuals as of the mass.

In what does it consist? First of all in a lessening of the strain imposed on individuals and on the mass by the struggle for existence. The establishment of as favourable conditions of living as possible for all is a demand which must be made partly for its own sake, partly with a view to the spiritual and moral perfecting of individuals, which is the ultimate object of civilization.

The struggle for existence is a double one: man has to assert himself in nature and against nature, and similarly also among his fellow-men and against them.

A diminution of the struggle is secured by strengthening the supremacy of reason over both external nature and human nature, and making it subserve as accurately as possible the ends proposed.

Civilization is then twofold in its nature: it realizes itself in the supremacy of reason, first, over the forces of nature, and, secondly, over the dispositions of men.

Which of these kinds of progress is most truly progress in civilization? The latter, though it is the least open to observation. Why? For two reasons. First, the supremacy which we secure by reason over external nature represents not unqualified progress, but a progress which brings with its advantages also disadvantages which may work in the direction of barbarism. The reason why the economic circumstances of our time endanger our civilization is to be sought for partly in the fact that we have pressed into our service natural forces which can be embodied in machines. But with that there must be such a supremacy of reason over the dispositions of men that they, and the nations which they form, will not use against one another the power which the control of these forces gives them, and thus plunge one another into a struggle for existence which is far more terrible than that between men in a state of nature.

A normal claim to be civilized can, then, only be reckoned as valid when it recognizes this distinction between what is essential in civilization and what is not.

Both kinds of progress can, indeed, be called spiritual in the sense that they both rest upon a spiritual activity in man, yet we may call the supremacy over natural forces material progress because in it material objects are mastered and turned to man's use. The supremacy of reason over human dispositions, on the other hand, is a spiritual achievement in another sense, in that it means the working of spirit upon spirit, *i.e.*, of one section of the power of reflexion upon another section of it.

And what is meant by the supremacy of the reason over human dispositions? It means that both individuals and the mass let their willing be determined by the material and spiritual good of the whole and the individuals that compose it; that is to say, their actions are ethical. Ethical progress is, then, that which is truly of the essence of civilization, and has only one significance; material progress is that which is much less essential and may have a good or bad effect on the development of civilization. This moral conception of civilization will strike some people as rationalistic and old-fashioned. It accords better with the spirit of our times to conceive of civilization as a natural manifestation of life in the course of human evolution, but one with most interesting complications. We are concerned, however, not with what is ingenious, but with what is true. In this case the simple is the true—the inconvenient truth with which it is our laborious task to deal.

*   *   *

The attempts to distinguish between civilization as what the Germans call "Kultur" and civilization as mere material progress aim at making the world familiar with the idea of an unethical form of civilization side by side with the ethical, and at clothing the former with a word of historical meaning. But nothing in the history of the word "civilization" justifies such attempts. The word, as commonly used hitherto, means the same as the German "Kultur", viz., the development of man to a state of higher organization and a higher moral standard. Some languages prefer one word: others prefer the other. The German usually speaks of "Kultur", the Frenchman usually of "civilisation", but the establishment of a difference between them is justified neither philologically nor historically. We can speak of ethical and unethical "Kultur" or of ethical and unethical "civilisation", but not of "Kultur" and "civilisation".

But how did it come about that we lost the idea that the ethical has a decisive meaning and value as part of civilization?

All attempts at civilization hitherto have been a matter of processes in which the forces of progress were at work in almost every department of life. Great achievements in art, architecture, administration, economics, industry, commerce, and colonization succeeded each other with a spiritual impetus which produced a higher conception of the universe. Any ebb of the tide of civilization made itself felt in the material sphere as well as in the ethical and spiritual, earlier, as a rule, in the former than in the latter. Thus in Greek civilization there set in as early as the time of Aristotle an incomprehensible arrest of science and political achievement, whereas the ethical movement only reached its completion in the following centuries in that great work of education which was undertaken in the ancient world by the Stoic philosophy. In the Chinese, Indian and Jewish civilizations ability in dealing with material things was from the start, and always remained, at a lower level than the spiritual and ethical efforts of these races.

In the movement of civilization which began with the Renaissance, there were both material and spiritual-ethical forces of progress at work side by side, as though in rivalry with each other, and this continued down to the beginning of the nineteenth century. Then, however, something unprecedented happened: man's ethical energy died away, while the conquests achieved by his spirit in the material sphere increased by leaps and bounds. Thus for several decades our civilization enjoyed the great advantages of its material progress while as yet it hardly felt the consequences of the dying down of the ethical movement. People lived on in the conditions produced by that movement without seeing clearly that their position was no longer a tenable one and preparing to face the storm that was brewing in the relations between the nations and within the nations themselves. In this way our own age, having never taken the trouble to reflect, arrived at the opinion that civilization consists primarily in scientific, technical and artistic achievements, and that it can reach its goal without ethics, or, at any rate, with a minimum of them.

Public opinion bowed down before this merely external conception of civilization because it was exclusively represented by persons whose position in society and scientific culture seemed to show them to be competent to judge in matters of the spiritual life.

* * *

What was the result of our giving up the ethical conception of civilization, and therewith all attempts to bring reasoned ethical ideals into effective relation with reality? It was that instead of using thought to produce ideals which fitted in with reality, we left reality without any ideals at all. Instead of discussing together the essential elements, such as population, State, Church, society, progress, which decide the character of our social development and that of mankind generally, we contented ourselves with starting from what is given by experience. Only forces and tendencies which were already at work were to be considered. Fundamental truths and convictions which ought to produce logical or ethical compulsion we would no longer acknowledge. We refused to believe that any ideas could be applicable to reality except those derived from experience. Thus ideals which had been knowingly and intentionally lowered dominated our spiritual life and the whole world.

How we glorified our practical common-sense, which was to give us such power in dealing with the world! Yet we were behaving, really, like boys who give themselves up exultingly to the forces of nature and whizz down a hill on their toboggan without asking themselves whether they will be able to steer their vehicle successfully when they come to the next bend or the next unexpected obstacle.

It is only a conviction which is based upon reasoned ethical ideals that is capable of producing free activity, *i.e.*, activity deliberately planned with a view to its object. In proportion as ideals taken from the workaday world are combined with it, reality influences reality. But then the human soul acts merely as an agent of debasing change.

Events which are to produce practical results within us are worked upon and moulded by our mentality. This mentality has a certain character, and on that character depends the nature of those value-judgments which rule our relation to facts.

Normally this character is to be found in the reasoned ideas which our reflexion upon reality brings into existence. If these disappear there is not left a void in which "events in themselves" can affect us, but the control of our mentality passes now to the opinions and feelings which hitherto have been ruled and kept under by our reasoned ideas. When the virgin forest is cut down, brushwood springs up where the big trees were formerly. Whenever our great convictions are destroyed their place is taken by smaller ones which carry out in inferior fashion the functions of the former.

With the giving up of ethical ideals which accompanies our passion for reality our practical efficiency is not, therefore, improved, but diminished. It does not make the man of to-day a cool observer and calculator such as he supposes himself to be, for he is under the influence of opinions and emotions which are created in him by facts. All unconsciously he mixes with what is the work of his reason so much of what is emotional that the one spoils the other. Within this circle move the judgments and impulses of our society, whether we deal with the largest questions or the smallest. Individuals and nations alike, we deal indiscriminately with real and imaginary values, and it is just this confused medley of real and unreal, of sober thought and capacity for enthusiasm for the unmeaning, that makes the mentality of the modern man so puzzling and so dangerous.

Our sense of reality, then, means this, that, as a result of emotional and short-sighted calculations of advantage, we let one fact issue immediately in another, and so on indefinitely. As we are not consciously aiming at any definitely planned goal, our activity may really be described as a kind of natural happening.

We react to facts in the most irrational way. Without plan or foundations we build our future into the circumstances of the time and leave it exposed to the destructive effects of the chaotic jostling that goes on amongst them. "Firm ground at last"! we cry, and sink helpless in the stream of events.

*　　*　　*

The blindness with which we endure this fate is made worse by our belief in our historical sense, which, in this connection, is nothing else than our sense of reality prolonged backwards.

We believe ourselves to be a critical generation which, thanks to its thorough knowledge of the past, is in a position to understand the direction which events are destined to take from the present to the future. We add to the ideals which have been taken from existing reality others which we borrow from history.

The achievements of historical science reached by the nineteenth century do, indeed, deserve our admiration, but it is another question whether our generation, for all its possession of an historical science, possesses a true historical sense.

Historical sense, in the full meaning of the term, implies a critical objectivity in the face of far-off and recent events alike. To keep this faculty free from the bias of opinions and interests when we are estimating facts is a power which even our historians do not possess. As long as they are dealing with a period so remote that it has no bearing on the present they are critical so far as the views of the school to which they belong allow it. But if the past stands in any real connection with "to-day", we can perceive at once in their estimate the influence of their particular standpoint, rational, religious, social or economic.

It is significant that while during the last few decades the learning of our historians has, no doubt, increased, their critical objectivity has not. Previous investigators kept this ideal before their eyes in much greater purity than have those of to-day; we have gone so far that we no longer seriously make the demand that in scientific dealings with the past there shall be a suppression of all prejudices which spring from nationality or creed. It is quite common nowadays to see the greatest learning bound up with the strongest bias. In our historical literature the highest positions are occupied by works written with propagandist aims.

So little educative influence has science had on our historians that they have often espoused as passionately as anyone the opinions of their own people instead of calling the latter to a thoughtful estimate of the facts, as was their duty to their profession; they have remained nothing but men of learning. They have not even started on the task for which they entered the service of civilization, and the hopes of civilization, which in the middle of the nineteenth century rested on the rise of a science of history, have been as little fulfilled as those which were bound up with the demand for national States and democratic forms of government.

The generation that has been brought up by teachers such as these has naturally not much idea of an elevated practical conception of events. Accurately viewed, its characteristic feature is not so much that we understand our past better than earlier generations understood theirs, but rather that we attribute to the past an extraordinarily increased meaning for the present. Now and again we actually substitute it for the latter. It is not enough for us that what has been is present in its results in what now is; we want to have it always with us, and to feel ourselves determined by it.

In this effort to be continually experiencing our historical process of becoming, and to acknowledge it, we replace our normal relation to the past by an artificial one, and wishing to find within the past the whole of our present, we misuse it in order to deduce from it, and to legitimize by an appeal to it, our claims, our opinions, our feelings and our passions. Under the very eyes of our historical learning there springs up a manufactured history for popular use, in which the current national and confessional ideas are unreservedly approved and upheld, and our school history books become regular culture beds of historical lies.

This misuse of history is a necessity for us. The ideas and dispositions which rule us cannot be justified by reason; nothing is left for us but to give them foundations in history.

It is significant that we have no real interest in what is valuable in the past. Its great spiritual achievements are mechanically registered, but we do not let ourselves be touched by them. Still less do we accept them as a heritage; nothing has any value for us except what can be squared with our plans, passions, feelings, and æsthetic moods of to-day. With these we live ourselves by lies into the past, and then assert with unshaken assurance that we have our roots in it.

This is the character of the reverence we pay to history. The fascination exercised upon us by earlier events is elevated to a religion. Blinded by what we consider or declare to be past and done with, we lose all sense for what is to happen. Nothing is any longer past for us; nothing is done and finished with. Again and again we let what is past rise up artificially in what is present, and endow bygone facts with a persistence of being which makes wholly impossible the normal development of our peoples. Just as our sense of reality makes us lose ourselves in present-day events, so does our historical sense compel us to do the same in those of the past.

* * *

From these two things, our sense of reality and historical sense, is born the nationalism to which we must refer the external catastrophe in which the decadence of our civilization finds its completion.

What is nationalism? It is an ignoble patriotism, exaggerated till it has lost all meaning, which bears the same relation to the noble and healthy kind as the fixed idea of an imbecile does to normal conviction.

How does it develop among us?

About the beginning of the nineteenth century the course of thought gave the national State its rightful position, starting for this from the axiom that it, as a natural and homogeneous organism, was better calculated than any other to make the ideal of the civilized State a working reality. In Fichte's addresses to the German nation the nation-State is summoned to the bar of the moral reason and learns that it has to submit in all things to the latter. It gives the necessary promise and straightway receives a commission to bring the civilized State into existence. It is given emphatically to understand that it must recognize as its highest task the continuous and steady development of the purely human element in the nation's life. It is to seek greatness by representing the ideas which can bring healing to the nations. Its citizens are urged to show their membership of it not through the lower, but through the higher, patriotism, that is, not to overvalue its external greatness and power, but to be careful to take for their aim "the unfolding of what is eternal and Godlike in the world", and to see that their objects coincide with the highest aims of humanity. Thus national feeling is placed under the guardianship of reason, morality and civilization. The cult of patriotism as such is to be considered as barbarism; it does, indeed, announce itself to be such by the purposeless wars which it necessarily brings in its train.

In this way the idea of nationality was raised to the level of a valuable ideal of civilization. When civilization began to decline, its other ideals all fell also, but the idea of nationality maintained itself because it had transferred itself to the sphere of reality. It incorporated henceforward all that remained of civilization, and became the ideal which summed up all others. Here, then, we have the explanation of the mentality of our age, which concentrates all the enthusiasm of which it is capable on the idea of nationality, and believes itself to possess in that all moral and spiritual good things.

But with the decay of civilization the character of the idea of nationality changed. The guardianship exercised over it by the other moral ideals to which it had hitherto been subordinate now ceased, since these were themselves on trial, and the nationalist idea began a career of independence. It asserted, of course, that it was working in the service of civilization, but it was, in truth, only an idea of reality with a halo of civilization round it, and it was guided by no ethical ideals, but only by the instincts which deal with reality.

That reason and morality shall not be allowed to contribute a word to the formation of nationalist ideas and aspirations is demanded by the mass of men to-day as a sparing of their holiest feelings.

If in earlier times the decay of civilization did not produce any such confusion in the sentiments of the various nations, this was because the idea of nationality had not then been raised in the same way to be the ideal of civilization. It was, therefore, impossible that it should insinuate itself into the place of the true ideals of civilization, and through abnormal nationalist conceptions and dispositions bring into active existence an elaborate system of uncivilization.

That in nationalism we have to do not so much with things as with the unhealthy way in which they are dealt with in the imagination of the crowd, is clear from its whole behaviour. It claims to be following a policy of practical results (Realpolitik);

in reality it by no means represents the uncompromisingly businesslike view of all the questions of home and foreign policy, but side by side with its egoism displays a certain amount of enthusiasm. Its practical policy is an over-valuation of certain questions of territorial economic interests, an over-valuation which has been elevated to a dogma and idealized, and is now supported by popular sentiment. It fights for its demands without having established any properly thought-out calculation of their real value. In order to be able to dispute the possession of millions of value, the modern State loaded itself with armaments costing hundreds of millions. Meaning to care for the protection and extension of its trade, it loaded the latter with imposts which imperilled its power of competing with its rivals much more than did any of the measures taken by those rivals.

Its practical politics were, therefore, in truth impracticable politics, because they allowed popular passion to come in, and thereby made the simplest questions insoluble. This style of politics put economic interests in the shop window, while it kept in the warehouse the ideas about greatness and conquest which belong to nationalism.

Every civilized State, in order to increase its power, gathered allies wherever it could. Thus half-civilized and uncivilized races were summoned by civilized ones to fight against the civilized neighbours of the latter, and these helpers were not content with the subordinate *rôle* which had been assigned to them. They acquired more and more influence on the course of events, till they were at last in a position to decide when the civilized nations of Europe should begin to fight each other about them. Thus has Nemesis come upon us for abandoning our dignity and betraying to the uncivilized world all that we still possessed of things that were of universal value.

It was significant of the unhealthy character of nationalism's "practical" politics that it tried in every possible way to deck itself out with a tinsel imitation of idealism. The struggle for power became one for right and civilization; the alliances for the promotion of their selfish interests which various nations made with one another against all the rest were made to appear to be friendships and spiritual affinities. As such they were dated back into the past, even though history had a great deal more to say about hereditary quarrels than about spiritual relationships.

*   *   *

Finally, nationalism was not content with putting aside, in the sphere of politics generally, all attempts to bring into existence a really civilized humanity; it distorted the very idea of civilization itself and talked of national civilization.

Once there was what was known just simply as civilization, and every civilized nation strove to possess it in its purest and most fully developed form. In this respect nationality had in the idea of civilization at that time something much more original and less spoilt than it has in the same idea to-day. If, in spite of this, there was no impulse among the nations to separate the spiritual life of each from that of its neighbours, we have a proof that nationality is not in itself the strong element in the people that demanded this. Such a claim as is made to-day to have a *national civilization* is an unhealthy phenomenon. It presupposes that the civilized peoples of to-day have lost their healthy nature, and no longer follow instincts, but theories. They percuss and sound their souls to such an extent that these are no longer capable of any natural action. They analyse and describe them so continuously that in thinking of what they ought to be they forget what they actually are. Questions of spiritual differences between races are discussed so subtly, and with such obstinacy and dogmatism, that the talk works like an obsession, and the peculiarities that are said to exist make their appearance like imaginary diseases.

In every department of life more and more effort is devoted to making clearly visible in the results which follow from them the emotions, the ideas, and the reasonings of the mass of the people. Any peculiarity preserved and fostered in this way shows that its natural counterpart has perished. The individual element in the personality of a people no longer, as something unconscious or half conscious, plays with varying lights on the totality of the nation's spiritual life. It becomes an artifice, a fashion, a self-advertisement, a mania. There is bred in the nation a mass of thought, the serious results of which in every department become more evident year by year. The spiritual life of some of the leading civilized nations has already, in comparison with earlier days, taken on a monotonous tone such as makes an observer feel anxious.

The unnatural character of this development shows itself not only in its results, but in the part which it allows to be played by conceit, self-importance, and self-deception. Anything valuable in a personality or a successful undertaking is attributed to some special excellence in the national character. Foreign soil is assumed to be incapable of producing the same or anything similar, and in most countries this vanity has grown to such a height that the greatest follies are no longer beyond its reach.

It goes without saying that there follows a serious decline of the spiritual element in the national civilization. The spirituality is, moreover, only a kind of disguise; it has in reality an avowedly materialist character. It is a distillation from all the external achievements of the nation in question and appears in partnership with its economic and political demands. While alleged to be grounded in the national peculiarities, nationalist civilization will not, as we should normally expect, remain limited to the nation itself; it feels called upon to impose itself upon others and make them happy! Modern nations seek markets for their civilization, as they do for their manufactures!

National civilization, therefore, is matter for propaganda and for export, and the necessary publicity is secured by liberal expenditure. The necessary phrases can be obtained ready-made and need only be strung together. Thus the world has inflicted on it a competition between national civilizations, and between these civilization itself comes off badly.

The nations of Europe entered the Middle Ages side by side as the heirs of the Greco-Roman world, and lived side by side with the freest mutual intercourse through the Renaissance, the period of the Illuminati, and of the philosophy of more recent times. But we no longer believe that they, with their offshoots in the other continents, form an indivisible unit of civilization. If, however, in this latest age, the differences in their spiritual life have begun to stand out more distinctly, the cause of it is that the level of civilization has sunk. When the tide ebbs, shallows which separate bodies of deep water become visible; while the tide is flowing they are out of sight.

How closely the nations which form the great body of civilized humanity are still interrelated spiritually is shown by the fact that they have all side by side suffered the same decadence.

*   *   *

With our sense of reality is bound up, further, the false confidence which we have in facts. We live in an atmosphere of optimism, as if the contradictions which show themselves in the world arranged themselves automatically so as to promote well-thought-out progress, and reconciled themselves in syntheses in which the valuable parts of the thesis and the antithesis coalesced.

In justification of this optimism appeal is made, both rightly and wrongly, to Hegel. It cannot be denied that he is the spiritual father of our sense of reality; he is the first thinker who tried to be just to things as they exist. We have been trained by him to realize the method of progress in thesis, antithesis, and synthesis as they show themselves in the course of events. But his optimism was not a simple optimism about facts, as ours is. He lived still in the spiritual world of rationalism, and believed in the power of ethical ideas worked out by reason; that was why he believed also in the certainty of uninterrupted spiritual progress. And it was because this was something upon which he could rely that he undertook to show how it was to be seen in the successive phases of events, and at the same time how it made itself a reality in the stream of outward facts. By emphasizing, however, the progressive purpose, which he finds immanent in the course of events, so strongly that it is possible to forget the ethical-spiritual presuppositions of his belief in progress, he is preparing the way for the despiritualized optimism about reality which has for decades been misleading us. Between the facts themselves there is nothing but an endless series of contradictions. The fresh mediating fact in which they counteract each other so as to make progress possible they cannot of themselves produce. This fact can only assert itself if the contradictions resolve themselves in a reasoned view in which there are ethical ideas about the condition of things which it is sought to realize. These are the formative principles for the new element which is to arise out of the contradictories, and it is only in this reasoned ethical view that the latter cease to be blind.

It was because we assumed the existence of principles, of progress, in the facts, that we viewed the advance of history, in which our future was being prepared, as progress in civilization, even though evolution condemned our optimism. And even now, when facts of the most terrible character cry out loudly against it, we shrink from giving up our creed. It no longer, indeed, gives us any real enlightenment, but the alternative, which bases optimism on belief in the ethical spirit, means such a revolution in our mode of thought that we find it difficult to take it into consideration.

With our reliance upon facts is bound up our reliance on organizations. The activities and the aims of our time are penetrated by a kind of obsession that if we could only succeed in perfecting or reforming in one direction or another the institutions of our public and social life, the progress demanded by civilization would begin of itself. We are, indeed, far enough from unanimity as to the plan needed for the reform of our arrangements: one section sketches out an anti-democratic plan; others believe that our mistake lies in the fact that democratic principles have not yet been applied consistently; others, again, see salvation only in a Socialist or Communist organization of society. But all agree in attributing our present condition, with its absence of true civilization, to a failure of our institutions; all look for the attainment of such civilization to a new organization of society; all unite in thinking that with new institutions there would arise a new spirit.

*　　*　　*

In this terrible confusion are entangled not only the unreflecting masses, but also many of the most earnest amongst us. The materialism of our age has reversed the relation between the spiritual and the actual. It believes that something with spiritual value can result from the working of facts. It was even expected that the war would bring us a spiritual regeneration! In reality, however, the relation between them works in the opposite direction. A spiritual element of real value can, if it is present, influence the moulding of reality so as to bring about desired results, and can thus produce facts in support of itself. All institutions and organizations have only a relative significance. With the most diverse social and political arrangements, the various civilized nations have all sunk to the same depth of barbarism. What we have experienced, and are still experiencing, must surely convince us that the spirit is everything and that institutions count for very little. Our institutions are a failure because the spirit of barbarism is at work in them. The best planned improvements in the organization of our society (though we are quite right in trying to secure them) cannot help us at all until we become at the same time capable of imparting a new spirit to our age.

The difficult problems with which we have to deal, even those which lie entirely in the material and economic sphere, are in the last resort only to be solved by an inner change of character. The wisest reforms in organization can only carry them a little nearer solution, never to the goal. The only conceivable way of bringing about a reconstruction of our world on new lines is first of all to become new men ourselves under the old circumstances, and then as a society in a new frame of mind so to smooth out the opposition between nations that a condition of true civilization may again become possible. Everything else is more or less wasted labour, because we are thereby building not on the spirit, but on what is merely external.

In the sphere of human events which decide the future of mankind reality consists in an inner conviction, not in given outward facts. Firm ground for our feet we find in reasoned ethical ideals. Are we going to draw from the spirit strength to create new conditions and turn our faces again to civilization, or are we going to continue to draw our spirit from our surroundings and go down with it to ruin? That is the fateful question with which we are confronted.

The true sense for reality is that insight which tells us that only through reasoned ethical ideals can we arrive at a normal relation to reality. Only so can man and society win all the power over events that they are able to use. Without that power we are, whatever we may choose to do, delivered over into bondage to them.

What is going on to-day between nations and within them throws a glaring illumination upon this truth. The history of our time is characterized by a lack of reason which has no parallel in the past. Future historians will one day analyse this history in detail, and test by means of it their learning and their freedom from prejudice. But for all future times there will be, as there is for to-day, only one explanation, viz., that we sought to live and to carry on with a civilization which had no ethical principle behind it.

Chapter 4

THE WAY TO THE RESTORATION

OF CIVILIZATION

Civilization-ideals have become powerless.

Ups and downs in the history of civilization.

The reform of institutions and the reform of convictions.

The individual as the sole agent of
the renewal of civilization.

Difficulties which beset the renewal of civilization.

THE ETHICAL CONCEPTION OF CIVILIZATION, THEN, IS THE ONLY one that can be justified.

But where is the road that can bring us back from barbarism to civilization? Is there such a road at all?

The unethical conception of civilization answers: "No." To it all symptoms of decay are symptoms of old age, and civilization, just like any other natural process of growth, must after a certain period of time reach its final end. There is nothing, therefore, for us to do, so it says, but to take the causes of this as quite natural, and do our best at any rate to find interesting the unedifying phenomena of its senility, which testify to the gradual loss of the ethical character of civilization.

In the thinking then which surrenders itself to our sense of reality, optimism and pessimism are inextricably intermingled.

If our optimism about reality is proved untenable, the optimism which thinks that continuous progress evolves itself among the facts as such, then the spirit which from above contemplates and analyses the situation turns without much concern to the mild pessimistic supposition that civilization has reached its Indian summer.

The ethical spirit cannot join in this little game of "Optimism or pessimism?" It sees the symptoms of decay as what they really are, viz., something terrible. It asks itself with a shudder what will become of the world if this dying process really goes on unchecked. The condition of civilization is a source of pain to it, for civilization is not an object which it is interesting to analyse, but the hope on which its thoughts fly out over the future existence of the race. Belief in the possibility of a renewal of civilization is an actual part of its life; that is why it can no longer quiet itself with what contents the sense of reality as it hovers between optimism and pessimism.

Those who regard the decay of civilization as something quite normal and natural console themselves with the thought that it is not civilization, but *a* civilization, which is falling a prey to dissolution; that there will be a new age and a new race in which there will blossom a new civilization. But that is a mistake. The earth no longer has in reserve, as it had once, gifted peoples as yet unused, who can relieve us and take our place in some distant future as leaders of the spiritual life. We already know all those which the earth has to dispose of. There is not one among them which is not already taking such a part in our civilization that its spiritual fate is determined by our own. All of them, the gifted and the ungifted, the distant and the near, have felt the influence of those forces of barbarism which are at work among us. All of them are, like ourselves, diseased, and only as we recover can they recover.

It is not the civilization of a race, but that of mankind, present and future alike, that we must give up as lost, if belief in a rebirth of our civilization is a vain thing.

But it need not be so given up. If the ethical is the essential element in civilization, decadence changes into renaissance as soon as ethical activities are set to work again in our convictions and in the ideas which we undertake to stamp upon reality. The attempt to bring this about is well worth making, and it should be world-wide.

It is true that the difficulties that have to be reckoned with in this undertaking are so great that only the strongest faith in the power of the ethical spirit will let us venture on it.

First among them towers up the inability of our generation to understand what is and must be. The men of the Renaissance and the Illuminati of the eighteenth century drew courage to desire the renewal of the world through ideas from their conviction of the absolute indefensibility of the material and spiritual conditions under which they lived. Unless with us, too, the many come to some such conviction, we must continue incapable of taking in hand this work, in which we must imitate them. But the many obstinately refuse to see things as they are, and hold with all their might to the most optimistic view of them that is possible. For this power, however, of idealizing with continually lowering ideals the reality which is felt to be ever less and less satisfying, pessimism also is partly responsible. Our generation, though so proud of its many achievements, no longer believes in the one thing which is all-essential: the spiritual advance of mankind. Having given up the expectation of this, it can put up with the present age without feeling such suffering as would compel it, for very pain, to long for a new one. What a task it will be to break the fetters of unthinking optimism and unthinking pessimism which hold us prisoners, and so to do what will pave the way for the renewal of civilization!

A second difficulty besetting the work which lies before us is that it is a piece of reconstruction. The ideals of civilization which our age needs are not new and strange to it. They have been in the possession of mankind already, and are to be found in many an antiquated formula. We have fundamentally nothing else to do than to restore to them the respect in which they were once held, and again regard them seriously as we bring them into relation with the reality which lies before us for treatment.

To make what is used up usable—is there a harder task? "It is an impossible one," says history. "Never hitherto have worn-out ideas risen to new power among the peoples who have worn them out. Their disappearance has always been a final one."

That is true. In the history of civilization we find nothing but discouragement for our task. Anyone who finds history speaking optimistically lends her a language which is not her own.

Yet from the history of the past we can infer only what has been, not what will be. Even if it proves that no single people has ever lived through the decay of its civilization and a rebirth of it, we know at once that this, which has never happened yet, must happen with us, and therefore we cannot be content to say that the reasoned ethical ideals on which civilization rests get worn out in the course of history, and console ourselves with the reflection that this is exactly in accordance with the ordinary processes of nature. We require to know why it has so happened hitherto, and to draw an explanation, not from the analogy of nature, but from the laws of spiritual life. We want to get into our hands the key of the secret, so that we may with it unlock the new age, the age in which the worn out becomes again unworn and the spiritual and ethical can no longer get worn out. We must study the history of civilization otherwise than as our predecessors did, or we shall be finally lost.

Why do not thoughts which contribute to civilization retain the convincing power which they once had, and which they deserve on account of their content? Why do they lose the evidential force of their moral and rational character? Why do traditional truths cease to be realities and pass from mouth to mouth as mere phrases?

*   *   *

Is this an unavoidable fate, or is the well drying up because our thinking did not go down to the permanent level of the water?

Moreover, it is not merely that the past survives among us as something valueless; it may cast a poisonous shade over us. There are thoughts on which we have never let our minds work directly because we found them ready formulated in history. Ideas which we have inherited do not let the truth which is in them come out into active service, but show it through a kind of dead mask. The worn-out achievements which pass over from a decadent civilization into the current of a new age often become like rejected products of metabolism, and act as poisons.

Granted that the Teutonic nations received a powerful stimulus to civilization at the Renaissance by reverting to the ideas of Greco-Roman thinkers, not less true is it that for many centuries they had been kept by that same Greco-Roman civilization in a condition of spiritual dependence which was wholly in contradiction to their native character. They took over from it decadent ideas which were for a long time a hindrance to their normal spiritual life, and thence came that strange mixture of strength and weakness which is the chief characteristic of the Middle Ages. The dangerous elements in the Greco-Roman civilization of the past still show themselves in our spiritual life. It is because Oriental and Greek conceptions which have had their day are still current among us that we bleed to death over problems which otherwise would have no existence for us. How much we suffer from the one fact that to-day and for several centuries past our thoughts about religion have been under the hereditary foreign domination of Jewish transcendentalism and Greek metaphysics, and, instead of being able to express themselves naturally, have suffered continual torture and distortion!

Because ideas get worn out in this way, and in this condition hinder the thinking of later generations, there is no continuity in the spiritual progress of mankind, but only a confused succession of ups and downs. The threads get broken, or knotted, or lost, or when tied up again get tied wrongly. Hitherto it has been thought possible to interpret this up-and-down movement optimistically because it was universally held that the Renaissance and the age of the Illuminati were quite natural successors of the Greco-Roman civilization, and it was assumed further that, as a permanent result of this, renewed civilizations would spring up in the place of exhausted ones, and thus continual progress be assured. But this generalization cannot justifiably be drawn from such observations. It was because new peoples came on the scene, who had been only superficially touched by the decadent civilizations and now produced others of their own, that it was possible to see this succession of ups and downs ending in an ascent. As a matter of fact, however, our newer civilization was not in any organic connection with the Greco-Roman, even if it did take its first steps with the help of the crutches which the latter provided; it may be described more truly as the reaction of a healthy spirit against the worn-out ideas which were thus offered to it. The essential element in the process was the contact of what was worn out with the fresh thought of young peoples.

To-day, however, all our thought is losing its power in its contact with the worn-out ideas of our expiring civilization, or —in the case of the Hindus and the Chinese—of our own and other expiring civilizations. The up-and-down movement will end, therefore, not in slow progress, but in unbroken descent—unless we can succeed in giving the worn-out ideas a renewal of their youth.

*　　*　　*

Another great difficulty in the way of the regeneration of our civilization lies in the fact that it must be an internal process, and not an external as well, and that, therefore, there is no place for healthy co-operation between the material and the spiritual. From the Renaissance to the middle of the nineteenth century the men who carried on the work of civilization could expect help toward spiritual progress from achievements in the sphere of external organization. Demands in each of these spheres stood side by side in their programme and were pushed on simultaneously. They were convinced that while working to transform the institutions of public life they were producing results which would call forth the development of the new spiritual life. Success in one sphere strengthened at once the hopes and the energies that were at work in the other. They laboured for the progressive democratization of the State with the idea of thereby spreading through the world the rule of grace and justice.

We, who have lived to see the spiritual bankruptcy of all the institutions which they created, can no longer work in this way simultaneously at the reform of institutions and the revival of the spiritual element. The help which such co-operation would give is denied us. We cannot even reckon any longer on the old co-operation between knowledge and thought. Once these two were allies. The latter fought for freedom and in so doing made a road for the former, and, on the other hand, all the results attained by knowledge worked for the general good of the spiritual life in that the reign of law in nature was more and more clearly demonstrated, and the reign of prejudice was becoming continually more restricted. The alliance also strengthened the thought that the well-being of mankind must be based upon spiritual laws. Thus knowledge and thought joined in establishing the authority of reason and the rational tone of mind.

To-day thought gets no help from science, and the latter stands facing it independent and unconcerned. The newest scientific knowledge may be allied with an entirely unreflecting view of the universe. It maintains that it is concerned only with the establishment of individual facts, since it is only by means of these that scientific knowledge can maintain its practical character; the co-ordination of the different branches of knowledge and the utilization of the results to form a theory of the universe are, it says, not its business. Once every man of science was also a thinker who counted for something in the general spiritual life of his generation. Our age has discovered how to divorce knowledge from thought, with the result that we have, indeed, a science which is free, but hardly any science left which reflects.

Thus we no longer have available for the renewal of our spiritual life any of the natural external helps which we used to have. We are called upon for a single kind of effort only, and have to work like men who are rebuilding the damaged foundations of a cathedral under the weight of the massive building. There is no progress in the world of phenomena to encourage us to persevere; an immense revolution has to be brought about without revolutionary action.

*   *   *

Again, the renewal of civilization is hindered by the fact that it is so exclusively the individual personality which must be looked to as the agent in the new movement.

The renewal of civilization has nothing to do with movements which bear the character of experiences of the crowd; these are never anything but reactions to external happenings.

But civilization can only revive when there shall come into being in a number of individuals a new tone of mind independent of the one prevalent among the crowd and in opposition to it, a tone of mind which will gradually win influence over the collective one, and in the end determine its character. It is only an ethical movement which can rescue us from the slough of barbarism, and the ethical comes into existence only in individuals.

The final decision as to what the future of a society shall be depends not on how near its organization is to perfection, but on the degrees of worthiness in its individual members. The most important, and yet the least easily determinable, element in history is the series of unobtrusive general changes which take place in the individual dispositions of the many. These are what precede and cause the happenings, and this is why it is so difficult to understand thoroughly the men and the events of past times. The character and worth of individuals among the mass and the way they work themselves into membership of the whole body, receiving influences from it and giving others back, we can even to-day only partially and uncertainly understand.

One thing, however, is clear. Where the collective body works more strongly on the individual than the latter does upon it, the result is deterioration, because the noble element on which everything depends, viz., the spiritual and moral worthiness of the individual, is thereby necessarily constricted and hampered. Decay of the spiritual and moral life then sets in, which renders society incapable of understanding and solving the problems which it has to face. Therefore, sooner or later, it is involved in catastrophe.

That is the condition in which we are now, and that is why it is the duty of individuals to rise to a higher conception of their capabilities and undertake again the function which only the individual can perform, that of producing new spiritual-ethical ideas. If this does not come about in a multitude of cases nothing can save us.

A new public opinion must be created privately and unobtrusively. The existing one is maintained by the Press, by propaganda, by organization, and by financial and other influences which are at its disposal. This unnatural way of spreading ideas must be opposed by the natural one, which goes from man to man and relies solely on the truth of the thoughts and the hearer's receptiveness for new truth. Unarmed, and following the human spirit's primitive and natural fighting method, it must attack the other, which faces it, as Goliath faced David, in the mighty armour of the age.

About the struggle which must needs ensue no historical analogy can tell us much. The past has, no doubt, seen the struggle of the free-thinking individual against the fettered spirit of a whole society, but the problem has never presented itself on the scale on which it does to-day, because the fettering of the collective spirit as it is fettered to-day by modern organizations, modern unreflectiveness, and modern popular passions, is a phenomenon without precedent in history.

* * *

Will the man of to-day have strength to carry out what the spirit demands from him, and what the age would like to make impossible?

In the over-organized societies which in a hundred ways have him in their power, he must somehow become once more an independent personality and so exert influence back upon them. They will use every means to keep him in that condition of impersonality which suits them. They fear personality because the spirit and the truth, which they would like to muzzle, find in it a means of expressing themselves. And their power is, unfortunately, as great as their fear.

There is a tragic alliance between society as a whole and its economic conditions. With a grim relentlessness those conditions tend to bring up the man of to-day as a being without freedom, without self-collectedness, without independence, in short as a human being so full of deficiencies that he lacks the qualities of humanity. And they are the last things that we can change. Even if it should be granted us that the spirit should begin its work, we shall only slowly and incompletely gain power over these forces. There is, in fact, being demanded from the will that which our conditions of life refuse to allow.

And how heavy the tasks that the spirit has to take in hand! It has to create the power of understanding the truth that is really true where at present nothing is current but propagandist truth. It has to depose ignoble patriotism, and enthrone the noble kind of patriotism which aims at ends that are worthy of the whole of mankind, in circles where the hopeless issues of past and present political activities keep nationalist passions aglow even among those who in their hearts would fain be free from them. It has to get the fact that civilization is an interest of all men and of humanity as a whole recognized again in places where national civilization is to-day worshipped as an idol, and the notion of a humanity with a common civilization lies broken to fragments. It has to maintain our faith in the civilized State, even though our modern States, spiritually and economically ruined by the war, have no time to think about the tasks of civilization, and dare not devote their attention to anything but how to use every possible means, even those which undermine the conception of justice, to collect money with which to prolong their own existence. It has to unite us by giving us a single ideal of civilized man, and this in a world where one nation has robbed its neighbour of all faith in humanity, idealism, righteousness, reasonableness, and truthfulness, and all alike have come under the domination of powers which are plunging us ever deeper into barbarism. It has to get attention concentrated on civilization while the growing difficulty of making a living absorbs the masses more and more in material cares, and makes all other things seem to them to be mere shadows. It has to give us faith in the possibility of progress while the reaction of the economic on ,the spiritual becomes more pernicious every day and contributes to an ever growing demoralization. It has to provide us with reasons for hope at a time when not only secular and religious institutions and associations, but the men, too, who are looked upon as leaders, continually fail us, when artists and men of learning show themselves as supporters of barbarism, and notabilities who pass for thinkers, and behave outwardly as such, are revealed, when crises come, as being nothing more than writers and members of academies.

All these hindrances stand in the path of the will to civilization. A dull despair hovers about us. How well we now understand the men of the Greco-Roman decadence, who stood before events incapable of resistance, and, leaving the world to its fate, withdrew upon their inner selves! Like them, we are bewildered by our experience of life. Like them, we hear enticing voices which say to us that the one thing which can still make life tolerable is to live for the day. We must, we are told, renounce every wish to think or hope about anything beyond our own fate. We must find rest in resignation.

The recognition that civilization is founded on some sort of theory of the universe, and can be restored only through a spiritual awakening and a will for ethical good in the mass of mankind, compels us to make clear to ourselves those difficulties in the way of a rebirth of civilization which ordinary reflection would overlook. But at the same time it raises us above all considerations of possibility or impossibility. If the ethical spirit provides a sufficient standing ground in the sphere of events for making civilization a reality, then we shall get back to civilization, if we return to a suitable theory of the universe and the convictions to which this properly gives birth.

The history of our decadence preaches the truth that when hope is dead the spirit becomes the deciding court of appeal, and this truth must in the future find in us a sublime and noble fulfilment.

Chapter 5

CIVILIZATION AND WORLD-VIEW

Renewal of world-view, and re-birth of civilization.

A thinking world-view. Rationalism and mysticism.

The optimistic-ethical world-view as the civilization world-view.

The renewal of our ideas by thinking about the meaning of life.

THE GREATEST OF ALL THE SPIRIT'S TASKS IS TO PRODUCE A THEORY of the universe (*Weltanschauung* [1]).

In that all the ideas, convictions and activities of an age have their roots, and it is only when we have arrived at one which is compatible with civilization that we are capable of holding the ideas and convictions which are the conditions of civilization at all.

What is meant by a theory of the universe? It is the content of the thoughts of society and the individuals which compose it about the nature and object of the world in which they live, and the position and the destiny of mankind and of individual men within it. What significance have the society in which I live and I myself in the world? What do we want to do in the world, what do we hope to get from it? What is our duty to it? The answer given by the majority to these fundamental questions about existence decides what the spirit is in which they and their age live.

[1] Translated "world-view" throughout the second part of these Lectures.

Is not this putting too high the value of a theory of the universe?

At present, certainly, the majority do not, as a rule, attain to any properly thought-out theory, nor do they feel the need of deriving their ideas and convictions from such a source. They are in tune, more or less, with all the tones which pervade the age in which they live.

But who are the musicians who have produced these tones? They are the personalities who have thought out theories of the universe, and drawn from them the ideas, more or less valuable, which are current amongst us to-day. In this way all thoughts, whether those of individuals or those of society, go back ultimately, in some way or other, to a theory of the universe. Every age lives in the consciousness of what has been provided for it by the thinkers under whose influence it stands.

Plato was wrong in holding that the philosophers of a State should also be its governors. Their supremacy is a different and a higher one than that which consists in framing and issuing laws and ordinances and giving effect to official authority. They are the officers of the general staff who sit in the background thinking out, with more or less clearness of vision, the details of the battle which is to be fought. Those who play their part in the public eye are the subordinate officers who, for their variously sized units, convert the general directions of the staff into orders of the day: namely, that the forces will start at such and such a time, move in this or that direction, and occupy this or that point. Kant and Hegel have commanded millions who had never read a line of their writings, and who did not even know that they were obeying their orders.

Those who command, whether it be in a large or a small sphere, can only carry out what is already in the thought of the age. They do not build the instrument on which they have to play, but are merely given a seat at it. Nor do they compose the piece they have to play; it is simply put before them, and they cannot alter it; they can only reproduce it with more or less skill and success. If it is meaningless, they cannot do much to improve it, but neither, if it is good, can they damage it seriously.

To the question, then, whether it is personalities or ideas

which decide the fate of an age, the answer is that the age gets its ideas from personalities. If the thinkers of a certain period produce a worthy theory of the universe, then ideas pass into currency which guarantee progress; if they are not capable of such production, then decadence sets in in some form or other. Every theory of the universe draws after it its own special results in history.

The fall of the Roman Empire in spite of that empire's having over it so many rulers of conspicuous ability, may be traced ultimately to the fact that ancient philosophy produced no theory of the universe with ideas which tended to that empire's preservation. With the rise of Stoicism, as the definitive result of the philosophic thought of antiquity, the fate of the Mediterranean peoples was decided. Thinking based on resignation, magnificent as it was, could not ensure progress in a world-wide empire. The efforts of its strongest emperors were useless. The yarn with which they had to weave was rotten.

In the eighteenth century, under the rule, in most places, of insignificant rococo-sovereigns and rococo-ministers, a progressive movement began among the nations of Europe which was unique in the history of the world. Why? The thinkers of the Aufklärung and of rationalism produced a worthy theory of the universe from which valuable ideas spread among mankind.

But when history began to shape itself in accordance with these ideas, the thought which had produced the progress came to a halt, and we have now a generation which is squandering the precious heritage it has received from the past, and is living in a world of ruins, because it cannot complete the building which that past began. Even had our rulers and statesmen been less short-sighted than they actually were, they would not in the long run have been able to avert the catastrophe which burst upon us. Both the inner and the outer collapse of civilization were latent in the circumstances produced by the prevalent view of the universe. The rulers, small and great alike, did not act in accordance with the spirit of the age.

With the disappearance of the influence exerted by the *Aufklärung,* rationalism, and the great philosophy of the early nineteenth century, the seeds were sown of the world-war to come. Then began to disappear also the ideas and convictions which would have made possible a solution on right lines of the controversies which arise between nations.

Thus the course of events brought us into a position in which we had to get along without any real theory of the universe. The collapse of philosophy and the rise and influence of scientific modes of thought made it impossible to arrive at an idealist theory which should satisfy thought. Moreover, our age is poorer in deep thinkers than perhaps any preceding one. There were a few strong spirits who, with varied knowledge and with devoted efforts, offered the world some patchwork thought; there were some dazzling comets; but that was all that was granted us. Their products in the way of world theories were good enough to interest a circle of academic culture, or to delight a few believing followers, but the people as a whole were entirely untouched.

We began, therefore, to persuade ourselves that it was, after all, possible to get through without any theory of the universe. The feeling that we needed to stir ourselves up to ask questions about the world and life, and to come to a decision upon them, gradually died away. In the unreflective condition to which we had surrendered ourselves, we took, to meet the claims of our own life and the nation's life, the chance ideas provided by our feeling for reality. During more than a generation and a half we had proof enough and to spare that the theory which consists in the result of absence of theory is the most worthless of all, involving not only ruin to the spiritual life, but ruin universal. For where there is no general staff to think out its plan of campaign for any generation its subordinate officers lead it, as in actual warfare so in the sphere of ideas, from one profitless adventure to another.

The reconstruction of our age, then, can begin only with a reconstruction of its theory of the universe. There is hardly anything more urgent in its claim on us than this which seems to be so far off and abstract. Only when we have made ourselves at home again in the solid thought-building of a theory which can support a civilization, and when we take from it, all of us in co-operation, ideas which can stimulate our life and work, only then can there again arise a society which can possess ideals with magnificent aims and be able to bring these into effective agreement with reality. It is from new ideas that we must build history anew.

For individuals as for the community, life without a theory of things is a pathological disturbance of the higher capacity for self-direction.

*   *   *

What conditions must a theory of the universe fulfil to enable it to create a civilization?

First, and defined generally, it must be the product of thought. Nothing but what is born of thought and addresses itself to thought can be a spiritual power affecting the whole of mankind. Only what has been well turned over in the thought of the many, and thus recognized as truth, possesses a natural power of conviction which will work on other minds and will continue to be effective. Only where there is a constant appeal to the need of a reflective view of things are all man's spiritual capacities called into activity.

Our age has an almost artistic prejudice against a reflective theory of the universe. We are still children of the Romantic movement to a greater extent than we realize. What that movement produced in opposition to the *Aufklärung* and to rationalism seems to us valid for all ages against any theory that would found itself solely on thought. In such a theory of the universe we can see beforehand the world dominated by a barren intellectualism, convictions governed by mere utility, and a shallow optimism, which together rob mankind of all human genius and enthusiasm.

In a great deal of the opposition which it offered to rationalism the reaction of the early nineteenth century was right. Nevertheless it remains true that it despised and distorted what was, in spite of all its imperfections, the greatest and most valuable manifestation of the spiritual life of man that the world has yet seen. Down through all circles of cultured and uncultured alike there prevailed at that time a belief in thought and a reverence for truth. For that reason alone that age stands higher than any which preceded it, and much higher than our own.

At no price must the feelings and phrases of Romanticism be

allowed to prevent our generation from forming a clear conception of what reason really is. It is no dry intellectualism which would suppress all the manifold movements of our inner life, but the totality of all the functions of our spirit in their living action and interaction. In it our intellect and our will hold that mysterious intercourse which determines the character of our spiritual being. The ideas about the world which it produces contain all that we can feel or imagine about our destiny and that of mankind, and give our whole being its direction and its value. The enthusiasm which comes from thought has the same relation to that which is produced by mere random feeling as the wind which sweeps the heights has to that which eddies about between the hills. If we venture once more to seek help from the light of reason, we shall no longer keep ourselves down at the level of a generation which has ceased to be capable of enthusiasm, but shall rise to the deep and noble passion inspired by great and sublime ideals. These will so fill and expand our being that that by which we now live will seem to be merely a poor kind of excitement, and will disappear.

Rationalism is more than a movement of thought which realized itself at the end of the eighteenth and the beginning of the nineteenth centuries. It is a necessary phenomenon in all normal spiritual life. All real progress in the world is in the last analysis produced by rationalism.

It is true that the intellectual productions of the period which we designate historically as the rationalistic are incomplete and unsatisfactory, but the principle, which was then established, of basing our views of the universe on thought and thought alone, is valid for all time. Even if the tree's earliest fruit did not ripen perfectly, the tree itself remains, nevertheless, the tree of life for the life of our spirit.

All the movements that have claimed to take the place of rationalism stand far below it in the matter of achievement. From speculative thought, from history, from feeling, from æsthetics, from science, they tried to obtain something like a world-view, grubbing at haphazard in the world around them instead of excavating scientifically. Rationalism alone chose the right place for its digging, and dug systematically, according to plan. If it found only metal of small value, that was because, with the means at its disposal, it could not go deep enough. Impoverished and ruined as we are because we sought as mere adventurers, we must make up our minds to sink another shaft in the ground where rationalism worked, and to go down through all the strata to see whether we cannot find the gold which must certainly be there.

To think out to the end a theory of the universe which has been produced by thought—that is the only possible way of finding our bearings amid the confusion of the world of thought to-day.

Philosophical, historical, and scientific questions with which it was not capable of dealing overwhelmed the earlier rationalism like an avalanche, and buried it in the middle of its journey. The new rational theory of the universe must work its way out of this chaos. Leaving itself freely open to the whole influence of the world of fact, it must explore every path offered by reflection and knowledge in its effort to reach the ultimate meaning of being and life, and to see whether it can solve some of the riddles which they present.

The ultimate knowledge, in which man recognizes his own being as a part of the All, belongs, they say, to the realm of mysticism, by which is meant that he does not reach it by the method of ordinary reflection, but somehow or other lives himself into it.

But why assume that the road of thought must suddenly stop at the frontier of mysticism? It is true that pure reason has hitherto called a halt whenever it came into that neighbourhood, for it was unwilling to go beyond the point at which it could still exhibit everything as part of a smooth, logical plan. Mysticism, on its side, always depreciated pure reason as much as it could, to prevent at all costs the idea from gaining currency that it was in any way bound to give an account to reason. And yet, although they refuse to recognize each other, the two belong to each other.

It is in reason that intellect and will, which in our nature are mysteriously bound up together, seek to come to a mutual understanding. The ultimate knowledge that we strive to acquire is knowledge of life, which intellect looks at from without, will from within. Since life is the ultimate object of knowledge, our ultimate knowledge is necessarily our thinking experience of life. But this does not lie outside the sphere of reason, but within reason itself. Only when the will has thought out its relation to the intellect, has come, as far as it can, into line with it, has penetrated it, and in it become logical, is it in a position to comprehend itself, so far as its nature allows this, as a part of the universal will-to-live and a part of being in general. If it merely leaves the intellect on one side, it loses itself in confused imaginings, while the intellect, which, like the rationalism of the past, will not allow that in order to understand life it must finally lose itself in thinking experience, renounces all hope of constructing a deep and firmly based theory of the universe.

Thus reflection, when pursued to the end, leads somewhere and somehow to a living mysticism, which is for all men everywhere a necessary element of thought.

Doubts whether the mass of men can ever attain to that level of reflection about themselves and the world which is demanded by a reflective theory of the universe, are quite justifiable if the man of to-day is taken as an example of the race. But he, with his diminished need of thought, is a pathological phenomenon.

In reality there is given in the mental endowment of the average man a capacity for thought which to the individual makes the creation of a reflective theory of things of his own not only possible, but under normal conditions even a necessity. The great movements of illumination in ancient and modern times help to maintain the confident belief that there is in the mass of mankind a power of thought on fundamentals which can be roused to activity. This belief is strengthened by observation of mankind and intercourse with the young. A fundamental impulse to reflect about the universe stirs us during those years in which we begin to think independently. Later on we let it languish, even though feeling clearly that we thereby impoverish ourselves and become less capable of what is good. We are like springs of water which no longer run because they have not been watched and have gradually become choked with rubbish.

More than any other age has our own neglected to watch the thousand springs of thought; hence the drought in which we are pining. But if we only go on to remove the rubbish which conceals the water, the sands will be irrigated again, and life will spring up where hitherto there has been only a desert.

Certainly there are guides and the guided in the department of world-theories, as in others. So far the independence of the mass of men remains a relative one. The question is only whether the influence of the guides leads to dependence or independence. The latter brings with it a development in the direction of truthfulness; the former means the death of that virtue.

Every being who calls himself a man is meant to develop into a real personality within a reflective theory of the universe which he has created for himself.

*   *   *

But of what character must the theory be if ideas and convictions about civilization are to be based on it?

It must be optimistic and ethical.

That theory of the universe is optimistic which gives existence the preference as against non-existence and thus affirms life as something possessing value in itself. From this attitude to the universe and to life results the impulse to raise existence, in so far as our influence can affect it, to its highest level of value. Thence originates activity directed to the improvement of the living conditions of individuals, of society, of nations and of humanity, and from it spring the external achievements of civilization, the lordship of spirit over the powers of nature, and the higher social organization.

Ethics is the activity of man directed to secure the inner perfection of his own personality. In itself it is quite independent of whether the theory of the universe is pessimistic or optimistic. But its sphere of action is contracted or widened according as it appears in connection with a theory of the first or the second type.

In the consistently pessimistic theory of the universe, as we have it in the thought of the Brāhmans or of Schopenhauer, ethics has nothing whatever to do with the objective world. It aims solely at securing the self-perfection of the individual as this comes to pass in inner freedom and disconnection from the world and the spirit of the world.

But the scope of ethics is extended in proportion as it develops and strengthens a connection with a theory of the universe which is affirmative toward the world and life. Its aim is now the inner perfection of the individual and at the same time the direction of his activity so as to take effect on other men and on the objective world. This freedom with its release from the world and its spirit ethics no longer holds up to man as an aim in itself. By its means man is to become capable of acting among men and in the world as a higher and purer force, and thus to do his part toward the actualization of the ideal of general progress.

Thus the optimistic-ethical theory of the universe works in partnership with ethics to produce civilization. Neither is capable of doing so by itself. Optimism supplies confidence that the world-process has somehow or other a spiritual and real aim, and that the improvement of the general relations of the world and of society promotes the spiritual-moral perfection of the individual. From the ethical comes ability to develop the purposive state of mind necessary to produce action on the world and society and to cause the co-operation of all our achievements to secure the spiritual and moral perfection of the individual which is the final end of civilization.

Once we have recognized that the energies which spring out of a theory of the universe, and impel us to create a civilization, are rooted in the ethical and the optimistic, we get light on the question why and how our ideals of civilization got worn out. This question is not to be answered by good or bad analogies from nature. The decisive answer is that they got worn out because we had not succeeded in establishing the ethical and optimistic elements on a sufficiently firm foundation.

If we should analyse the process in which the ideas and convictions that produce civilization reveal themselves, it would be found that whenever an advance has been registered, either the optimist or the ethical element in the theory of the universe has proved more attractive than usual, and has had as its consequence a progressive development. When civilization is decaying there is the same chain of causation, but it works negatively. The building is damaged or falls in because the optimist element or the ethical, or both, give way like a weak foundation.

No amount of inquiry will give any other reason for the changes. All imaginable ideas and convictions of that character spring from optimism and the ethical impulse. If these two pillars are strong enough, we need have no fears about the building.

The future of civilization depends, therefore, on whether it is possible for thought to reach a theory of the universe which will have a more secure and fundamental hold on optimism and the ethical impulse than its predecessors have had.

* * *

We Westerners dream of a theory of the universe which corresponds to our impulse to action and at the same time clarifies it. We have not been able to formulate such a theory definitely. At present we are in the state of possessing merely an impulse without any definite orientation. The spirit of the age drives us into action without allowing us to attain any clear view of the objective world and of life. It claims our toil inexorably in the service of this or that end, this or that achievement. It keeps us in a sort of intoxication of activity so that we may never have time to reflect and to ask ourselves what this restless sacrifice of ourselves to ends and achievements really has to do with the meaning of the world and of our lives. And so we wander hither and thither in the gathering dusk formed by lack of any definite theory of the universe like homeless, drunken mercenaries, and enlist indifferently in the service of the common and the great without distinguishing between them. And the more hopeless becomes the condition of the world in which this adventurous impulse to action and progress ranges to and fro, the more bewildered becomes our whole conception of things and the more purposeless and irrational the doings of those who have enlisted under the banner of such an impulse.

How little reflection is present in the Western impulse to action becomes evident when this tries to square its ideas with those of the Far East. For thought in the Far East has been constantly occupied in its search for the meaning of life, and forces us to consider the problem of the meaning of our own restlessness, the problem which we Westerners shirk so persistently. We are utterly at a loss when we contemplate the ideas which are presented to us in Indian thought. We turn away from the intellectual presumption which we find there. We are conscious of the unsatisfying and incomplete elements in the ideal of cessation from action. We feel instinctively that the will-to-progress is justified not only in its aspect as directed to the spiritual perfecting of personality, but also in that which looks toward the general and material.

For ourselves we dare to allege that we adventurers, who take up an affirmative attitude toward the world and toward life, however great and even ghastly our mistakes may be, can yet show not only greater material, but also greater spiritual and ethical, achievements than can those who lie under the ban of a theory of the universe which leads to cessation from action.

And yet, all the same, we cannot feel ourselves completely justified in the face of these strange Eastern theories. They have in them something full of nobility which retains its hold on us, even fascinates us. This tinge of nobility comes from the fact that these convictions are born of a search for a theory of the universe and for the meaning of life. With us, on the other hand, activist instincts and impulses take the place of a theory of the universe. We have no theory affirming the world and life to oppose to the negative theory of these thinkers, no thought which has found a basis for an optimistic conception of existence to oppose to this other, which has arrived at a pessimistic conception.

The reawakening of the Western spirit must thus begin by our people, educated and simple alike, becoming conscious of their lack of a theory of the universe and feeling the horror of their consequent position. We can no longer be satisfied to make shift with substitutes for such a theory. What is the basis of the will-to-activity and progress which impels both to great actions and to terrible deeds, and which tries to keep us from reflection? We must bend all our energies to the solution of this problem.

There is only one way in which we can hope to emerge from the meaningless state in which we are now held captive into one informed with meaning. Each one of us must turn to contemplate his own being, and we must all give ourselves to cooperative reflection so as to discover how our will to action and to progress may be intellectually based on the way in which we interpret our own lives and the life around us, and the meaning which we give to these.

The great revision of the convictions and ideals in which and for which we live cannot be brought about by preaching to our contemporaries ideas and thoughts other and better than those by which they are dominated at the moment. It can start if the many come to reflect about the meaning of life and to re-orientate, revise and make over again their ideals of action and of progress, asking themselves whether these have a meaning in accord with that which we attribute to life itself. This personal reflection about final and elemental things is the one and only reliable way of measuring values. My willing and doing have real meaning and value only in proportion as the aims which action sets before itself can be justified as being in direct accord with my interpretation of my own and of other life. All else, however much it may pass current as approved by tradition, usage, and public opinion, is vain and dangerous.

It seems, indeed, little better than mockery that we should urge men to anything so remote as a return to reflection about the meaning of life at a time when the passions and the follies of the nations have become so intense and so extended, when unemployment and poverty and starvation are rife, when power is being used on the powerless in the most shameless and senseless way, and when organized human life is dislocated in every direction. But only when the general population begins to reflect in this way will forces come into being which will be able to effect something to counterbalance all this chaos and misery. Whatever other measures it is attempted to carry out will have doubtful and altogether inadequate results.

When in the spring the withered grey of the pastures gives place to green, this is due to the millions of young shoots which sprout up freshly from the old roots. In like manner the revival of thought which is essential for our time can only come through a transformation of the opinions and ideals of the many brought about by individual and universal reflection about the meaning of life and of the world.

But are we sure of being able to think out that affirmation of the world and of life, which is such a powerful impulse in us, into a theory of the world and of life from which a stream of energy productive of intelligible life and action may convincingly and constantly proceed? How are we to succeed in doing what the spirit of the Western world during past generations has in vain toiled to accomplish?

Even if thought, once more awakened, should only attain to an incomplete and unsatisfying theory of the universe, yet this, as the truth to which we have ourselves worked through, would be of more value than a complete lack of any theory at all, or, alternatively, than any sort of authoritative theory to which, neglecting the demands of true thought, we cling on account of its supposed intrinsic value without having any real and thorough belief in it.

The beginning of all spiritual life of any real value is courageous faith in truth and open confession of the same. The most profound religious experience, too, is not alien to thought, but must be capable of derivation from this if it is to be given a true and deep basis. Mere reflection about the meaning of life has already value in itself. If such reflection should again come into being amongst us, the ideals, born of vanity and of suffering, which now flourish in rank profusion like evil weeds among the convictions of the generality of people, would infallibly wither away and die. How much would already be accomplished toward the improvement of our present circumstances if only we would all give up three minutes every evening to gazing up into the infinite world of the starry heavens and meditating on it, or if in taking part in a funeral procession we would reflect on the enigma of life and death, instead of engaging in thoughtless conversation as we follow behind the coffin! The ideals, born of folly and passion, of those who make public opinion and direct public events, would have no more power over men if they once began to reflect about infinity and the finite, existence and dissolution, and thus learnt to distinguish between true and false standards, between those which possess real value and those which do not. The old-time rabbis used to teach that the kingdom of God would come if only the whole of Israel would really keep a single Sabbath simultaneously! How much more is it true that the injustice and violence and untruth, which are now bringing so much disaster on the human race, would lose their power if only a single real trace of reflection about the meaning of the world and of life should appear amongst us!

But is there not a danger in challenging men with this question about the meaning of life and in demanding that our impulse to action should justify and clarify itself in such reflection as that of which we have spoken? Shall we not lose, in acceding to this demand, some irreplaceable element of naïve enthusiasm?

We need not thus be anxious as to how strong or how weak our impulse to action will prove to be when it shall have arrived, as the result of intellectual reflection, at an interpretation of life. The impulse to action is meaningless apart from the meaning which we can find and feel in our own life. It is not the quantity, but the quality, of activity that really matters. What is needed is that our will-to-action should become conscious of itself and should cease to work blindly.

But perhaps, it may be objected, we shall end in the resignation of agnosticism, and shall be obliged to confess that we cannot discover any meaning in the universe or in life.

If thought is to set out on its journey unhampered, it must be prepared for anything, even for arrival at intellectual agnosticism. But even if our will-to-action is destined to wrestle endlessly and unavailingly with an agnostic view of the universe and of life, still this painful disenchantment is better for it than persistent refusal to think out its position at all. For this disenchantment does, at any rate, mean that we are clear as to what we are doing.

There is, however, no necessity whatever for such an attitude of resignation. We feel that a position of affirmation regarding the world and life is something which is in itself both necessary and valuable. Therefore it is at least likely that a foundation can be found for it in thought. Since it is an innate element of our will-to-live, it must be possible to comprehend it as a necessary corollary to our interpretation of life. Perhaps we shall have to look elsewhere than we have done hitherto for the real basis of that theory of the universe which carries with it affirmation of the world and of life. Previous thought imagined that it could deduce the meaning of life from its interpretation of the universe. It may be that we shall be obliged to resign ourselves to abandon the problem of the interpretation of the universe and to find the meaning of our life in the will-to-live as this exists in ourselves.

The ways along which we have to struggle toward the goal may be veiled in darkness, yet the direction in which we must travel is clear. We must reflect together about the meaning of life; we must strive together to attain to a theory of the universe affirmative of the world and of life, in which the impulse to action which we experience as a necessary and valuable element of our being may find justification, orientation, clarity and depth, may receive a fresh access of moral strength, and be retempered, and thus become capable of formulating, and of acting on, definite ideals of civilization, inspired by the spirit of true humanitarianism.

Part II

CIVILIZATION AND ETHICS

TO

MY WIFE

THE MOST LOYAL OF COMRADES

REVISER'S NOTE

THOUGH HE IS SO COMPLETELY BI-LINGUAL THAT ONE OF HIS WORKS was first written in French, Dr. Schweitzer, being an Alsatian, habitually writes in German, a dialect of which, interspersed with a few French words, is the common tongue of his country. For those who are totally unacquainted with the German language, it may make what follows easier to grasp if I explain a few of the expressions which Dr. Schweitzer frequently uses, expressions which, familiar and simple in the original—for he avoids the technical phrases of the philosophers—have in English no exact equivalent.

DIE ETHIK. Very simple in German. But some critics have said that in English the use of the word "ethics" to denote anything but "the science of morality" is wrong, and that it is impossible to speak of "an ethic." Then, again, there is divergence of opinion in dictionaries as to whether the word is singular or plural, so that writers have a habit of avoiding its use when a verb must follow.

The *Oxford English Dictionary* among its meanings adds to "the science of morality":

"The moral principles or system of a particular leader or school of thought";

"The moral principles by which a person is guided";

"The rules of conduct recognized in certain associations or departments of human life";

"The whole field of moral science," and quotes Bentham (1789):

"Ethics at large may be defined as the art of directing men's actions to the production of the greatest possible quantity of happiness."

[67]

As for "an ethic," the same authority gives its meaning as "The science of morals"; "A scheme of moral science," and quotes its use from Spencer's *Data of Ethics* in the words, "an attempt to construct an ethic apart from theology . . ."

AUSEINANDERSETZUNG and its verb. This is a very favourite word with Dr. Schweitzer and occurs very frequently throughout the original of this volume. No single English word can give its meaning, which is, roughly, the taking of a subject to pieces, the spreading out of the details for thorough examination and discussion, and following on this the arrival at some kind of agreement or compromise. It has been translated as "trying conclusions," "discussion," "conflict," "agreement," etc., as best suits the context.

WELTANSCHAUUNG. Many writers, for want of an English word that conveys exactly the same very wide meaning, use the German word to express what it stands for. But to the general reader unfamiliar with a foreign language nothing is more annoying than to be constantly encountering a word he cannot even pronounce. Dr. Schweitzer himself defines "Weltanschauung" as the sum-total of the thoughts which the community or the individual think about the nature and purpose of the universe and about the place and destiny of mankind within the world.

Mr. Campion, for reasons which he explains in a footnote, has invariably translated the word as "world-view." I have ventured to vary the monotony of this in English rather odd-sounding word, by the use of "outlook on life," "conception of the universe," "philosophy," etc. It should be noted that the one German word "Welt" does duty for our two words, universe and world.

GEIST and GEISTIG. Here again the Germans have only one word where we have two. We say mind and spirit, mental and spiritual, where they say only spirit and spiritual. The translator almost always uses the latter terms, comprising both senses in the one word, but it must be remembered that the meaning is wider than that we often attach to spiritual, and the word may therefore sometimes appear not quite appropriate.

WORLD- AND LIFE-AFFIRMATION. This means that man has an inner conviction that life is a real thing, that the world in itself and life in itself have great value, that life is for each individual infinitely worth while, that the human spirit can dominate nature, and that man must never admit defeatism. It is the characteristic European attitude to human life.

WORLD- AND LIFE-NEGATION is the contrary belief, that life is an illusion, that nothing really matters because all is vanity, that the individual in his short span of life can achieve nothing of value, that the supreme good is to make an end of it. This is the characteristic Indian attitude to life.

CIVILIZATION. The exceptionally wide and comprehensive meaning attached to this word should also be kept in mind throughout. Dr. Schweitzer defines it as the sum-total of all progress made by mankind in every sphere of action and from every point of view, in so far as this progress is serviceable for the spiritual perfecting of the individual. Its essential element is, he says, the ethical perfecting of the individual and of the community.

REVERENCE FOR LIFE. This phrase too is immensely wide in its meaning, embracing as it does the whole span and the whole scale, in all its degrees, of a single and constant attitude toward all life as such, including even those forms of life which are injurious to our lives.

L.M.R.

1945.

PREFACE

MY SUBJECT IS THE TRAGEDY OF THE WESTERN WORLD-VIEW.[1]
While still a student I was surprised to find the history of
thought always written merely as a history of philosophical
systems, never as the history of man's effort to arrive at a conception of the universe. Later, when reflecting on the current of
civilization in which I found myself living, I was struck by the
strange and inexorable connections which exist between civilization and our view of the world as a whole. Next I felt a still
stronger compulsion to put to Western thought the question
what it has been aiming at, and what result it has reached in the
matter of a philosophy of life. What is there left of the achievements of our philosophy when it is stripped of its tinsel of
learning? What has it to offer when we demand from it those
elemental ideas which we need, if we are to take our position in
life as men who are growing in character through the experience
given by work?

So I came to an unsparing effort to come to an understanding
with Western thought. I recognized and admitted that it has
sought for that outlook on life from which alone a deep and

[1] [*Translator's Note*—Weltanschauung. This compound word may be translated
"theory of the universe," "world-theory," "world-conception," or "world-view."
The first is misleading as suggesting, wrongly, a scientific explanation of the
universe; the second and third as suggesting, less ambitiously but still wrongly,
an explanation of how and why our human world is what it is. The last indicates
a sufficiently wide knowledge and consideration of our corner of the universe to
allow all factors to be taken into consideration which bear on the question at
issue.

There may be passages in which it is desirable to vary the translation, and
others in which it is possible to give the meaning in more elegant English, for
good English style does not take kindly to such compound words. But this latter
consideration can be only a secondary one in the translation of a philosophical
work, the first object of which must be to ensure that the author's meaning shall
be reproduced as clearly as possible.]

[71]

comprehensive civilization can come. It has wanted to reach a position of world- and life-affirmation and with that as a foundation decree that it is our duty to be active, to strive for progress of all kinds, and to create values. It has wanted to reach an ethical system and on that foundation establish that for the sake of serviceable activity we have to place our life at the service of ideas and of the other life around us.

But it did not succeed in grounding its world- and life-affirming ethical world-view convincingly and permanently in thought. Our philosophy did nothing more than produce again and again unstable fragments of the serviceable outlook on life which hovered before its mind's eye. Consequently our civilization also has remained fragmentary and insecure.

It was a fatal mistake that Western thought never admitted to itself the unsatisfying result of its search for a stable and serviceable outlook on the universe. Our philosophizing became less and less elemental, losing all connection with the elementary questions which man must ask of life and of the world. More and more it found satisfaction in the handling of philosophic questions that were merely academic, and in expert mastery of philosophical technique. It became more and more the captive of secondary things. Instead of real music it produced again and again mere bandmaster's music, often magnificent of its kind, but still only bandmaster's music.

Through this philosophy which did nothing but philosophize instead of struggling for a world-view founded on thought and serviceable for life, we came to be without any world-view at all, and therefore lacking in civilization.

Signs of an awakening of thought on this point are beginning to be visible. It is admitted here and there that philosophy must again try to offer a conception of the universe. This is generally expressed by saying that people are encouraging it to venture once more on "metaphysics," that is to say, to put forward definitive views about the spiritual nature of the world, whereas hitherto it has been occupied with the classification of scientific facts and the emission of cautious hypotheses.

Not only in philosophy, but in thought generally, this awakening of the need for a world-view expresses itself as a need for "metaphysics." Fantastic systems of "metaphysics" are sought

for and offered. Individuals who believe that they have at their
disposal peculiar psychic experiences, and assert that with their
aid they can look behind the actual nature of phenomena, come
forward as producers of a world-view.

But neither the cautious academic, nor the much-claiming
fantastic, "metaphysics," can really give us a world-view. That
the road to this leads through "metaphysics" is a fatal error
which has already enjoyed too long a span of life in our Western
thought. It would be tragic if we renewed its vigour just now,
when we are faced by the necessity of working our way out of
that shortage of a philosophy of life in which our misery, both
spiritual and material, is grounded. No further wandering along
the traditional roads that lead nowhere can save us, whether
we advance as the successors of our fathers or on adventurous
lines of our own. Only in a deep conception of, and experience
in, the problems of world-view lies for us any possibility of
advance.

That is why I am undertaking what has never been attempted
in this way before, namely, so to pose the problem of Western
philosophy as to make the Western search for a world-view come
to a halt and take account of itself. There are two points on
which it must be clear before it proceeds to further exertion.
The first is the overwhelming importance in the search for a
world-view of the quality of that which is sought. What is it we
want? We want to find the world- and life-affirmation, and the
ethical system which we need for that serviceable activity which
gives our life a meaning, based on such thought about the world
and life as finds a meaning in them also. If our search for a
world-view is once thoroughly permeated by the recognition
that everything turns upon these two fundamental questions, it
is thereby saved from betaking itself to by-paths, thinking that
by some happy disposition of fortune it can reach its goal along
them. It will then not search for a "metaphysic," thinking by
means of it to reach a world-view, but it will search for a world-
view and accept with it anything "metaphysical" that may turn
up. From every point of view it will remain elemental.

The second task which the conscious search for a conception
of the universe must not shirk, is the consideration of what is
the real and ultimate nature of the process by which it has

hitherto attempted to secure that serviceable world-view which hovered before it. Reflection on this is necessary that it may make up its mind whether further advance along the road it has hitherto followed gives any prospect of success. Our philosophy ought to have been philosophizing long ago about the road along which it was going in search of a world-view. It never did so, and therefore was always running uselessly round and round in a circle.

The process by which Western thought has hitherto sought for a world-view is doomed to be fruitless. It has consisted simply in interpreting the world in the sense of world- and life-affirmation, that is to say, in attributing to the world a meaning which allowed it to conceive the aims of mankind and of individual men as having a meaning within that world. This interpretation is acted upon by all Western philosophy. A few thinkers who venture to be un-Western, and resolutely allow world- and life-negation and ethics to be made subjects of discussion, are side-currents which do not affect the main course of the river.

That this process followed by Western thought consists in adopting an optimistic-ethical interpretation of the world will not be clear without further explanation, for it is, indeed, not always openly followed. The optimistic-ethical interpretation is often found imbedded in the results of investigations into the nature of knowledge; it often appears beneath a veil of "metaphysics"; it is often so delicately shaded that it produces none of its usual effects. It is only when one has clearly grasped the fact that Western thought has nothing else in mind than to establish for itself a world-view based on world- and life-affirmation and ethical in character, that one can realize how in its theory of knowledge, in its metaphysics, and in all its movements generally in the game of life, it is guided, consciously or unconsciously, by the effort to interpret the world in some way or other, and in some measure, in the sense of world- and life-affirmation and ethics. Whether in this attempt it goes to work openly or secretly, skilfully or unskilfully, honourably or craftily, does not matter. Western thought needs this interpretation in order that it may be able to give a meaning to human life. Its view of life is to be a result of its view of the world. It has never considered any other course.

But this awakening of Western thought will not be complete until that thought steps outside itself and comes to an understanding with the search for a world-view as this manifests itself in the thought of mankind as a whole. We have too long been occupied with the developing series of our own philosophical systems, and have taken no notice of the fact that there is a world-philosophy of which our Western philosophy is only a part. If, however, one conceives philosophy as being a struggle to reach a view of the world as a whole, and seeks out the elementary convictions which are to deepen it and give it a sure foundation, one cannot avoid setting our own thought face to face with that of the Hindus, and of the Chinese in the Far East. The latter looks strange to us because in much it has remained till now naïve and embodied in myth, while on the other hand it has spontaneously advanced to refinements of criticism and to artificialities. But this does not matter. The essential thing is that it is a struggle for a philosophy of life: the form it takes is a secondary matter. Our Western philosophy, if judged by its own latest pronouncements, is much naïver than we admit to ourselves, and we fail to perceive this only because we have acquired the art of expressing what is simple in a pedantic way.

Among the Hindus we encounter the world-view which is based on world- and life-negation, and the way in which it has laid its foundations in thought is calculated to leave us not knowing what to make of our prejudice in favour of world- and life-affirmation, which, as Westerners, we are inclined to assume to be more or less self-evident.

The attraction and tension which in Hindu thought govern the relations between world- and life-negation and ethics afford us glimpses into the problem of ethics for which Western thought offers us no comparable opportunities.

Nowhere, again, has the problem of world- and life-affirmation, both in itself and in its relation to ethics, been felt in so elemental and comprehensive a fashion as in Chinese thought. Lao-tse, Chwang-tse, Kung-tse (Confucius), Meng-tse, Lie-tse and the rest are thinkers in whom the problems of world-view with which our Western thought is wrestling encounter us in a form, strange indeed, but compelling our attention. Discussing these problems with them means that we ourselves are wrestling with them as well.

That is why I bade our search for a world-view seek to reach clear ideas about itself, and come to a halt in order to fix its attention on the thought of mankind as a whole.

My solution of the problem is that we must make up our minds to renounce completely the optimistic-ethical interpretation of the world. If we take the world as it is, it is impossible to attribute to it a meaning in which the aims and objects of mankind and of individual men have a meaning also. Neither world- and life-affirmation nor ethics can be founded on what our knowledge of the world can tell us about the world. In the world we can discover nothing of any purposive evolution in which our activities can acquire a meaning. Nor is the ethical to be discovered in any form in the world-process. The only advance in knowledge that we can make is to describe more and more minutely the phenomena which make up the world and their implications. To understand the meaning of the whole—and that is what a world-view demands!—is for us an impossibility. The last fact which knowledge can discover is that the world is a manifestation, and in every way a puzzling manifestation, of the universal will to live.

I believe I am the first among Western thinkers who has ventured to recognize this crushing result of knowledge, and the first to be absolutely sceptical about our knowledge of the world without at the same time renouncing belief in world- and life-affirmation and ethics. Resignation as to knowledge of the world is for me not an irretrievable plunge into a scepticism which leaves us to drift about in life like a derelict vessel. I see in it that effort of honesty which we must venture to make in order to arrive at the serviceable world-view which hovers within sight. Every world-view which fails to start from resignation in regard to knowledge is artificial and a mere fabrication, for it rests upon an inadmissible interpretation of the universe.

When once thought has become clear about the relation in which world-view and life-view stand to each other, it is in a position to reconcile resignation as to knowledge with adherence to world- and life-affirmation and ethics. Our view of life is not dependent on our view of the world in the way that uncritical thought imagines. It does not wither away if it cannot send its roots down into a corresponding world-view, for it does not originate in knowledge although it would like to base itself thereon. It can safely depend upon itself alone, for it is rooted in our will-to-live.

World- and life-affirmation and ethics are given in our will-to-live, and they come to be clearly discerned in it in proportion as it learns to think about itself and its relation to the world. The rational thought of other times aimed at getting to know the world, and at being able in that knowledge to conceive of the highest impulses of our will-to-live as purposive in view of the universe and its evolution. But that aim was unattainable. We are not meant to unite the world and ourselves in such harmony with one another. We were naïve enough to assume that our view of life must be contained in our view of the world, but the facts do not justify this assumption. The result is that our thought finds itself involved in a dualism with which it can never be reconciled. It is the dualism of world-view and life-view, of knowing and willing.

To this dualism all the problems with which human thought has busied itself ultimately go back. Every fragment of the thought of mankind which has any bearing on man's conception of the universe—whether in the world-religious or in philosophy —is an attempt to resolve this dualism. It is sometimes softened down, but only to let a unitary, monistic world-view be adopted in its place; at other times it is left standing, but is transformed into a drama with a monistic issue.

Innumerable are the expedients which thought has used in trying to get rid of dualism. Everything it has undertaken commands respect, even the staggering *naïvetés* and the meaningless acts of violence to which it committed itself, for it has always been acting under the compulsion of inner necessity: it wanted to rescue a serviceable world-view from the abyss of dualism.

But from this continuous mishandling of the problem there could issue no solution capable of satisfying thought. We were to be taken over the abyss on tottering bridges of snow.

Instead of going on bridging this abyss with forced logic and imaginative ideas, we must make up our minds to get to the root of the problem and let it bring its influence to bear as it directly encounters us in the facts. The solution is, not to try to get rid of dualism from the world, but to realize that it can no longer do us any harm. This is possible, if we leave behind us all the artifices and unveracities of thought and bow to the fact that, as we cannot harmonize our life-view and our world-view, we must make up our minds to put the former above the latter. The volition which is given in our will-to-live reaches beyond our knowledge of the world. What is decisive for our life-view is not our knowledge of the world but the certainty of the volition which is given in our will-to-live. The eternal spirit meets us in nature as mysterious creative power. In our will-to-live we experience it within us as volition which is both world- and life-affirming and ethical.

Our relation to the world as it is given in the positive certainty of our will-to-live, when this seeks to comprehend itself in thought: that is our world-view. World-view is a product of life-view, not vice versa.

The rational thought of to-day, therefore, does not pursue the phantom of getting to know the world. It leaves knowledge of the world on one side as something for us unattainable, and tries to arrive at clear ideas about the will-to-live which is within us.

The problem of world-view, then, brought back to facts and tackled by rational thought without formulating any hypothesis, may be put thus: "What is the relation of my will-to-live, when it begins to think, to itself and to the world?" And the answer is: "From an inner compulsion to be true to itself and to remain consistent with itself, our will-to-live enters into relations with our own individual being, and with all manifestations of the will-to-live which surround it, that are determined by the sentiment of reverence for life."

Reverence for life, *veneratio vitæ*, is the most direct and at the same time the profoundest achievement of my will-to-live.

In reverence for life my knowledge passes into experience. The simple world- and life-affirmation which is within me just because I am will-to-live has, therefore, no need to enter into controversy with itself, if my will-to-live learns to think and yet does not understand the meaning of the world. In spite of the negative results of knowledge, I have to hold fast to world-

and life-affirmation and deepen it. My life carries its own meaning in itself. This meaning lies in my living out the highest idea which shows itself in my will-to-live, the idea of reverence for life. With that for a starting-point I give value to my own life and to all the will-to-live which surrounds me, I persevere in activity, and I produce values.

Ethics grow out of the same root as world- and life-affirmation, for ethics, too, are nothing but reverence for life. That is what gives me the fundamental principle of morality, namely, that good consists in maintaining, promoting, and enhancing life, and that destroying, injuring, and limiting life are evil. Affirmation of the world, which means affirmation of the will-to-live that manifests itself around me, is only possible if I devote myself to other life. From an inner necessity, I exert myself in producing values and practising ethics in the world and on the world even though I do not understand the meaning of the world. For in world- and life-affirmation and in ethics I carry out the will of the universal will-to-live which reveals itself in me. I live my life in God, in the mysterious divine personality which I do not know as such in the world, but only experience as mysterious Will within myself.

Rational thinking which is free from assumptions ends therefore in mysticism. To relate oneself in the spirit of reverence for life to the multiform manifestations of the will-to-live which together constitute the world is ethical mysticism. All profound world-view is mysticism, the essence of which is just this: that out of my unsophisticated and naïve existence in the world there comes, as a result of thought about self and the world, spiritual self-devotion to the mysterious infinite Will which is continuously manifested in the universe.

This world-affirming, ethical, active mysticism has always been hovering as a vision before Western thought, but the latter could never adopt it because in its search for a world-view it always turned into the wrong road of optimistic-ethical interpretation of the world, instead of reflecting directly on the relation which man assumes to the world under the inner compulsion of the profoundest certainty of his will-to-live.

From my youth onwards, I have felt sure that all thought

which thinks itself out to an issue ends in mysticism. In the stillness of the African jungle I have been able to work out this thought and give it expression.

I come forward therefore with confidence as a restorer of that rational thought which refuses to make assumptions. I know indeed that our time will have absolutely no connection with anything that is in any way rationalistic, and would like to know it renounced as an aberration of the eighteenth century. But the time will come when it will be seen that we must start again where that century came to a stop. What lies between that time and to-day is an intermezzo of thought, an intermezzo with extraordinarily interesting and valuable moments, but nevertheless unhappy and fatal. Its inevitable end was our sinking into a condition in which we had neither a philosophy of life nor civilization, a condition which contains in itself all that spiritual and material misery in which we languish.

The restoration of our world-view can come only as a result of inexorably truth-loving and recklessly courageous thought. Such thinking alone is mature enough to learn by experience how the rational, when it thinks itself out to a conclusion, passes necessarily over into the non-rational. World- and life-affirmation and ethics are non-rational. They are not justified by any corresponding knowledge of the nature of the world, but are the disposition in which, through the inner compulsion of our will-to-live, we determine our relation to the world.

What the activity of this disposition of ours means in the evolution of the world, we do not know. Nor can we regulate this activity from outside; we must leave entirely to each individual its shaping and its extension. From every point of view, then, world- and life-affirmation and ethics are non-rational, and we must have the courage to admit it.

If rational thought thinks itself out to a conclusion, it arrives at something non-rational which, nevertheless, is a necessity of thought. This is the paradox which dominates our spiritual life. If we try to get on without this non-rational element, there result views of the world and of life which have neither vitality nor value.

All valuable conviction is non-rational and has an emotional character, because it cannot be derived from knowledge of the world but arises out of the thinking experience of our will-to-live, in which we stride out beyond all knowledge of the world. This fact it is which the rational thought that thinks itself out to a conclusion comprehends as the truth by which we must live. The way to true mysticism leads up through rational thought to deep experience of the world and of our will-to-live. We must all venture once more to be "thinkers," so as to reach mysticism, which is the only direct and the only profound world-view. We must all wander in the field of knowledge to the point where knowledge passes over into experience of the world. We must all, through thought, become religious.

This rational thought must become the prevailing force among us, for all the valuable ideas that we need develop out of it. In no other fire than that of the mysticism of reverence for life can the broken sword of idealism be forged anew.

In the disposition to reverence for life lies enclosed an elementary conception of responsibility to which we must surrender ourselves; in it there are forces at work which drive us to revision and ennoblement of our individual social and political disposition.

It is the disposition to reverence for life, too, which alone is capable of creating a new consciousness of law. The misery prevailing under our political and social condition is due to a great extent to the fact that neither jurists nor laity have in their minds a living and direct conception of law. During the age of rational thought there was a search made for such a conception, and effort was made to establish fundamental laws which were held to be given in the nature of man, and to get them generally recognized. Later on, however, this endeavour was given up, and laws passed at definite dates displaced natural law. Finally we got to the stage of being satisfied with purely technical law. This was the intermezzo which followed the period of rational thought in the sphere of law.

We have entered on a period in which the feeling for law is hopelessly bereft of force, of soul, and of sense of moral obligation. It is a period of lawlessness. Parliaments produce with easy readiness statutes which contradict the idea of law. States deal arbitrarily with their subjects without regard to the maintenance of any feeling for law. Those, indeed, who fall into the power of a foreign nation are outlaws. No respect is shown for their natural right to a fatherland, or freedom, or dwelling-place, or property, or industry, or food, or anything else. Belief in law is to-day an utter ruin.

This state of things was in preparation from the moment when the search for the natural conception of law, grounded on rational thought, was given up.

The only thing to be done, then, is to make a new connection in the sphere of law also, at the point where the thread of the rational thought of the eighteenth century got broken. We must search for a conception of law that is founded on an idea which grows directly and independently out of a world-view. We have to re-establish human rights which cannot be infringed, human rights which guarantee to each person the greatest possible freedom for his personality within the entity of his own nation, human rights which protect his existence and his human dignity against any foreign violence to which he may be subjected.

Jurists have allowed law and the feeling for law to be ruined. They could not help it, however, for there was no idea provided by the thought of the time to which a living conception of law could have anchored itself. In the complete absence of any world-view, law collapsed entirely, and it is only out of a new world-view that it can be built up again. It is from a fundamental idea about our relation to all that lives, as such, that it must flow in future, as from a spring which can never dry up and never become a swamp. That spring is reverence for life.

Law and ethics spring up together from the same idea. Law is so much of the principle of respect for life as can be embodied in an external code; ethics are what cannot be so embodied. The foundation of law is humanity. It is folly to wish to put out of action the links between law and world-view.

In this way a world-view is the germ of all ideas and dispositions which are determinative for the conduct of individuals and of society.

Aeroplanes carry men to-day through the air over a world in which hunger and brigandage have a place. It is not in China only that one recognizes the grotesque character of such progress: it is almost typical for mankind generally, and such grotesque progress cannot be changed to the normal until there prevails a general disposition capable of bringing order again into the chaos of human life through ethics. In the last resort the practical can be realized only through the ethical.

What a remarkable circle! Rational thought which thinks itself out arrives at something non-rational and subjective which is a necessity of thought, namely the ethical affirmation of world and life. On the other hand, what for the purpose of moulding the conditions of existence for individual men and mankind as a whole is rational, that is to say, what is objectively practical in this regard, can only be brought about by individuals perseveringly putting into action the above-mentioned non-rational and subjective. The non-rational principle underlying our activity, a principle which is provided for us by rational thought, is the sole rational and practical principle underlying all the happenings which are to be produced through human action. Thus the rational and the non-rational, the objective and the subjective, proceed each from the other, and return each into the other again. Only when the play of this mutual interchange is in full activity do normal conditions of existence arise for men and mankind. Let it be disturbed, and the abnormal develops.

So in this book I have written the tragedy of the search for a world-view, and have myself trodden a new path to the same goal. Whereas Western thought has not arrived at any goal because it would not venture resolutely into the desert of scepticism about knowledge of the world, I make my way through this desert with calm confidence. It is, after all, only a narrow strip, and it lies in front of the ever-green oasis of an elemental philosophy of life which grows out of thought about the will-to-live. In my attempt, however, to reach a philosophy of life by this new method, I am conscious of having done no more than put together and think out to conclusions many gropings after this new method which were made by other seekers during the period covered.

But I also put into this book my conviction that mankind must renew itself in a new temper of mind, if it is not to be ruined. I entrust to it, further, my belief that this revolution will come about, if only we can make up our minds to become thinking men.

A new Renaissance must come, and a much greater one than that in which we stepped out of the Middle Ages; a great Renaissance in which mankind discovers that the ethical is the highest truth and the highest practicality, and experiences at the same time its liberation from that miserable obsession by what it calls reality, in which it has hitherto dragged itself along.

I would be a humble pioneer of this Renaissance, and throw the belief in a new humanity, like a torch, into our dark age. I make bold to do this because I believe I have given to the disposition to humanity, which hitherto has ranked only as a noble feeling, a firm foundation in a philosophy of life which is a product of elementary thinking and can be made intelligible to everyone. Moreover, it has gained thereby a power of attracting and convincing which it has not had hitherto; and is capable now of trying conclusions in energetic and consistent fashion with reality, and of proving its full value within it.

                              ALBERT SCHWEITZER

July 1923

The two instalments of my Philosophy of Civilization which are now ready—*The Decay and Restoration of Civilization* and *Civilization and Ethics*—will be followed by two others. In the next, which will be entitled *The World-view of Reverence for Life,* I elaborate this world-view, which so far I have only sketched for a conclusion to my discussion of the search for a world-view, as carried on down to the present day. The fourth and last will treat of the Civilized State.

Chapter 6

THE CRISIS IN CIVILIZATION AND ITS

SPIRITUAL CAUSE

The material and spiritual elements in civilization.

Civilization and world-view.

OUR CIVILIZATION IS GOING THROUGH A SEVERE CRISIS.
Most people think that the crisis is due to the war,[1] but they
are wrong. The war, with everything connected with it, is only
a phenomenon of the condition of uncivilization in which we
find ourselves. Even in States which took no part in the war,
and on which the war had no direct influence, civilization is
shaken, only the fact is not so clearly evident in them as in those
which were hard hit by the consequences of its peculiarly cruel
spiritual and material happenings.

Now, is there any real, live thought going on among us about
this collapse of civilization, and about possible ways of working
our way up out of it? Scarcely any! Clever men stumble about
in seven-league boots in the history of civilization and try to
make us understand that civilization is some kind of natural
growth which blossoms in definite peoples at definite times and
then of necessity withers, so that new peoples with new civilizations must keep replacing those which are worn out. When they
are called upon, indeed, to complete their theory by telling us
what peoples are destined to be our heirs, they are somewhat
embarrassed. There are, in fact, no peoples to be seen whom one
could imagine to be capable of even a portion of such a task.
All the peoples of the earth have been in large measure under

[1] I.e. the war of 1914–18.

[85]

the influence both of our civilization and of our lack of it, so that they more or less share our fate. Among none of them are to be found thoughts which can lead to any considerable original movement of civilization.

Let us put on one side ingenious theories and interesting surveys of the history of civilization, and busy ourselves in a practical way with the problem of our own endangered civilization. What is the nature of this degeneration in our civilization, and why has it come about?

To begin with, there is one elementary fact which is quite obvious. The disastrous feature of our civilization is that it is far more developed materially than spiritually. Its balance is disturbed. Through the discoveries which now place the forces of Nature at our disposal in such an unprecedented way, the relations to each other of individuals, of social groups, and of States have undergone a revolutionary change. Our knowledge and our power have been enriched and increased to an extent that no one would have thought possible. We have thereby been enabled to make the conditions of human existence incomparably more favourable in numerous respects, but in our enthusiasm over our progress in knowledge and power we have arrived at a defective conception of civilization itself. We value too highly its material achievements, and no longer keep in mind as vividly as is necessary the importance of the spiritual element in life. Now come the facts to summon us to reflect. They tell us in terribly harsh language, that a civilization which develops only on its material side, and not in corresponding measure in the sphere of the spirit, is like a ship with defective steering gear which gets out of control at a constantly accelerating pace, and thereby heads for catastrophe.

The essential nature of civilization does not lie in its material achievements, but in the fact that individuals keep in mind the ideals of the perfecting of man, and the improvement of the social and political conditions of peoples, and of mankind as a whole, and that their habit of thought is determined in living and constant fashion by such ideals. Only when individuals work in this way as spiritual forces brought to bear on themselves and on society is the possibility given of solving the problems which have been produced by the facts of life, and of attaining to a general progress which is valuable in every respect. Whether there is rather more or rather less of material achievement to record is not what is decisive for civilization. Its fate depends on whether or not thought keeps control over facts. The issue of a voyage does not depend on whether the vessel's speed is a little faster or a little slower, but on whether it follows the right course, and its steering gear keeps in good condition.

Revolutions in the relations of life between individuals, society, and peoples, as they follow in the train of our great material achievements, if they are to show real progress in the sense of valuable civilization, make higher demands on the habit of thought of civilized people, just as the increased speed of a ship presupposes greater reliability in rudder and steering gear. Advances in knowledge and power work out their effects on us almost as if they were natural occurrences. It is not within our power so to direct them that in every respect they influence favourably the relations in which we live, but they produce for individuals, for society, and for nations, difficult and still more difficult problems, and bring with them dangers which it is quite impossible to estimate in advance. Paradoxical as it may seem, our progress in knowledge and power makes true civilization not easier but more difficult. Judging by the events of our own and the two preceding generations, one might even say that we are almost entitled to doubt whether in view of the way in which these material achievements have been showered upon us, true civilization is still possible.

The most widespread danger which material achievements bring with them for civilization consists in the fact that through the revolutions in the conditions of life men become in greater numbers unfree, instead of free. The type of man who once cultivated his own bit of land becomes a worker who tends a machine in a factory; manual workers and independent tradespeople become employees. They lose the elementary freedom of the man who lives in his own house and finds himself in immediate connection with Mother Earth. Further, they no longer have the extensive and unbroken consciousness of responsibility of those who live by their own independent labour. The conditions of their existence are therefore unnatural. They no longer carry on the struggle for existence in comparatively normal relations in which each one can by his own ability make good his position whether against Nature or against the competition of his fellows, but they see themselves compelled to combine together and create a force which can extort better living conditions. They acquire thereby the mentality of unfree men, in which ideals of civilization can no longer be contemplated with the needful clarity, but become distorted to correspond with the surrounding atmosphere of struggle.

To a certain extent we have all of us, under modern conditions, become unfree men. In every rank of life we have from decade to decade, if not from year to year, to carry on a harder struggle for existence. Overwork, physical or mental or both, is our lot. We can no longer find time to collect and order our thoughts. Our spiritual dependence increases at the same rate as our material dependence. In every direction we are the victims of conditions of dependence which in former times were never known in such universality and such strength. Economic, social, and political organizations, which are steadily becoming more and more complete, are getting us more and more into their power. The State with its increasingly rigid organization holds us under a control which is growing more and more decisive and inclusive. In every respect, therefore, our individual existence is depreciated. It is becoming ever more difficult to be a personality.

Thus it is that the progress of our external civilization brings with it the result that individuals, in spite of all the advantages they get, are thereby in many respects injured both materially and spiritually in their capacity for civilization.

It is our progress in material civilization, too, which intensifies in so disastrous a way our social and political problems. Modern social problems involve us in a class struggle which shakes and shatters economic and national relations. If we go down to rock-bottom, it was machinery and world commerce which brought about the world war, and the inventions which put into our hands such mighty power of destruction made the war of such a devastating character that conquered and conquerors alike are ruined for a period of which no one can see the end. It was also our technical achievements which put us in a position to kill at such a distance, and to annihilate men in such masses, that we sank so low as to push aside any last impulse to humanity, and were mere blind wills which made use of perfected lethal weapons of such destructive capacity that we were unable to maintain the distinction between combatants and non-combatants.

Material achievements, then, are not civilization, but become civilization only so far as the mental habit of civilized peoples is capable of allowing them to aim at the perfecting of the individual and the community. Fooled, however, by our advances in knowledge and power, we did not reflect on the danger to which we were exposing ourselves by the diminished value we put on the spiritual elements in civilization. We surrendered completely to a naïve satisfaction at our magnificent material achievements, and went astray into an incredibly superficial conception of civilization. We believed in a progress which was a matter of course, because contained in the facts themselves. Instead of harbouring in our thought ideals approved by reason, and undertaking to mould reality into accordance with them, we were deluded by a vain conception of reality, and wanted to live with lowered ideals borrowed from it. By taking this course we lost all control over the facts.

Accordingly, just when it was necessary that the spiritual element in civilization should be present in unparalleled strength, we allowed it to waste away.

*   *   *

But how could it come about that the spiritual element in civilization became so lost to us?

To understand that, we must return to the time when it was at work among us in a direct and living way, and this leads us back into the eighteenth century. Among the Rationalists, who approach everything through reason, and would regulate everything in life by rational considerations, we find expression given in elemental strength to the conviction that the essential element in civilization is a habit of thought. It is true that they are already impressed by modern achievements in discovery and invention, and do allow to the material side of civilization a corresponding importance. But they nevertheless regard it as self-evident that the essential and valuable element in civilization is the spiritual. Their interest is focused first of all on the spiritual progress of men and humanity, and in this they believe with vigorous optimism.

The greatness of these men of the period of the "Aufklärung" lies in the fact that they set up as ideals the perfecting of the individual, of society, and of mankind, and devote themselves to these ideals with enthusiasm. The force on which they count for realizing them is the general habit of thought; they demand of the human spirit that it shall transform men and the relations in which they live, and they trust to it to prove itself stronger than the facts of life.

But whence came the impulse to set up such high ideals of civilization, and their confidence that they would be able to realize them? It came from their conception of the world—from their Weltanschauung.

The Rationalist world-view is optimistic and ethical. Its optimism consists in that it assumes as ruling in the world a general purpose directed to the achievement of perfection, and that from this purposiveness the efforts of individual men and of mankind in general to secure material and spiritual progress derive meaning and importance, and in addition a guarantee of success.

This conception is ethical because it regards the ethical as something in accordance with reason, and on that ground demands from man that, putting egoistic interests behind him, he shall devote himself to all ideals that are waiting for realization, taking the ethical as in everything the standard by which to judge. A habit of humane thought is for the Rationalist an ideal which they can by no consideration be induced to resign.

When, at the close of the eighteenth century and the beginning of the nineteenth, the reaction against rationalism set in and criticism began to play upon it, its optimism was reproached as superficial and its ethics as sentimental. But the spiritual movements which criticize it and take its place cannot develop on the same lines what it accomplished, in spite of its manifold imperfections, by inspiring men with ideals of civilization grounded in reason. The energy of thought about civilization dwindles imperceptibly but steadily. In proportion as the world-view of rationalism is left behind, the feeling for actuality makes its influence felt, until at last, from the middle of the nineteenth century onwards, ideals are borrowed no longer from reason but from actuality, and we therewith sink still further into a state of uncivilization and lack of humanity. This is the clearest and the most important of all the facts which can be established in the history of our civilization.

What has it to tell us? It tells us that there is a close connection between civilization and world-view. Civilization is the product of an optimistic-ethical conception of the world. Only in proportion as the prevalent philosophy is world- and life-affirming and at the same time ethical, do we find ideals of civilization put forward and kept influential in the habits of thought of individuals and of society.

That this inner relation between civilization and the world-view of civilized peoples has never received the attention that it deserves, is the result of there having been among us so little real meditation on the essential nature of civilization.

What then is civilization? It is the sum total of all progress made by men and the individual man in every sphere of action and from every point of view, in so far as this progress helps towards the spiritual perfecting of individuals as the progress of all progress.

The impulse to strive for progress in all spheres of action and from every point of view comes to men from an optimistic philosophy which affirms the world and life to be valuable in themselves, and consequently bears within itself a compulsion to raise to its highest possible value all that exists in so far as it can be influenced by us. Hence come will and hope, and effort directed to the improvement of the condition of individuals and of society, of peoples and of mankind. This leads to a lordship of the spirit over the powers of Nature, to the perfecting of the religious, social, economic, and practical association of men, and the spiritual perfecting of individuals and of the community.

Just as the world- and life-affirming, that is to say, the optimistic philosophy of life, is alone capable of stirring men to effort aimed at promoting civilization, so in an ethical world-view alone is there latent the power to make men, after renouncing altogether their selfish interests, persevere in such effort, and to keep them always bent on the spiritual and moral perfecting of the individual as the essential object of civilization. Bound the one to the other, then, world- and life-affirming world-view and ethics think out in harmony the ideals of true, complete civilization and set to work at realizing them.

If civilization remains incomplete or its level falls, this rests in the last resort on the fact that either the world- and life-affirmation of the world-view, or its ethics, or both, have remained undeveloped or have declined. And that is the case with us. It is evident that the ethics required for civilization have gone out of use.

For decades we have been accustoming ourselves increasingly to measure with relative ethical standards, and no longer to allow ethics to have their say in all questions alike. We regard this renunciation of consistent ethical judgment as an advance in practicality.

But our world- and life-affirmation also have become shaky. The modern man no longer feels under any compulsion to think about and to will ideals of progress. To a large extent he has come to terms with actuality. He is much more resigned than he admits to himself, and in one respect he is even outspokenly pessimistic. For he really no longer believes in the spiritual and ethical progress of men and of mankind, which is nevertheless the essential element in civilization.

This stunting of our world- and life-affirmation and of our ethics has its cause in the character of our world-view, in regard to which we have been going through a crisis since the middle of the nineteenth century. It is no longer possible for us to arrive at a conception of the universe in which the meaning of the existence of men and of mankind can be recognized, and in which, therefore, there are also contained the ideals which flow from thoughtful world- and life-affirmation and from ethical volition. We are falling more and more into a condition of having no world-view at all, and from this deficiency comes our lack of civilization.

The great question for us is, therefore, whether we have to renounce permanently the world-view which carries within it in all their strength the ideal of the perfecting of individual men and of mankind, and the ideal of ethical effort. If we succeed in re-establishing a world-view in which world- and life-affirmation is given in convincing fashion, we shall master the decay of civilization which is in progress, and reach again a true and living civilization. Otherwise we are condemned to see the wreck of all attempts to arrest the degeneration. Only when the truth that renewal of civilization can only come by a renewal of our outlook on life becomes a universal conviction, and when a new longing for a world-view sets in, shall we find ourselves on the right path. But this is not yet in prospect. The modern man is still without any correct feeling for the full significance of the fact, that he is living with an unsatisfactory philosophy, or without any at all. The unnatural and dangerous character of this condition must first be brought home to his consciousness, just as those persons who exhibit disturbances of the stability of their nervous system have to be clearly told that their vitality is threatened although they feel no pain. Similarly, we have to stir up the men of to-day to elementary meditation upon what man is in the world, and what he wants to make of his life. Only when they are impressed once more with the necessity of giving meaning and value to their existence, and thus come once more to hunger and thirst for a satisfying world-view, are the preliminaries given for a spiritual condition in which we again become capable of civilization.

But in order to learn the way to a satisfactory philosophy of life, we must see clearly why the struggle undertaken by the European spirit to secure it was for a time successful, but during the second half of the nineteenth century came to an unfortunate end.

Because our thinking is too little occupied with civilization, it has been insufficiently noticed that the essential aspect of the history of philosophy is the history of man's struggle for a satisfactory world-view. Thus regarded, this history unrolls itself like a tragic drama.

Chapter 7

THE PROBLEM OF THE OPTIMISTIC

WORLD-VIEW

The Western and the Indian conceptions of civilization.

The struggle for the optimistic world-view.

Optimism and pessimism.

Optimism, pessimism and ethics.

FOR US WESTERNERS CIVILIZATION CONSISTS IN THIS: THAT WE WORK simultaneously for the perfecting of ourselves and of the world.

But do the activities that are directed outwards and inwards necessarily belong together? Cannot the spiritual and moral perfecting of the individual, which is the ultimate aim of civilization, also be secured if he works for himself alone, and leaves the world and its circumstances to themselves? Who gives us any guarantee that the course of the world can be influenced so as to promote the special aim of civilization, the perfecting of the individual? Who tells us that it has any meaning at all which can be further developed? Is not any action of mine which is directed on the world a diversion of what could be directed on myself, on whom finally everything depends?

Moved by these doubts, the pessimism of the Hindus and of Schopenhauer refuses to allow any importance to the material and social achievements which form the outward and visible part of civilization. About society, nation, mankind, the individual is not to trouble himself; he is only to strive to experience in himself the sovereignty of spirit over matter.

[94]

This, too, is civilization, in that it pursues its own final object, namely, the spiritual and ethical perfecting of the individual. If we Westerners pronounce it incomplete, we must not do so too confidently. Do the outward progress of mankind and the moral and spiritual perfecting of the individual really belong together as we imagine? Are we not, under an illusion, forcing together things which are different in kind? Does the victory of the spirit in one kind of action actually bring about some gain for the other?

What we set up as our ideal, we have not realized. We have lost ourselves in outward progress, allowing all advance in the moral life and inwardness of the individual to come to a standstill. So we have not been able to produce practical proof of the correctness of our view of what civilization is. We cannot, therefore, simply put aside that other narrower conception, but must come to terms with it.

There will come a time—it is already being prepared for—when pessimistic and optimistic thought, which have hitherto talked past each other almost as strangers, will have to meet for practical discussion. World-philosophy is just dawning. It will shape itself in a struggle as to whether its philosophy of life shall be optimistic or pessimistic.

*   *   *

The history of Western philosophy is the history of the struggle for an optimistic outlook on life. If in antiquity and in modern times the peoples of Europe have managed to produce a civilization, it is because the optimistic world-view was dominant in their thought, and held the pessimistic permanently in subjection, although it was not able to suppress it altogether.

The accessions of knowledge which have come in the course of our philosophy have been nothing in themselves: they always stand in the service of one world-view or the other, and only in it attain to their real significance.

But the characteristic thing about the way in which the dispute is conducted on each occasion is that it never is settled in the open. The two world-views are never brought face to face and the case of each heard. That the optimistic alone is in the right is a conviction which is accepted as more or less self-evident. The only thing felt as a problem is how to marshal all possible knowledge in the triumphal procession of proof to defeat the other, and how to knock on the head anything that may still wish to rise in its defence.

Since the pessimistic world-view has never made its presence properly felt, Western thought manifests a lofty unwillingness to understand it, though it has a splendid flair for detecting it. Where it finds, as in Spinoza, too little interest for activity directed upon the world, it reacts immediately by rejecting it. Yet all objectively thinking investigation of the reality of nature is disliked in the West because it may lead to the central position of the human spirit in the universe being insufficiently emphasized. It is because materialism seems likely to be the last ally of pessimism, that Western thought carries on so embittered a struggle against it.

In the discussion of the problem of the theory of knowledge from Descartes to Kant and beyond him, it is really the cause of the optimistic world-view which is being maintained. That is why the theoretical possibility of a depreciation or a denial of the world of sense is attacked with such obstinacy. By proving the ideality of space and time, Kant hopes to make finally secure the optimistic world-view of rationalism with all its ideals and demands. Only thus can it be explained that the most penetrating examinations of the theory of knowledge are carried through with the most naïve conclusions about world-view. The great post-Kantian systems of thought, however much they differ from one another in their subject-matter and the process of the speculation with which they deal with it, are all united in this, that in their cloud-castles they crown the optimistic world-view as the ruler of the universe.

To fit in the aims of mankind with those of the universe in a logically convincing fashion: that is the endeavour in which European philosophy serves the optimistic world-view. Anyone who does not help, or who is indifferent about it, is an enemy.

In its prejudice against scientific materialism philosophy was right. Materialism has done much more to shake the position of the optimistic world-view than has Schopenhauer, although it never proceeded against it with outspoken hostility. When, after the collapse of the great systems, it was allowed to seat itself at table with philosophy, which had now become more modest, it even exerted itself to find out in what tone the latter would like the conversation to be carried on. In dealing with Darwin and others, philosophizing natural science made touchingly naïve attempts so to extend and stretch out the history of zoological development which led up to man, that mankind and with it the spiritual should appear again as the goal of the world-process, as in the speculative systems. But in spite of these well-meant efforts of materialism, the proletarian guest, the conversation could no longer be carried on in the old spirit. Of what use was it for this guest to try to be better than his reputation? He brought with him more respect for nature and facts than was consistent with the convincing establishment of the optimistic world-view. He therefore shook it, even when he did not intend to.

To such a disregard of nature and science as was shown by the earlier philosophy we can never return. Nor can we expect the return of a system of thought which makes it possible to discover in any convincing way in the universe the aims and objects of mankind, as was allowed by the old methods. The optimistic world-view ceases, therefore, to be self-evident to us, or to be demonstrable by the arts of philosophy. It must renounce the attempt to find for itself a solid foundation.

* * *

Confusion is caused by the fact that in the history of human thought the optimistic and pessimistic world-views seldom come forward pure and unadulterated. Their relations are usually such that the one is predominant, while the other has a voice in the matter without being officially recognized. In India a tolerated world- and life-affirmation maintains for pessimism something of interest in the external civilization which pessimism nominally denies. With us it slips in and gnaws at the civilizing energies of the optimistic view, with the result that belief in the spiritual progress of mankind has left us. From pessimism, too, comes the fact that we everywhere conduct the business of life with lowered ideals.

Pessimism is depreciated will-to-live, and is to be found wherever man and society are no longer under the pressure of all those ideals of progress which must be thought out by a will-to-live that is consistent with itself, but have sunk to the level of letting actuality be, over wide stretches of life, nothing but actuality.

It is where pessimism is at work in this anonymous fashion, that it is most dangerous to civilization. It attacks then the most valuable ideas belonging to life-affirmation, leaving the less valuable untouched. Like some concealed source of magnetic power, it disturbs the world-view's compass, so that it takes a wrong course without suspecting it. Thus the unavowed mixture of optimism and pessimism in our thought has the result that we continue to approve the external blessings given us by civilization, things which to thinking pessimism are a matter of indifference, while we abandon that which alone it holds to be valuable, the pursuit of inner perfection. The desire for progress which is directed to objects of sense, goes on functioning because it is nourished by actuality, while that which reaches after the spiritual becomes exhausted, because it is thrown back upon the inner stimulus which comes from the thinking will-to-live. As the tide ebbs, objects which reach deep down are left stranded, while flat ones remain afloat.

Our degeneration, then, traced back to our world-view and what resulted from it, is due to the fact that true optimism, without our noticing it, has disappeared from among us. We are by no means a race weakened and decadent through excessive enjoyment of life, and needing to pull ourselves together to show vigour and idealism amid the thunderstorms of history. But although we have retained our vigour in most departments of the direct activities of life, we are spiritually stunted. Our conception of life with all that depends on it has been lowered both for individuals and for the community. The higher forces of volition and influence are impotent in us, because the optimism from which they ought to draw their strength has become imperceptibly permeated with pessimism.

A characteristic feature of the presence at the same time of optimism and pessimism as lodgers in "Thoughtless House" is that each goes about in the other's clothes, so that what is really pessimism gives itself out among us as optimism, and vice versa. What passes for optimism with the mass of people is the natural or acquired faculty of seeing things in the best possible light, this being the result of lowered ideals for the future no less than for the present. A person ill with consumption is brought by the poison of the disease into the condition which is called Euphoria, so that he experiences an imaginary feeling of health and strength. Similarly there is an external optimism present in individuals and in society just in proportion as they are, without realizing it, infected with pessimism.

True optimism has nothing to do with any sort of lenient judgment. It consists in contemplating and willing the ideal in the light of a deep and self-consistent affirmation of life and the world. Because the spirit which is so directed proceeds with clear vision and impartial judgment in the valuing of all that is given, it wears to ordinary people the appearance of pessimism. That it wishes to pull down the old temples in order to build them again more magnificently, is by vulgar optimism put down to its discredit as sacrilege.

The reason, then, why the only legitimate optimism, that of volition inspired by imagination, has to carry on such a hard struggle with pessimism is that it always has first to track the latter down in vulgar optimism and unmask it. That is a task which optimism has never finished. Never must it think it is at an end. For so long as it allows the enemy to emerge in any shape whatever, there is danger for civilization. When that happens, activity in promoting the special aims of civilization always diminishes, even if satisfaction with its material achievements remains as strong as before.

Optimism and pessimism, therefore, do not consist in counting with more or less confidence on a future for the existing state of things, but in what the will desires the future to be. They are qualities not of the judgment, but of the will. The fact that up to now the inadmissible definition of optimism and pessimism was current side by side with the correct one, so that there were four items to deal with instead of two, made the game easier for the unthinking by deceiving us about what true optimism is. Pessimism of the will they passed off as optimism of the judgment, and optimism of the will they put aside as pessimism of the judgment. These false cards must be taken from them, so that they may not continue to deceive the world in such a fashion.

*   *   *

In what relation do optimism and pessimism stand to ethics?

That close and peculiar relations do exist between them is clear from the fact that in the thought of mankind the two struggles, that for optimistic or pessimistic world-view and that about ethics, are usually involved in each other. It is the general belief that when the one issue is being fought out the other is being fought as well.

This mutual connection is very convenient for thought. When a foundation for ethics is being laid, optimistic or pessimistic arguments are unconsciously pressed into the service, as are ethical arguments when optimism or pessimism have to be established. In this process Western thought lays most stress on justifying a life-affirming—that is to say an activist—ethical system and thinks that merely by doing so it has proved the case for optimism in its world-view. For Indian thought the most important thing is to find a logical foundation for pessimism; and the justifying of a life-denying—that is to say a passivist—ethical system, is rather a derivative from that.

The confusion which resulted from the struggles for optimism and pessimism and for ethics not being kept distinct, has contributed almost more than anything else to prevent the thought of mankind from attaining to clarity.

It was an easy mistake to make. For the question whether it is to be affirmation or negation of life and the world, crops up in ethics in the same way as in the dispute between optimism and pessimism. Things which by their nature belong together feel themselves drawn together, so that optimism naturally thinks it can support itself on an affirmative ethical system, and pessimism thinks the same about a negative one. Nevertheless, the result has hitherto always been that neither of these two closely-related entities could stand firm, because neither of them chose to depend on itself alone.

Chapter 8

THE ETHICAL PROBLEM

The difficulties of ethical perception.

The importance of thought about ethics.

The search for a basic principle of morality.

Religious and philosophical ethics.

HOW CAME MANKIND TO REFLECT ON MORALITY AND TO MAKE progress in that sphere of thought?

It is a picture of confusion that unrolls itself before the eyes of anyone who undertakes a journey through the history of man's search for the ethical. Progress in moral thought is inexplicably slow and uncertain. That the scientific view of the world could be delayed in its rise and development is to a certain extent intelligible, for its advance depended more or less on the chance of there existing gifted observers, whose discoveries in the realm of the exact sciences and the knowledge of nature was needed, to begin with, to provide new horizons and to point out new paths for thought.

But in ethics thought is thrown back entirely on itself: it has to do only with man himself and his self-development, which goes on by a process of causation from within. Why, then, does it not make better progress? Just because man himself is the material which has to be investigated and moulded.

Ethics and æsthetics are the step-children of philosophy. They both deal with a subject which is coy about submitting itself to reflection, for they both treat of spheres in which man exercises his purely creative activities. In science man observes and describes the course of nature, and tries to penetrate its mysteries. In practical matters he uses and moulds it by applying what he has grasped of it outside his own person. But in his moral and artistic activities he uses knowledge and obeys impulses, perceptions, and laws which originate in himself. To establish these firmly and from them to create ideals, is an undertaking which can be successful to a certain extent only. Thought lags behind the material on which it exercises itself.

This is evident from the fact that the examples with which ethics and æsthetics try to work upon reality are usually not quite consistent and are often foolish. And how far from simple are their assertions! How they contradict each other! The guidance that an artist can get for his activities from the best works on æsthetics is but small. Similarly, a business man who seeks in a work on ethics advice as to how, in any given case, he is to bring the demands of his business into harmony with those of ethics, can seldom find any satisfactory information.

The inadequacy of æsthetics is not of great importance for the spiritual life of mankind. Artistic activity is always the peculiar affair of individuals, whose natural gifts are developed more by the study of actual works of art than by consideration of the conclusions arrived at by æsthetic theorizing.

With ethics, however, it is a matter of the creative activity of the mass of men, an activity which is largely determined by the principles which are current in the general thought of the time. The absence of that progress which is still possible in ethics is tragic.

Ethics and æsthetics are not sciences. Science, as the description of objective facts, the establishment of their connection with one another, and the drawing of inferences from them, is only possible when there is a succession of similar facts to be dealt with, or a single fact in a succession of phenomena, when, that is to say, there is subject matter which can be reduced to order under a recognized law. But there is no science of human willing and doing, and there never can be. Here there are only subjective and infinitely various facts to be studied, and their mutual connection lies within the mysterious human ego.

It is only the history of ethics that can be regarded as a science, and that only in so far as a history of man's spiritual life is scientifically possible.

*   *   *

There is, therefore, no such thing as a scientific system of ethics; there can only be a thinking one. Philosophy must give up the illusion which it has cherished even down to the present day. As to what is good and what is bad, and about the considerations in which we find strength to do the one and avoid the other, no one can speak to his neighbour as an expert. All that one can do is to impart to him so much as one finds in oneself of that which ought to influence everybody, though better thought out perhaps, and stronger and clearer, so that noise has become a musical note.

Is there, however, any sense in ploughing for the thousand and second time a field which has already been ploughed a thousand and one times? Has not everything which can be said about ethics already been said by Lao-tse, Confucius, the Buddha, and Zarathustra; by Amos and Isaiah; by Socrates, Plato, and Aristotle; by Epicurus and the Stoics; by Jesus and Paul; by the thinkers of the Renaissance, of the "Aufklärung," and of Rationalism; by Locke, Shaftesbury, and Hume; by Spinoza and Kant; by Fichte and Hegel; by Schopenhauer, Nietzsche, and others? Is there a possibility of getting beyond all these contradictory convictions of the past to new beliefs which will have a stronger and more lasting influence? Can the ethical kernel of the thoughts of all these men be collected into an idea of the ethical, which will unite all the energies to which they appeal? We must hope so, if we are not to despair of the fate of the human race.

Does thought about ethics bring more ethics into the world? The confused picture offered us by the history of ethics is enough to make one sceptical. On the other hand, it is clear that ethical thinkers like Socrates, Kant, or Fichte had a moralizing influence on many of their contemporaries. From every revival of ethical reflection there went forth ethical movements which made the contemporary generation fitter for its tasks. If any age lacks the minds which force it to reflect about the ethical, the level of its morality sinks, and with it its capacity for answering the questions which present themselves.

In the history of ethical thought we wander in the innermost circles of world-history. Of all the forces which mould reality, morality is the first and foremost. It is the determining knowledge which we must wring from thought. Everything else is more or less secondary.

For this reason everyone who believes that he can contribute something to help forward the ethical self-consciousness of society and of individuals has the right to speak now, although it is political and economic questions that the present day prescribes for study. For what is inopportune is really opportune. We can accomplish something lasting in the problems of political and economic life only if we approach them as men who are trying to think ethically. All those who in any way help forward our thought about ethics are working for the coming of peace and prosperity in the world. They are engaged in the higher politics, and the higher national economics, and even if all they can do is nothing more than to bring ethical thinking to the fore, they have nevertheless done something valuable. All reflection about ethics has as one result a raising and rousing of the general disposition to morality.

*   *   *

But however certain it is that every age lives by the energies which have sprung from its thought about ethics, it is equally certain that up to now the ethical thoughts which have become current after a longer or shorter period have lost their power of convincing. Why has the establishment of an ethical system never met with more than a partial and temporary success, and never become a permanency? Why is the history of the ethical thinking of mankind the history of inexplicable stoppages and retrogressions? Why has there been no organic progress to allow one period to build upon the achievements of preceding ones? Why in the sphere of ethics do we live in a city of ruins, in which, to provide for its barest needs, one generation builds for itself here, and another there.

"To preach morality is easy, to give it a foundation is hard," says Schopenhauer, and that saying shows the nature of the problem.

In every effort of thought about ethics there is to be seen, distinctly or indistinctly, the search for a basic principle of morality, which needs no support outside itself, and unites in itself the sum total of all moral demands. But no one has ever succeeded in really formulating this principle. Only elements of it have been brought to light and given out to be the whole, until the difficulties which emerged destroyed the illusion. The tree, however finely it sprouted, did not live to grow old, because it was unable to send its roots down into the permanently nourishing and moisture-giving earth.

The chaos of ethical views becomes to some extent intelligible as soon as one sees that we are concerned with differing and mutually contradictory opinions about fragments of the basic principle. The contradiction lies in their incompleteness. There is ethical matter in what Kant objects to in the ethics of rationalism, as also in what he puts in its place; in that part of Kant's writings where his conception of the moral is opposed by Schopenhauer, as also in what is to take its place in the ethical system of the latter. Schopenhauer is ethical in the points on which Nietzsche attacks him, and Nietzsche is ethical in his opposition to Schopenhauer. What is wanted is to find the fundamental chord in which the dissonances of these varied and contradictory ethical ideas unite in producing harmony.

The ethical problem, then, is the problem of a basic principle of morality founded in thought. What is the common element of good in the manifold things which we feel to be good? Is there such a universally valid conception of the good? If there is, in what does it consist, and how far is it real and necessary for me? What influence has it over my general disposition and my actions? Into what relations with the world does it bring me?

It is, then, on the basic principle of the moral that the attention of thought has to be fixed. The mere giving of a list of virtues and duties is like striking notes at random on the piano and thinking it is music. And when we come to discuss the works of earlier moralists, it is only the elements in them which can help the establishment of an ethical system that will interest us, not the way in which any system has been advocated.

Otherwise there can be no success for any attempt to bring order into chaos. How utterly at sea is Friedrich Jodl [1] in his history of ethics, the most important existing work in this de-

---

[1] Friedrich Jodl: *A History of Ethics as Philosophical Science*, 2nd ed., 2 vols. (Vol. I., 1906; Vol. II., 1912). It treats of the ethics of Western philosophy only.

partment, when he tries to estimate the relative values of the various ethical standpoints! Failing to judge them directly by their distance from an initial basic principle of morality, he is unable to establish a standard of comparison. He gives us, therefore, only a survey of ethical views, not a history of the ethical problem.

*   *   *

In the search for the fundamental principle of morality, are we concerned only with the direct attempts of philosophy to find it? No, we are concerned with every attempt of the kind, those of religion as well as others. We must pass through the whole experience of mankind in its search for the ethical.

The raising of a dividing wall between philosophical ethics and religious ethics is based on the mistaken idea that the former are scientific and the latter non-scientific. But neither of them is either: they are both alike simply thought; only the one has freed itself from acceptance of the traditional religious world-view, while the other still maintains its connection with it.

The difference, however, is merely relative. Religious ethics appeal, indeed, to a supernatural authority, but that is rather the form which they assume. As a matter of fact, however high they rise, they will seek to find an independent basic principle of morality. In every religious genius there lives an ethical thinker, and every really deep philosophical moralist is in some way or other religious.

How indeterminate is the border-line, is shown by Indian ethics. Are they religious, or are they philosophical? Originating in the thought of the priests, they claim to be a deeper exposition of the demands of religion, but in essential nature they are philosophical. With the Buddha and others, they venture to make the step from pantheism to atheism, but without giving up their claim to be religious. Spinoza and Kant, however, who are counted among philosophical moralists, do, if we judge by the general direction of their thought, belong at the same time to the realm of religious ethics.

It all depends on a relative difference in methods of thought. The one group works towards the basic principle of ethics by a more intuitive process, the other by a process which is more analytical. It is the depth, not the method of the thought, which decides the matter. The more intuitive thinker produces his ethical thought like an artist who with the production of an important work of art opens up new horizons. In deep-reaching moral sayings, like the beatitudes of Jesus, the basic principle of morality shines out. There comes progress in the recognition of what is moral, even if the provision of a foundation for it fails to advance in the same way.

On the other hand, the search for the basic principle of the moral by a process of critical analysis may lead to an impoverished system of ethics, because there runs through it the effort to take into account only what is connected with the idea that seems to be what is being sought for. That is why philosophical ethics are as a rule so far behind practical ethics, and have so little direct influence. While religious moralists with one mighty word can get down to the waters flowing far below the surface, philosophical ethics often dig out nothing but a slight hollow in which a puddle forms.

Nevertheless, it is rational thinking alone which is able to pursue the search for the basic principle with perseverance and hope of success. It must find it at last, if it only goes deep enough, and is sufficiently simple.

The weakness of all ethics hitherto, whether philosophical or religious, has lain in this, that they have not shown individuals how to deal directly and naturally with reality. To a large extent they merely talk "about it and about." They do not touch a man's daily experience, and therefore they exert no permanent pressure upon him. The result is lack of ethical thought, and mere platitudes about ethics.

The true basic principle of the ethical must be not only something universally valid, but something absolutely elementary and inward, which, once it has dawned upon a man, never relinquishes its hold, which as a matter of course runs like a thread through all his meditation, which never lets itself be thrust aside, and which continually challenges him to try conclusions with reality.

For centuries men who navigated the seas guided themselves by the stars. In time they rose above this imperfect method through the discovery of the magnetic needle, which by its natural principle of activity pointed them to the north. Now they can tell where they are in the darkest night on the most distant sea. That is the kind of progress that we have to seek in ethics. So long as we have nothing but an ethical system of ethical sayings, we direct our course by stars, which, however brilliant their radiance, give us only more or less reliable guidance, and can be hidden from us by rising mist. During a stormy night, as we know by recent experiences, they leave mankind in the lurch. If, however, we have in our possession a system of ethics which is a necessity of thought and a principle which comes to clearness within ourselves, there begins a far-reaching ethical deepening of the consciousness of individuals, and steady ethical progress in mankind.

Chapter 9

RELIGIOUS AND PHILOSOPHICAL

WORLD-VIEWS

The world-views of the world-religions.

*The world-views of the world-religions and that
of Western thought.*

IN THE WORLD-RELIGIONS WE CAN SEE POWERFUL ATTEMPTS TO
establish an ethical world-view.

The religious thinkers of China, Lao-tse (born 604 B.C.),
Kung-tse (Confucius, 551–479 B.C.), Meng-tse (372–289 B.C.),
and Chwang-tse (fourth century B.C.), all try to base the ethical
on a world- and life-affirming nature-philosophy. In so doing
they arrive at a world-view which, because it is optimistic-ethical,
contains incentives to inward and outward civilization.

The religious thinkers of India also, the Brahmans, the
Buddha (560–480 B.C.), and the Hindus, start, like the Chinese,
from reflection on existence, that is to say, from nature-philosophy. They do not, however, take a world- and life-affirming, but
a world- and life-denying, view of it. Their world-view is pessimistic-ethical, and contains, therefore, incentives only to the
inward civilization of the heart, not to outward civilization as
well.

Chinese and Indian piety recognize but a single world-
principle. They are monistic and pantheistic. Their world-view
has to solve the problem of how far we can recognize the original
source of the world as ethical, and how far, correspondingly, we
become ethical by the surrender to it of our will.

[109]

In contrast to these monistic-pantheistic world-views, we find a dualistic outlook on life in the religion of Zarathustra (sixth century B.C.), in that of the Jewish prophets (from the eighth century B.C. onwards), and in those of Jesus and Mohammed, this last, however, showing itself to be in all points unoriginal and decadent. These religious thinkers do not start from an investigation of the existence which manifests itself in the universe, but from a view of the ethical which is quite independent. They put it in opposition to natural happenings. Accordingly they assume the existence of two world-principles, the natural and the ethical. The first is in the world, and has to be overcome; the other is incorporated in an ethical personality which is outside the world and endowed with final authority.

If among the Chinese and the Hindus the basic principle of morality was life in harmony with the world-will, so among dualists it is an attempt to be different from the world in harmony with an ethical divine personality outside and above the world.

The weakness of dualistic religions is that their world-view, because it rejects every kind of nature-philosophy, is always naïve. Their strength lies in the fact that they have the ethical within themselves, directly present and with undiminished force. They have no need to strain it and explain it, as must the monists, in order to be able to conceive it as an effluence from the world-will which reveals itself in nature.

The world-views of the dualistic world-religions, taken as a whole, are optimistic. They live in the confident belief that ethical force will prove superior to natural, and so raise the world and mankind to true perfection. Zarathustra and the older Jewish prophets represent this process as a kind of world-reform. The optimistic element in their world-view asserts itself in a quite natural way. They have the will, and the hope, of being able to transform human society and make the races of the world fit for their higher destiny. Progress in any department of life means for them something gained, for they think of inward and outward civilization together.

With Jesus the value of the optimistic element in his world-view is impaired by the fact, that he looks forward to the perfected world as the result of a catastrophic end to the natural one, and while with Zarathustra and the older Jewish prophets the Divine intervention is to a certain extent only the completion of the human activities which have been directed to the perfecting of the world, it is with Jesus the only thing which has to be taken into account. The kingdom of God is to appear in a supernatural way; it is not prepared for by any effort made by mankind to attain to civilization.

The world-view of Jesus, because it is fundamentally optimistic, accepts the ends aimed at by outward civilization. But biased by the expectation of the end of the world, it is indifferent to all attempts made to improve the temporal, natural world by a civilization which organizes itself on lines of outward progress, and concerns itself only with the inward ethical perfecting of individuals.

Just in proportion, however, as the Christian world-view realizes the consequences of the fact that the world has not come to an end, and accepts the idea that the kingdom of God must be established by a process of development which transforms the natural world, it begins to understand and be interested in the completing of social organization, and in all such progress in outward civilization as contributes to it. The optimistic element in the world-view can again work unhindered side by side with the ethical. Thus we get an explanation of the fact that Christianity, which in the ancient world showed itself hostile to civilization, seeks in modern times with more or less success to conduct itself as the world-view of true progress in every sphere of activity.

*   *   *

The questions which press for an answer from the world-religions in their struggle to reach an ethical and an optimistic-ethical world-view, are the same as those which present themselves also to Western philosophy. The great problem is to think out a connection between the universe and ethics.

The three types of world-view which show themselves in the world-religions, recur also in Western philosophy. The latter, too, attempts to find an ethical code either in a world- and life-affirming, or in a world- and life-denying, nature-philosophy, or it attempts, more or less completely setting aside all nature-philosophy, to reach a world-view which is in itself ethical. Only, it at the same time does its best to avoid acknowledging, and indeed to conceal, the naïve and dualistic element which is inevitably encountered when this last method of procedure is followed.

The world-views, then, of the world-religions, and of Western philosophy, do not belong to different worlds, but stand in close inward relations to one another. After all, the distinction between a religious world-view and a philosophical is quite superficial. The religious world-view which seeks to comprehend itself in thought becomes philosophical, as is the case among the Chinese and the Hindus. On the other hand a philosophical world-view, if it is really profound, assumes a religious character.

Although Western thought does, in principle, approach the problem of world-view without any presuppositions, it has not been able to keep itself entirely uninfluenced by religious conceptions of the universe. From Christianity it has received impulses of a decisive character, and the attempt to transform the naïve-ethical world-view of Jesus into a philosophical system has cost it more attention and effort than it admits to itself. With Schopenhauer and his successors the pessimistic monism of India finds expression, and it enriches their reflection upon the nature of the ethical.

Thus the energies of all the great world-views stream into Western thought. Through the co-operation of these varied forms of thought and energy it is enabled to exalt into a universal conviction the optimistic-ethical concept which hovers before its mind, and that too in a strength which it has never displayed in any previous age or in any other part of the world. And that is why the West has advanced farthest both in inward and outward civilization.

To give a real foundation to the optimistic-ethical world-view, Western thought is indeed as little able as were any of the world-religions. Because the West experiences the problem of world-view in its most universal and most pressing form, it is the scene of the greatest advances made by the civilized mind, but also of its greatest catastrophes. It experiences portentous changes in its world-view, and is familiar, too, with terrible periods when it has no philosophy of life at all.

It is because Western thought is so sensitive in all directions, that it reveals most clearly the questions and difficulties amid which the search for an optimistic world-view moves.

To what extent does the history of our thought give to us Westerners the explanation of our fate? What road does it indicate to us as the best for our future search for a world-view in which the individual can find inwardness and strength, and mankind progress and peace?

Chapter 10

CIVILIZATION AND ETHICS IN THE

GRÆCO-ROMAN PHILOSOPHY

The beginnings: Socrates.

Epicureanism and Stoicism. The ethic of resignation.

Plato's abstract basic principle of the ethical. The ethic of world-negation.

Aristotle. Instruction about virtue in place of ethics.

The ideal of the civilized state in Plato and Aristotle. Seneca, Epictetus and Marcus Aurelius.

The optimistic-ethical world-view of the later Stoicism.

IN THE SEVENTH CENTURY BEFORE CHRIST THE GREEK SPIRIT BEGINS to free itself from the conception of the universe which underlay the traditional religion, and undertakes to base its world-view on a foundation of knowledge and thought.

First there comes a nature-philosophy, the result of investigation of Being and reflection upon what it really is. Then criticism begins its work. Belief in the gods is found unsatisfying, not only because the course of nature is not made intelligible by the rule of dwellers in Olympus, but also because these personalities no longer answer to the demands of feeling which is thoughtful and moral. These two elements, nature-philosophy and criticism, are found united in Xenophanes and Heraclitus in the sixth century B.C.

In the course of the fifth century B.C. the Sophists appear, and begin to concern themselves critically with the accepted standards of value current for social life and individual activities.[1] The result is annihilating. The more moderate of these "Enlighteners" proclaim the overwhelming majority of these standards which pass for moral to be merely claims made by society on its members, leaving open thereby the possibility that a small remainder may be able to prove themselves to rational consideration as moral in themselves. But the younger radical Sophists maintain the position that all morality, like all current law, has been invented by organized society in its own interest. Hence the thinking man who is freeing himself from this tutelage will make his own moral standards, and will follow in them nothing but his own pleasure and his own interests. Thus Western philosophical thought about the problem of ethics and civilization starts with shrill dissonance.

What was Socrates (470–399 B.C.) able to contribute, when he came forward to oppose this tendency?

In the place of the simply pleasurable he put the rationally pleasurable.

By rational consideration, he asserts, it is possible to establish a standard of action in which the happiness of the individual, rightly understood, is in harmony with the interests of society. Virtue consists in right knowledge.

That the rationally moral is that which procures for the person concerned true pleasure, or, what means the same thing, true profit, Socrates draws out into the most diverse applications in the simple everyday discussions which Xenophon has transmitted to us in his *Memorabilia*.[2] The dialogues of Plato show

[1] Very important for our knowledge of the old philosophy and ethics are the ten books entitled *The Lives and Teaching of Famous Philosophers*, composed by Diogenes Laertius in the third century after Christ. Just because they are purely anecdotal, they have preserved for us much information and many views which otherwise—for the works of the philosophers treated of have all been lost —we should not possess.

[2] Xenophon, one of the generals who led the ten thousand back from Asia, wrote down his recollections of Socrates after the latter's death. By his report of the simple conversations of the Master, he seeks to render impotent for all time the accusation that he corrupted youth and taught atheism, for even after his

him going beyond this primitive utilitarianism, and seeking a conception of the good which has been made inward and aims at the well-being of the soul; which stands, too, in relationship with the beautiful.[3] How much of this more advanced view is actually the Master's own, and how much of his own thoughts his pupil has in this way put into his mouth, cannot now be decided.

That Socrates spoke of an inner, mysterious voice, the "daimonion," as being the highest moral authority in man is indeed certain, for it is mentioned in his indictment. His utilitarian rationalism is therefore completed by a kind of mysticism. An empirical ethic—that is to say, an ethic founded on past experience and with future experience in view—and an intuitive ethic live in him side by side and undistinguished from one another, to be separated later and developed in contrast to one another in his pupils, the Cynics and Cyrenaics on the one hand, and Plato on the other.

Was Socrates at all conscious that with the bringing back of the moral to that which is rationally pleasurable he builds the road only a short way further, and stops exactly at the point where the real difficulty makes its appearance, namely, that of defining the most general content of the moral as given by reason? Or was he so naïve as to regard the general formula he had arrived at as the solution of the difficulty?

The confidence which he displays in all his public life leads us to suppose the latter. In his unaffected simplicity lies his strength. In that perilous hour when Western thought comes to the point of having to philosophize about the moral in order to arrest the dissolution of Greek society which has been begun by a body of unstable and disputatious teachers, the wise man of Athens shatters all scepticism by the mighty earnestness of his conviction that what is moral can be determined by thought. Beyond that general statement he does not go, but he is the

---

death teachers of rhetoric did in fact draw up formal complaints against him. Xenophon's straightforward, realistic portrait of Socrates is extraordinarily valuable.

3 The most important dialogues in this connection are the *Protagoras*, the *Gorgias*, the *Phædrus*, the *Symposium*, the *Phædo*, and the *Philebus*.

course of that serious spirit in which antiquity after his day busied itself with the problem. What would that ancient world have become without him?

Characteristic for this prologue to Western philosophizing about the moral is the indifference with which Socrates stands aloof from the philosophic endeavour to reach a complete world-view. He troubles himself neither about the results of natural science, nor about inquiries into the nature of knowledge, but is busied simply with man in his relation to himself and to society. Lao-tse, Confucius, the Indian philosophers, the Jewish prophets, and Jesus seek to comprehend ethics as somehow or other derived from, or forming part of, a world-view. Socrates gives them no foundation but themselves. On this stage, which has no scenery to form a background, there will appear in succession to him the utilitarians of every age.

And here a remarkable prospect opens before us. To all efforts to determine the content of the moral, more help is afforded by the ethic which keeps clear of all connection with a complete world-view than by any other. Such an ethic is the most practical. And yet this isolation is unnatural. The idea that ethics are rooted in a complete world-view, or must find their completion in one—that is, the idea that one's relations to one's fellowmen and to society are in the last resort rooted in some relation to the world—never loses its natural claim. Hence again and again—already in Plato, then in Epicurus and in the Stoic philosophy—ethics have felt the need of resuming connection with world-view, and the same process continues in modern thought. But the practical search for the content of the ethical remains the prerogative of those who are busied with ethics as such.

In Socrates the ethical mysticism of devotion to the inner voice takes the place of the complete world-view, which was in future to be the foundation of the ethical destiny of man.

*   *   *

Three tasks were left by Socrates to his successors: to determine more exactly the content of the rationally useful; to give the world the most universal general notion of the good; and to think ethics into a complete world-view.

What conclusions are come to by those who concern themselves with the first question, and seek to determine the rationally useful from a corresponding experience of pleasure?

As soon as the notion of pleasure is brought into connection with ethics, it shows disturbances, as does the magnetic needle in the neighbourhood of the poles. Pleasure as such shows itself incapable in every respect of being reconciled with the demands of ethics, and it is therefore given up. Enduring pleasure is called on to take its place, but this retreat does not suffice, for lasting pleasure, interpreted seriously, can be nothing but pleasure of the mind. Even this position, however, is not tenable. Reflection upon the ethic which is to produce happiness is compelled at last to give up the positive notion of pleasure in any form. It has to reconcile itself to the negative notion which conceives pleasure as somehow or other a liberation from the need of pleasure. Thus the individualistic, utilitarian ethic, also called Eudæmonism, destroys itself as soon as it ventures to be consistent. This is the paradox which reveals itself in the ethics of antiquity.

Instead of coming to maturity in the following generations, the ethically-rational life-ideal put forward by Socrates succumbs to an incurable decline, because the notion of pleasure, which lives in it, denies itself as soon as it makes any attempt to think itself out.

Aristippus (c. 435–355 B.C.), the founder of the Cyrenaic school, Democritus of Abdera (c. 450–360 B.C.), the author of the atomic theory, and Epicurus (341–270 B.C.) seek to retain as much as possible of the positive notion of pleasure. The Cynic school of Antisthenes (born c. 440 B.C.), and the Stoicism which originated with Zeno, a native of Kittium in Cyprus (c. 336–264 B.C.), withdraw from the very beginning to the negative notion.[4] But the final result is the same in both cases. Epicurus sees him-

---

4 Of the writings of the Cyrenaics and the Cynics, of Democritus, Epicurus, Zeno, and the older Stoics hardly anything has come down to us. Our knowledge of them is derived mostly from Diogenes Laertius.

The Cyrenaics were known as the philosophers of pleasure because Aristippus, the first preacher of the world-wisdom of joy, hailed from Cyrene. The Cynics, or dog-philosophers, derived their name from the fact that they despised the amenities of life and often delighted in a coarse naturalness. The best known of them is Diogenes of Sinope (died 323 B.C.).

Zeno's philosophy was called Stoicism because he taught at Athens in a colonnaded portico (Stoa).

self compelled at last to exalt the absence of desire for pleasure as being itself the purest pleasure, landing thereby on the shore of resignation where the Stoics take their exercise. The fundamental difference between the two great philosophical schools of antiquity does not lie in what they offer to men as ethical. About what the "wise man" does and leaves undone, they both frequently express themselves almost in the same way. What separates them is the world-view with which their ethic is combined. Epicureanism accepts the atomistic materialism of Democritus, is atheistic, asserts that the soul perishes, and is in every respect irreligious. Stoicism is pantheistic.

With Epicurus and Zeno ethics no longer trust themselves, as with Socrates, to maintain an independent existence. They see the necessity of attaching themselves to some sort of world-view. Travelling along this road, Epicurus is guided solely by the effort to retain veracity. He leaves the last word to the purely scientific knowledge of the world, not allowing ethics to join in the investigation of Being and introduce into it what might be of advantage to itself. How poor, or how rich, it will finally become is to him a matter of indifference. The one thing he is concerned about is that the world-view be a true one, and therein lies the greatness of Epicurus and his claim to our respect.

Stoicism seeks to satisfy the need for an inward, stable philosophy of life; like the Chinese monists it tries to find a meaning in the world. It tries to widen out the ethical rationalism of Socrates into cosmic rationalism. The moral is to show itself to be conduct agreeable to the pronouncements of world-reason.

Stoicism has a vision of an optimistic-ethical affirmation of life, grounded in the nature of the cosmos, but it fails to reach it.

It is not untutored enough to acquiesce in the ethical simplicity of a nature-philosophy such as can be seen in Lao-tse and in the older philosophical Taoism. It is ever struggling to discover in world-reason the notion of purposive activity, and is ever mercilessly thrust back upon that of activity pure and simple. Hence the ethic with which it is operating never has a sufficiently universalist character to let it form a natural connection with world-reason. As might be expected from its origin, it is dominated by the problem of pleasure and not-pleasure, and therefore no longer possesses any efficacious instinct for effort. Its horizons, because still determined by the questions arising out of ancient citizenship and the ancient city-state, are narrow. It is, therefore, not advanced enough to engage in thought on scientific lines, concerned with both the world and man, although it does feel the inner necessity for doing so.

The vacillation which is characteristic of Stoicism comes, then, from the fact that the results it attains do not match its aspirations, but are much poorer than these. The spirit of antiquity tries to find an optimistic-ethical life-affirmation in nature-philosophy, and to find in it also the justification of those instincts for reliable activity which it has possessed since the days when it was entirely unsophisticated, but it cannot do so. Whenever it acknowledges what has happened, it sees clearly that thinking about the universe leads only to resignation, and that a life in harmony with the world means quiet surrender to being carried along in the flood of world-happenings, and, when the hour comes, sinking into it without a murmur.

Stoicism talks, it is true, with deep earnestness of responsibility and duty, but since it cannot draw either from nature-philosophy or from ethics a well-established and living notion of activity, it lays out in these words nothing but beautiful corpses. It is impotent to command anything whatever that is bound up with voluntary activity which is conscious of its aim. Again and again evidence breaks through that its thinking has been pushed aside on to the track of passivity. Nature-philosophy only provides the cosmic background for the resignation to which ethics have come. The ideal, which gives life to Chinese Monism, of the perfecting of a world through ethical and ethically organized mankind, is not really discerned, much less securely grasped.

One watches with dismay the shaping of the fate of ancient ethics in Epicureanism and Stoicism. In place of the vigorous life-affirming ethic which Socrates expects from rational thinking, resignation steps in. An inconceivable impoverishment takes place in the representation of the moral. The notion of action cannot be worked out to completion. Even so much of it as, thanks to tradition, still survives in the simple thought-methods of the Greek world in general, is lost.

The ancient Greek was more citizen than man. Active devotion to the cause of the community was to him a matter of course. Socrates takes it for granted. In the conversations which

Xenophon hands down to us in the *Memorabilia,* he is ever insisting that the individual must make himself fit in order to become an active citizen. The natural course would have been that the thought which originated with him should deepen this mentality by setting before it the highest social aims. It was, however, never at all in a position to maintain the mentality as it received it. More and more it leads the individual to withdraw himself from the world and from all that goes on in it.

By a never-ceasing process of change, the ethics of Greek thought become in Epicureanism and Stoicism ethics of decadence. Not being capable of producing ideals of progressive development for collective bodies, they are also impotent to become really ethics of civilization. In place of the ideal of the man who works for civilization they set the ideal of the "wise man." It is only the inward individual civilization of refined and reflective self-liberation from the world that now floats before their eyes, but this in all its depth.

It is true that there is power in the preaching of resignation which ancient thought, no longer ignorant about life, allows to go forth to mankind. Resignation is the lofty porch through which one enters upon ethics. But Epicurus and the Stoics stay on in this porch. Resignation becomes for them an ethical worldview. Hence they are incapable of leading ancient society from its ingenuous life- and world-affirmation to a philosophy based on thought.

The conception of the rationally pleasurable, which was the legacy of Socrates, is not productive enough to keep a world alive. It is impossible to develop from it the ideas of a utilitarianism directed to the welfare of the community, although he believed he found them in it. Ethical thought remains confined within the circle of the *ego.* Every attempt to ennoble the rationally pleasurable ends in life-affirmation changing into life-negation. On this logical fact was wrecked the ancient West, which, after the critical awakening of the Greek spirit, could have been saved only by means of a reflective optimistic-ethical outlook on life. It was able to take seriously what Socrates gave it, but not to make it capable of producing life and civilization.

* * *

Plato, too (427–347 B.C.), and Aristotle (384–322 B.C.), the two great independent thinkers of antiquity, are incapable of producing an ethic of action, and so giving civilization a firm foundation.

Plato seeks the general notion of the Good, but he abandons the path which was pointed out, even if not followed to the end, by Socrates, namely the determination of the Good by a process of induction. He gives up trying to arrive at the nature of the Good by considerations of the kind, the object, and the results of action, that is to say, by its content. He wants to establish it by a purely formal process, by abstract logical thinking.

In order to arrive at an ethic he uses a detour through the theory of ideas. All similar phenomena, he says, are to be conceived of as varying copies of an original—to express which he uses the word "idea." In trees there is to be seen the idea of tree, in horses, that of horse. The idea does not come to us, as we are inclined to think, by our abstracting from trees the idea of tree, and from horses that of horse. We have it within us already. It originates, not in our experience of the empirical world, but in the recollection which our soul brought with it from the supra-sensuous, pure world of ideas, when it began its existence in a body. In the same way we have brought with us the idea of the Good.

Thus in a tortured doctrine which is disfigured everywhere with fancies and obscurities, Plato tries to found ethics on a theory about the character of our knowledge of the world of sense, and he is encouraged to this undertaking by the consideration, that it is not from reflection that we obtain our conception of the Beautiful, which is closely allied with that of the Good: that conception also we bring with us, ready made.

Plato is the first of all thinkers who feels that the presence of the ethical idea in man is what it is: something profoundly mysterious. That is his great distinction. Hence he cannot profess to be satisfied with the attempt of the historic Socrates to explain the Good as that which is rationally pleasure-giving. It is clear to him that it must be something absolute, with a compelling force of its own, and to preserve for it this character seems to him, as later to Kant, to be the great task of thought.

But what is the result of his undertaking? A fundamental

principle of ethics which is devoid of content. In order to secure its lofty character, it is supposed to be born of abstract considerations in the country of the supra-sensuous. It can, therefore, never find itself at home in reality or become familiar with it, nor can any rules for concrete ethical conduct be developed from it. Thus Plato, when he treats of ethics on practical lines, is compelled to abide by the chief virtues as popularly conceived. In the *Republic* he names four of them: wisdom, courage, temperance, and justice, and he founds them, not on his general idea of the Good, but on psychology.

But the characteristic ethic of Plato has nothing whatever to do with such virtues. If the conception of the Good is supra-sensible and the immaterial world is the only real one, then it is only thought and conduct which deal with the immaterial that can have any ethical character. In the world of appearance there is nothing of value to be made actual. Man is simply compelled to be an impotent spectator of its shadow-play. All willing must be directed to enabling oneself to turn away from this, and discover that true activity which goes on in the light.

The true ethic, then, is world-negation. To this view Plato was committed the moment he allowed the ethical to find its home in the world of pure Being. Thoughts of ascetic inactivity find expression in him side by side with the Greek feeling for reality, and it is confusing that he does not recognize the conflict between them, but speaks now in one sense, now in the other. His ethic is a chaos, and he himself an expert in inconsistency.

Plato's ethic of world-negation is not an original creation; he takes it over in the Indian setting in which it is offered to him by Orphism and Pythagoreanism. By what route there found its way into Greek thought this pessimism which had been thought out to a system and equipped with the doctrine of re-incarnation, we do not know, and shall probably never learn. The presence side by side in Greek thought of an artless optimism and a mature pessimism will always remain for us the great puzzle of Greek civilization. But if the pessimism had not been there, Plato must have introduced it. The abstract basic principle of morality, which he adopts in order to preserve the absolute character of morality which he was the first to pronounce a necessity, precludes any other content than the denial of the world of the senses and of natural life.

*   *   *

Plato's fate alarms Aristotle. He refuses to soar to the heights where Plato lost himself. How then does he fare?

His object is the establishment of a serviceable ethic which is in harmony both as to extent and content with reality. What he accomplished lies before us in the so-called *Nicomachean Ethics,* the comprehensive work which he composed for the benefit of his son, Nicomachus. The general thought of Socrates, that ethics are a striving after happiness, he acknowledges. But at the same time he is clear that activity plays a much greater part in ethics than is given to it by Plato or the other post-Socratics. Aristotle feels that the crux of the question is the conception of activity, and this he wants to save. He therefore avoids Plato's paths of abstract thinking, and rejects the ethic of pleasure and not-pleasure over which the Cyrenaics and Cynics work so hard. In his ethical thinking the vitality of the ancient world tries to find expression.

In magnificent fashion he lays down the hypotheses which are necessary for the accomplishment of his undertaking. He finds the motive to activity in the conception of pleasure, a thing he can do because his whole philosophy has indeed for its aim and object the conceiving of Being as formative activity. Hence the essential element in human nature also is activity. Happiness is to be defined as activity in accordance with the law of excellence. Rational pleasure is experience of the perfecting of activity.

Starting from the conception of pleasure which experiences itself as activity, Aristotle is on the way to comprehend ethics as deepened life-affirmation, and to attack the problem of leading the ancient world up from a naïve to a reflecting world-affirmation. But on the way he diverges from the high-road.

When he has to ask the decisive question as to what makes activity moral, he shrinks from discussing the problem of the basic principle of the moral. Ethics are not some sort of knowledge which gives a content to activity, he says in opposition to Socrates. The content of the will is already given. No reflection and no knowledge can put anything new into it, or alter it.

Ethics consist, then, not in a guiding of the will by aims and objects which knowledge puts before it, but in the will's own regulation of itself. The right thing to do is to establish the correct balance between the different elements in the given contents of the will. Left to itself, the will rushes to extremes. Rational reflection keeps it in the correct middle path. Thus brought to a state of harmony, human activity can be conceived as motived and ethical. Virtue, therefore, is readiness to observe the correct mean which is to be acquired by practice.

Instead of creating an ethic, Aristotle contents himself with a doctrine of virtue. This depreciation of the ethical is the price he pays in order to reach an ethic which ends neither in the abstract nor in resignation. While he shirks the problem of the basic principle of the moral, he still remains able to establish an ethic of activity, though the latter contains indeed no live forces, only dead ones.

Aristotle's ethic is therefore an æsthetic of the impulses of the will. It consists in a catalogue of virtues and in the demonstration that they are to be conceived as a mean. Thus courage lies between rashness and cowardice, temperance between sensuality and insensibility, modesty between boastfulness and bashfulness, liberality between prodigality and avarice, high-mindedness between conceit and small-mindedness, gentleness between quarrelsomeness and characterless good-nature.

On this excursion through the field of the ethical, there open up many interesting views. In an acute and living discussion, Aristotle lets his readers survey the questions of the relations of man to his fellow-men and to society. How much that is deep and true there is in the chapter on moral excellence and in that on friendship! How he wrestles with the problem of justice!

No one can fail to feel the charm of the *Nicomachean Ethics*. There is revealed in them a noble personality with abundant experience of life, depicted with a magnificent simplicity. But just in proportion as the method followed is technically advantageous, it is valueless in itself. The ethical tries conclusions with reality without having first endeavoured to come to clear understanding of itself. It is in the course of this disputation that understanding is to be found, Aristotle thinks, but he is mistaken. His mind is seduced through his having observed that some virtues—but even these more or less under compulsion—allow themselves to be conceived as real means between two extremes, and he is misled into developing on these lines the whole of his ethical system.

But a more or less natural quality, which in ordinary speech is called a virtue, is one thing; virtue in the really ethical sense is another. The middle quality between prodigality and avarice is not the ethical virtue of liberality, but the quality of rational economy. The middle quality between rashness and cowardice is not the ethical virtue of courage, but the quality of rational prudence. The combination of two qualities only produces a single one. But virtue, in the ethical sense, means a quality guided by an ideal of self-perfection, and serviceable for some object which looks towards the universal. Liberality as an ethical virtue means a process of spending which serves some object recognized by the person practising it as valuable in principle, and serving it in such a way that any natural tendency to prodigality, should there be such in the giver, plays no part, while the tendency to avarice is paralysed.

Courage is daring to risk my life for an object I recognize as altogether valuable: the natural disposition to foolhardiness which I possibly possess plays no part in it, and natural timidity is invalidated.

Devotion of one's property or one's life to an object which is valuable in principle is under all circumstances ethical, while prodigality and avarice, rashness and cowardice, being simple qualities not inspired by any higher aim, have never any ethical character; they are merely natural. Whether the devotion of one's property or of one's life for an object valuable in principle is made more completely than need be, or exactly to the extent required by the circumstances, does not alter in any way the ethical character of the determination and the action. Such excess or defect only shows how much or how little the ethical will has allowed itself to be influenced by considerations of prudence.

Aristotle's representation, then, rests on the fact that he allows virtue in the ordinary sense and virtue in the ethical sense to get mixed up. He smuggles in the really ethical, and then offers it as the resultant of two natural qualities, each of which is an extreme.

In the chapter on temperance—in the third Book of the *Nicomachean Ethics*—he has to admit that the theory which makes the ethical a mean between two extremes cannot be completely developed. The love of beauty, he says plainly, however strong it becomes, remains what it is; there can never be any question of excess. He throws out this admission without seeing that he thereby undermines his feeble definition of the ethical as the appropriate relative mean, and, like Socrates and Plato, acknowledges that there can be something which its content allows to be reckoned as good in itself.

Aristotle is so firmly resolved not to have anything to do with the problem of the basic principle of ethics, that he will allow nothing to lead him to discuss it. He means to voyage along the coast, keep to facts, and deal with ethics as if they were a branch of natural science. Only he forgets that in science we can confine ourselves to venturing from definite given happenings through hypotheses to the nature of the Being which lies behind them, while in ethics, on the contrary, we have to establish a basic principle through the application of which we secure our happenings.

It is because he misunderstands their nature that Aristotle cannot help ethics forward. Plato goes beyond Socrates and loses himself in abstractions. Aristotle, in order to maintain the connection with reality, aims lower than Socrates. He brings together material for a monumental building, and runs up a wooden shack. Among teachers of virtue he is one of the greatest. Nevertheless, the least of those who venture on the search for the basic principle of the ethical is greater than he.

Ethical theory is no more ethics than cartilage is bone. But how strange is this inability to establish the basic principle of ethical action which Socrates regarded as from the outset the certain product of thoughtful reflection on the ethical! Why do all the ancient thinkers who in succession to Socrates search for it, always miss it? Why does Aristotle cease to concern himself with it, and so condemn himself to a doctrine of virtue in which, as a matter of fact, there is hardly any more living ethical force than there is in the abstract ethical system of Plato or in the ethics of resignation of other thinkers?

* * *

How little Plato and Aristotle are capable of establishing an ethic of action can be seen from the way in which they sketch their ideal of the civilized State. Plato develops his in the *Republic,* Aristotle his in the *Politics.* At this very time, Mencius (Meng-tse) is putting before the princes of China a doctrine of the civilized State.

That the State must be something more than a union which regulates in the most practical way the common life of a number of persons whom natural conditions compel to depend upon one another, is quite clear to both of them. They also agree in demanding that the State shall promote the true prosperity of its citizens. This is, however, unthinkable and impossible without virtue, so the State must develop into an ethical institution. "Honourable and virtuous conduct is the object at which the political community aims," is the way Aristotle puts it.

The State, evolved by history, is therefore to come under the influence of a representation of its nature as a political body which is both ethical and rational. In the *Republic* Plato puts in the mouth of Socrates the following sentiment: "Unless it happen that either philosophers acquire the kingly power in States, or those who are to-day called kings and potentates cultivate philosophy truly and sufficiently, and thus political power and philosophy become as one . . . there can be no deliverance from evil for States, nor even, I think, for the human race."

When, however, it comes to a more detailed carrying out of the ideal of the civilized State, Plato and Aristotle betray remarkable embarrassment. To begin with, their vision of the State of the future is not that of a community which embraces a whole nation, but is always just a copy of the Greek city-republic with appropriate improvements. That they think out their ideal within such narrow limits is historically intelligible, but for the development of the philosophical idea of the civilized State it is deplorable.

One result of these narrow limits is that both are anxiously concerned to provide that the well-being of the city-republic shall not be endangered by the increase of the population. The number of the inhabitants is to be kept as far as possible always near the same figure. Aristotle is not alarmed by the proposal that weakly children shall be allowed to die of hunger, and that unborn children shall be disposed of by intentional abortion. That the Spartan State, on the contrary, regards the increase of the population as desirable, and exempts a citizen from all imposts as soon as he has four children, does not seem to him reasonable.

Again, just as these two thinkers cannot rise to a general idea of a national State, so they are unable to reach the idea of mankind. They draw a strict line of division between the unfree on the one side, and the free on the other. The former they regard merely as creatures made for work, who are to maintain the material well-being of the State. What becomes of them as human beings is to them a matter of very little interest. Such beings as they, are not meant to have any share in the growth towards perfection which is to be brought about by means of the civilized State.

Slavery was, indeed, attacked now and again by the Sophists from their point of view, not, however, on the ground of humanity, but from a desire to raise doubts about the accepted justification of existing institutions. Aristotle defends it as a natural arrangement, but recommends kindly treatment.

Artisans, and in general all who earn their living by the labour of their hands, are not to be allowed to be citizens. "One cannot practise virtue, if one leads the life of an artisan, or of one who labours for wages," says Aristotle. An ethical valuation of labour as such is still a thing unknown to him, even though he conceives of happiness as "activity in accordance with the law of excellence." Plato and he are still entirely under the influence of the ancient opinion that only the "free" man can have full value as a man.

In details of the ideal of the State, however, the two part company, and Aristotle argues against Plato. Unfortunately, just those parts of the *Politics* in which he sketches his ideal State have not come down to us complete. The main difference is that Aristotle keeps closer than Plato to the historically given. He builds his State upon the family; Plato makes the State into a family. In his *Republic* the free men live with property, wives, and children owned in common. They are to possess nothing as their own, so that they may not by private interests be held back from working for the general welfare. Moreover, the general welfare allows the State to breed its citizens systematically. He prescribes the connections which men and women are to form, and permits only such as allow the expectation of a new generation which is sound both in body and mind. The offspring of unions not approved by the authorities are either to be killed before birth, or removed from the world by starvation.

Aristotle contents himself with guaranteeing the quality of the offspring by legal regulation of the age for marriage. Women may marry at eighteen, men not till they are thirty-seven. Moreover, marriages are to take place preferably in winter, and as far as possible, when the wind is in the north.

In what, then, does the good consist which is to be realized by the civilized State? To this decisive question Aristotle and Plato have in reality only the answer that it is meant to make it possible for a number of its members, namely the "free" men, released from material cares, to devote themselves entirely to their own bodily and mental culture, and to take the lead in public affairs. The State is not established with a view to the production of anything ethical in any deeper sense, nor for the sake of an ideal of progress on lines which could be described as great and noble. Nowhere do the characteristic limitations of ancient ethics reveal themselves so clearly as in the inadequacy of the ideal of the State.

The ethical valuation of man as man has not yet been reached. Hence the State has for its object, not the growth to perfection of all, but only that of a particular class.

The nation, too, is not yet recognized as a great natural and ethical entity, and therefore no consideration is given to the question of uniting the various city communities for the joint pursuit of higher objects. Each remains isolated. Plato thinks he has satisfied the claims arising from membership of the same nation by requiring that in wars waged by Greek cities against one another the houses shall not be destroyed nor the fields laid waste, as would be done if the war were against barbarians.

The idea of humanity as a whole has not yet come in sight. It is, therefore, not possible for Plato and Aristotle to make their State work in co-operation with others to promote the general progress of mankind.

So they establish their civilized State on a political organism which is hemmed in in every direction by narrow horizons. Moreover, the political community which they adopt as the typical State at the very time when they are writing is already a dying entity. While Aristotle is writing the *Politics,* his pupil, Alexander the Great, is founding an empire, and Rome is beginning to subject Italy to her rule.

More important still than all external faults in their ideal of the civilized State, is the fact that these two thinkers are unable to introduce into the community the energies which are needed for its maintenance. The idea of the civilized State is present with the vitality needed only when the individual is by the impulse contained in his world-view moved so far as to devote himself to organized society with enthusiastic activity. Without civic idealism no civilized State! But to assume anything of that kind in the members of their State is impossible for Plato and Aristotle, since both have already arrived at the ideal of the wise man who withdraws himself prudently and gracefully from the world.

Plato admits this. His wise citizens who are destined to be rulers devote themselves to the service of the State only when their turn comes, and are glad when they are relieved and in retirement can once more concern themselves, as wise men among wise men, with the world of pure Being.

When Aristotle raises in the *Politics* the question whether the contemplative life is not to be preferred to that of political activity, he decides in theory in favor of the latter. "It is a mistake," he says, "to value inactivity higher than activity, since happiness consists in activity." But in the doctrine of virtue in the *Nicomachean Ethics* there is nothing which could lead the individual to place his life at the service of the community.

Plato and Aristotle undoubtedly cherish the ancient conviction that the individual ought to devote himself to the State, but they cannot find a foundation for it in their philosophy. Like Epicurus and the adherents of the Porch, they are under the spell of an ethic in which there is present no will to attempt a transformation of the world.

How much greater than the two Greeks is Meng-tse (Mencius), when he is thinking out the ideal of the civilized State! He can make it as large as he likes and take men into its service with their best thoughts, because it results in the most natural way from a large-scale philosophy of ethical activity.

Plato and Aristotle, lacking such a world-view, can do no more than guess at the nature of a civilized State, and invent one for themselves. Plato's *Republic* is a mere curiosity. Aristotle's *Politics* is valuable, not on account of the theory of the civilized State which is there presented, but only for his magnificent practical analysis of the advantages and disadvantages of the various State-constitutions, and of their economic problems.

The decadence of antiquity does not begin, then, with the suppression of the individual by the Empire, and its destruction of the normal mutual relations between the individual and the community. It sets in immediately after Socrates, because the ethical thinking which started with him cannot really lead the individual beyond himself, and set him as an effective force in the service of the moralization and the perfecting of social relations.

There is no middle term between the ethic of enthusiasm and the ethic of resignation. But an ethic of resignation cannot think out, much less bring into existence, a system of social relations which can be called really civilized.

*   *   *

"In imperial times Stoicism shrivels up into a moralizing popular philosophy" is what we are usually told in works on ancient philosophy. As a matter of fact there is by no means a shrivelling up, but a serious struggle for a living ethic which begins unexpectedly in the later period of Græco-Roman thought, and leads to an optimistic-ethical nature-philosophy.

The pillars of this movement are L. Annæus Seneca (4 B.C. –A.D. 65), Nero's teacher, who at the command of his pupil had to open his veins; the Phrygian slave, Epictetus (born *c.* A.D. 50), who in A.D. 94 was banished from Rome by Domitian with all the other philosophers; the Emperor Marcus Aurelius (A.D. 121–180) who, brought up by pupils of Epictetus, defended the Empire at a time of great danger, and wrote his philosophical *Meditations* in camp.[5]

In their classical period Greek ethics offer us either egoistic considerations of advantage, or cold doctrines of virtue, or ascetic renunciation of the world, or resignation. In whichever direction they turn, they never really lead men out beyond themselves.

In Seneca, Epictetus, and Marcus Aurelius, ethics lose this self-regarding character. Renouncing the spirit of the earlier time, they develop to an ethic of universal brotherhood, and are concerned with the direct, altruistic relations of man to man.

Whence comes this understanding for humanity, which is never seen in classical antiquity?

The older Greek moralists are concerned with the State. Their interest is absorbed in the maintenance of the organization of society which is embodied in the city-republic, so that the free citizens can continue to live the life of freedom. The type of complete manhood is to be realized. All around are toiling men who receive no consideration except in so far as they are means to this end.

But amid the mighty political and social revolutions which lead to the creation of the Empire, this mentality ceases to be accepted as a matter of course. The fearful experiences it goes through cause feeling to become more humane, and the horizons of ethics are widened. The city-republic, on which ethical thinking had been focused, has disappeared, but an empire now oppresses the lives of all men alike. Thus the individual man as such becomes the object of reflection and of ethics. The concep-

[5] Of Seneca quite a series of ethical treatises have come down to us. We mention here: *On Clemency (De Clementia,* addressed to Nero); *On Benefits (De Beneficiis); On Tranquillity of Soul (De Tranquillitate Animi); On Anger (De Ira).*

Our knowledge of the teachings of Epictetus we owe to his pupil, Flavius Arrianus, the historian. The latter has recorded a number of his master's lectures in eight books, of which four have survived. In addition to these he collected and published a number of his sayings on morality in the *Enchiridion.*

In the popular philosophizings of Cicero (106–43 B.C.) as well, we can see an attempt to produce a new ethic which is really living.

tion of the brotherhood of all men appears. A disposition to humanity makes itself heard, and Seneca condemns the gladiatorial shows. Nay more: even the inner relationship between mankind and the animal world is recognized.

So now, when mankind as a whole and man as such have come into view, ethics reach such a depth and breadth as allows them to be comprehended in a universal world-will. Henceforth nature-philosophy and ethics can work together. Stoicism from the very beginning had a vision of this, but had not been able to make it a reality, since it had not at its disposal the living and universal ethic which was needed.

But there is another reason why optimism and ethics can now in nature-philosophy come into power. The old school of the Porch was crushed down into resignation just in proportion as it submitted to the necessity for critical thinking. But as time goes on, the practical and religious instincts which were always present in its world-view, gain in strength. The antiquity which is passing away is no longer critical, but either sceptical or religious, and therefore the later school of the Porch can submit it to the guidance of the ethical demands of its world-view much more completely than could the old one. It becomes at once deeper and more simple than the latter, and, like Chinese ethical monism, rises to such freedom from limitations as to be able to interpret the world-will as ethical. So now Stoics appear who, like Confucius, like Mencius, and like Chwang-tse, and indeed, like the Rationalists of the eighteenth century, preach ethics as grounded in the nature of the universe and the nature of mankind. They cannot prove the truth of this world-view any better than could Zeno and his pupils, who also resorted to it, but they announce it with an inner conviction which these could not command, and produce their results by means of an enthusiasm which was denied to their predecessors.

When the later school of the Porch reaches the stage of exalting the world-principle more and more to the status of a personal and ethical god, it is following laws which are at work also in Hinduism.

Yet it never succeeds in rendering entirely impotent the world-view of resignation, which it had inherited from the older school. In Seneca and Epictetus this is still strongly maintained side by side with the ethical conception of the universe. It is only in Marcus Aurelius that the optimistic motives victoriously ring out.

Stoicism was from the beginning a multiform elemental philosophy, and it is because it ventured to be this in such comprehensive measure that the Later Stoicism is so rich and so full of life.

Moral Sayings of Seneca

No man is nobler than his fellow, even if it happen that his spiritual nature is better constituted and he is more capable of higher learning. The world is the one mother of us all, and the ultimate origin of each one of us can be traced back to her, whether the steps in the ladder of descent be noble or humble. To no one is virtue forbidden; she is accessible to all; she admits everyone, she invites everyone in: free men and freedmen, slaves, kings, and exiles. She regards neither birth nor fortune; the man alone is all she wants.

It is a mistake to think that the status of a slave affects the whole of a person's nature; the nobler part of it is not touched thereby.

Every single person, even if there is nothing else to recommend him, I must hold in regard, because he bears the name of man.

In the treatment of a slave we have to consider not how much we can do to him without being liable to punishment, but how much the nature of right and of justice allows us to do, seeing that these bid us treat gently even prisoners and purchased slaves. Although in the treatment of a slave everything is allowed, there is nevertheless something which through the common right of every living being is stigmatized as not permissible in the treatment of a man, because he is of the same nature as thyself.

This, in fact, is the demand which is laid upon each man, namely that he works, when possible, for the welfare of many; if that is impracticable, that he works for the welfare of a few; failing that, for the welfare of his neighbours, and if that is impossible, for his own.

It is through untiring benevolence that the bad are won over, and there is no disposition so hard and so hostile to loving treatment . . . as to refuse love to the good people whom it will in the end have to thank again for something more. "Not a word of thanks did I get! What am I now to begin to do?" What the gods do, . . . who begin to shower benefits on us before we are aware of it, and continue them even though we do not thank them.

Moral Sayings of Epictetus

Nature is wonderful, and full of love for all creatures.

Wait upon God, ye men. When He calls you, and releases you from service, then go to Him; but for the present remain quietly in the position in which He has placed you.

You carry a god about with you, and do not know it, unhappy one! You have him within yourself, and do not notice it when you defile him with unclean thoughts or foul deeds.

Cultivate the will to satisfy yourself, and to stand right before God. Strive to become pure, one with yourself and one with God.

Think silence best; say only what is necessary, and say it shortly. Above all, do not talk about thy fellow-men, either to praise them, or to blame them, or to compare them with others. Do not swear; never, if possible, or at any rate as seldom as possible. Your bodily wants—food, drink, clothing, housing, service—satisfy in the simplest way. Avoid unseemly joking, for there is always a danger of becoming vulgar, and joking away the respect of your fellow-men.

As you are careful when walking not to tread on a nail or to sprain your ankle, so take care not to let your soul get hurt.

Moral Sayings from the Meditations *of Marcus Aurelius*

Everything that happens, happens right, and if you can observe things carefully, you will recognize that it is so. I do not mean only in accordance with the course of nature, but much more that they happen in accordance with the law of righteousness, and as if controlled by a Being who orders all things according to merit.

If I am active, I am so with due regard to the general welfare. If anything happens to me, I accept it and consider it in relation to the gods and the universal source from which, in close connection, come all our happenings.

He who commits unrighteousness is godless, for universal nature created rational beings for one another; to help each other where there is need, but never to injure one another.

Love mankind; obey the godhead.

If thou art unwilling to get up in the morning, reflect thus: I am waking in order to go and work as a man.

Seek all thy joy and contentment in advancing, mindful always of God, from one generally useful deed to another.

The best way to avenge oneself on anyone is to avoid returning evil for evil.

It is a privilege of man to love even those who do him wrong. One can reach this level by reflecting that all men are of one family with oneself; that their shortcomings are due to ignorance, and against their will; that in a short time both of you will be dead.

What is good is necessarily useful, and that is why the good and noble man must be concerned about it.

Nobody gets tired of seeking his own advantage. But doing so procures us an activity which is natural. Never get tired, then, of seeking thine own advantage, provided thou procurest thus the advantage of others also.

Treat as befits a man endowed with reason, that is magnanimously and nobly, the animals which are not so endowed, and indeed all creatures whatever that can feel but have no reason. But other men, since they are endowed with reason, treat with friendly affection.

Thou has existed till now as a fragment of the universe, and wilt some day be absorbed in thy creator, or rather, thou wilt suffer a transformation and reappear as a new germ of life.

Many grains of incense are destined for the same altar. Some fall soon into the flame, others later, but that makes no difference.

*   *   *

In their optimistic-ethical world-view the Later Stoics find those impulses to effort which were not available for the ancient ethics of the classical age. Marcus Aurelius is an enthusiastic utilitarian like the Rationalists of the eighteenth century, because, like them, he is convinced that nature itself has bound up together what is ethical and what is advantageous both to the individual and to the community.

That being so, the classical question of ancient ethics, whether the thinking man is to busy himself with public affairs or not must again be discussed. Epicurus taught that "the wise man has nothing to do with State affairs unless exceptional circumstances arise." Zeno's decision was that "he will take part in the business of the State unless obstacles prevent it." Both schools leave the retirement into oneself to the decision of the wise man, only one lets the grounds for the decision be given somewhat earlier, the other somewhat later. The thought of a devotion to the general good which is to be kept active for its own sake and under all circumstances is beyond the horizon of their ethic.

With the Later Stoics it emerges, because the conception of "mankind" has come in sight. Man, as Seneca works out in his treatise on Leisure (*De Otio*), belongs to two republics. One is large and universal, extends as far as the sun shines, and embraces both gods and men; the other is that into which through the fate assigned us by our birth, we have been adopted as citizens. Circumstances may bring it about that the wise man cannot dedicate himself to the service of the State, but, to escape the storm, must "take refuge in the harbour." It may happen—and Seneca has in mind his own time—that not one of the existing States is of such a character as to tolerate the activity of the wise man. Nevertheless, the latter does not wholly withdraw into himself, but serves the great republic by working to improve the general outlook of mankind and hasten the coming of a new age.

In Epictetus also this deepened and widened conception of duty is to be found. Marcus Aurelius does not even consider that it might be impossible to take part in public life. In him there speaks the ruler who feels himself to be the servant of the State. His ideal is the citizen who "from one activity which makes his fellow-citizens happier goes on to another, and undertakes with alacrity anything whatever that the State lays upon him." "Do what is needed, and what is bidden by the reason of a being who is destined by nature to membership of a State, and do it as it is bidden."

In the middle of the second century A.D. ancient thought arrives at an optimistic-ethical world-view which offers living ideals of civilization, and therefore anticipates that which later on in the eighteenth century will bring into activity so mighty and universal a movement of civilization. But for the men of the Græco-Roman world it comes too late. It does not permeate the masses, but remains the private possession of an *élite*.

It cannot permeate the masses, because there are forces at work among them with which it cannot combine. It is true, indeed, that the ethic of the later Stoicism is so near akin to the universal charity of the Christian ethic, that by the tradition of later times Seneca is declared to be a Christian, and that the

Church father, Augustine, holds up the life of the heathen emperor, Marcus Aurelius, as an example for Christians.

Yet the two movements cannot amalgamate, but have to oppose each other. Marcus Aurelius is responsible for most terrible persecutions of Christians, and Christianity on its side declares war to the death against the Porch.

Why this strange fatality? Because Christianity is dualistic and pessimistic, whilst the ethic of Stoicism is monistic and optimistic. Christianity abandons the natural world as evil, the later Stoics idealize it. It helps not at all that their ethical teaching is almost identical. Each appears as part of a philosophy which is irreconcilable with that of the other. All contradictions in the world may be concealed, but not that between two world-views, and the struggle ends with the annihilation of the optimistic-ethical philosophy of the Stoics, which is defended by officers without an army. The attempt that was undertaken as the ancient world was coming to an end, to restore the Empire and make it embrace the whole of mankind, was a failure.

The horizons of the philosophy of the ancient world had remained narrow too long. No ethical thinkers had appeared who at the right time might have led that world to an ethical optimism about reality. It was a calamity, too, that the natural sciences, which had made such a promising start, came to a standstill, partly through the fault of fate, partly because philosophy turned away from them, before mankind discovered the laws governing the forces of nature, and thereby obtained control over them. Hence the men of antiquity never acquired that self-consciousness which in their descendants of modern times has kept alive, even through the darkest periods of history, the belief in progress—even though it be sometimes progress of the most superficial kind. This psychological factor is of great importance.

It is true that artistic ability, which in the Greek spirit meets us in such abundant measure, is also control over the material, but this creative power was unable to draw the man of antiquity up to a higher life-affirmation and to belief in progress. It served only to let him express himself, in words and in form, in the antagonism between unsophisticated world- and life-affirmation, and reflective world- and life-negation. It is the mysterious intermixture of serenity and melancholy which constitutes the tragic charm of Hellenic art.

From every point of view, vigorous ethical world- and life-affirmation is made difficult for the ancient world. That is why it falls more and more a prey to pessimistic conceptions of the universe, which draw its thoughts away from reality, and celebrate the liberation of the spiritual from its bondage to the material in a succession of cosmic dramas. Gnosticism, Oriental and Christian, Neo-Pythagoreanism, which arose as early as the first century B.C., the Neo-Platonism which originated with Plotinus (A.D. 204–269), and the great Mystery-religions, all come to meet the religious, world-shunning disposition of the masses during the break-up of antiquity, and offer it that deliverance from the world of which it is in search. In this chaos of ideas Christianity emerges victorious because it is the most robust religion of redemption, because as a community it possesses the strongest organization, and because beneath its pessimistic world-view it has at its disposal living ethical ideas.

The optimistic-ethical monism of the later Stoics is like a sunbeam breaking through in the evening of the long, gloomy day of antiquity while the darkness of the middle ages is already drawing on, but it has no power to waken any civilization to life. The time for that is past. The spirit of antiquity, having failed to reach an ethical nature-philosophy, has become the prey of a pessimistic dualism in which no ethic of action is any longer possible; there can only be an ethic of purification.

The thoughts of Seneca, Epictetus, and Marcus Aurelius are the winter seed of a coming civilization.

Chapter II

OPTIMISTIC WORLD-VIEW

AND ETHICS IN THE RENAISSANCE

AND POST-RENAISSANCE PERIODS

Belief in progress and ethics.

Christian and Stoic elements in modern ethics.

THE ESSENTIAL CHARACTERISTIC OF THE MODERN AGE IS THAT IT thinks and acts in the spirit of a world- and life-affirmation which has never before appeared in such active strength.

This world-view breaks through in the Renaissance, beginning at the end of the fourteenth century, and it arises as a protest against the mediæval enslavement of the human spirit. The movement is helped to victory by the increasing knowledge of Greek philosophy in its original form, which is the result of the migration to Italy about the middle of the fifteenth century of learned Greeks from Constantinople. Among the thinking men of that time there arises the belief that philosophy must be something more elemental and more living than Scholasticism taught.

But the thought of antiquity would not have been sufficient by itself to keep alive this new world- and life-affirmation which appealed to it as a precedent. It had not, in truth, the mentality required. But another kind of fuel is in time brought for the fire. Taking refuge from book-learning in nature, the men of that time discover the world. As mariners they reach countries whose very existence was not suspected, and they measure the size of the earth. As inquirers they press on into the infinite and the secrets of the universe, and learn by experience that forces governed by uniform laws are at work, and that man has power to make them serviceable to himself. The knowledge and power won by Leonardo da Vinci (1452–1519), Corpernicus (1473–1543), Kepler (1571–1630), Galileo (1564–1642), and others are decisive for the current world-view.

As a movement which draws its life solely from spiritual forces, the Renaissance passes its blossoming-time comparatively quickly, and without forming much fruit. With Paracelsus (1493–1541), Bernardino Telesio (1508–1588), Giordano Bruno (1548–1600), and others, an enthusiastic nature-philosophy is announced. But it does not reach full growth. The Renaissance has not strength enough to bring to birth a world- and life-affirming philosophy which can rise to the height of these men's intellects. Here and there their thought surges for a time, like a rough sea, against the world-denying philosophy of the Church. Then all is still. What we know definitely as the philosophy of modern times begins almost without any reference to the Renaissance. It springs, not from any nature-philosophy, but from the problem of the theory of knowledge which was raised by Descartes, and from that starting-point philosophy has once more had laboriously to seek its way to a nature-philosophy.

It is not, then, because it was enlarged during the Renaissance into a fully thought out theory of the universe that world- and life-affirmation made good its position in the modern age. If it was able to hold out right into the eighteenth century, when it triumphs against the world- and life-negation which mediæval thought and Christianity kept in action in opposition to it, it owed this to the circumstance that progress in knowledge and power never ceased. In them the new mentality had a support which never wavered, but became continually stronger. Since the new scientific knowledge cannot be suppressed nor its progress arrested, belief in the sovereignty of truth becomes firmly established. Since it becomes more and more evident that nature works with a uniformity which never misses its aim, there grows up a confidence that the circumstances of society and of mankind can also be so organized as to secure definite objects. Since man is ever obtaining greater power over nature, he takes it more and more as self-evident that the reaching of perfection in other spheres is only a question of a sufficiency of will-power and a no less correct method of grappling with problems.

Under the steadily active influence of the new mentality, the world-view of Christianity changes, and becomes leavened with the yeast of world- and life-affirmation. It gradually begins to be accepted as self-evident that the spirit of Jesus does not renounce the world, but aims at transforming it. The early Christain conception of the Kingdom of God, which was born of pessimism and, thanks to Augustine, prevailed through the Middle Ages, is rendered impotent, and its place is taken by a conception which is the offspring of modern optimism. This new orientation of the Christian world-view, which is accomplished by a slow and often interrupted process of change between the fifteenth century and the end of the eighteenth, is the decisive spiritual event of the modern age. During this period Christianity takes no account of what is happening to itself. It believes that it is remaining unaltered, whereas in reality, by this change from pessimism to optimism, it is surrendering its original character.

The modern man, then, becomes optimistic, not because deepened thought has made him understand the world in the sense of world- and life-affirmation, but because discovery and invention have given him power over the world. This enhancement of his self-reliance and the consequent strengthening of his will and his hopes, determine his will-to-live in a correspondingly pronounced and positive sense.

In the ancient world, man's natural disposition to world- and life-affirmation could not be worked out to a complete world-view, because at that time deep thought about the world and life pressed resignation upon him as a necessity of thought. In the man of the modern age the mentality produced by discovery and invention unites with his natural disposition to world- and life-affirmation, and establishes him in an optimistic world-view without leading him to deeper thought about the world and life.

The spirit of the modern age is not the work of any one great thinker. It wins its way gradually by reason of the unbroken series of triumphs won by discovery and invention. Hence it is not a result of chance that an almost unphilosophic and more-over somewhat worm-eaten personality like Francis Bacon, Lord Verulam (1561–1626), is the man who drafts the programme of the modern world-view. He founds it upon the sentence: "Knowledge is power." He develops his picture of the future in his *New Atlantis,* in which he describes how the inhabitants of an island, through the practical application of all known discoveries and inventions and all possible rational reflection on the purposive organization of society, find themselves in a position to lead the happiest possible lives.[1]

*   *   *

What is the relation between ethics and the mentality of belief in progress, and how were ethics influenced by this belief?

When the ethical thought of antiquity wanted to come to clearness about itself, it fell a victim to resignation, because it tried to determine the moral as that which is rationally profitable and pleasurable to the individual. It remained shut up within the circle of the egoistic, and never reached the idea of social utilitarianism. From such a fate modern ethics are protected in advance. They have no need to produce from their own resources the thought that the ethical is action directed to promoting the welfare of others, for they find it already accepted as true. That is the gift of Christianity. The thought of Jesus that the ethical is the individual's active self-devotion to others has won its way to acceptance. Ethics, whilst becoming independent of religion, as a result of their passage through Christianity, retain a pronouncedly active and altruistic mode of thought. All they have to do is to provide this possession with a rational foundation.

It is extraordinarily significant that in the Later Stoicism there comes to meet modern ethics a philosophical ethical system in which, as the result of rational thinking, there appear thoughts which closely approach Christian morality. There is now coming up for the benefit of modern times the seed sown

1 Bacon was Lord Chancellor under James I. of England, but was in 1621 deprived of his office because found guilty of corruption. His two chief works are the *Novum Organum Scientiarum* (1620) and *De Dignitate et Augmentis Scientiarum* (1623). Of the *New Atlantis* only a fragment has survived.

by Seneca, Epictetus, and Marcus Aurelius. Cicero, too, counts for so much, because modern thinkers find in his writings noble morality based upon thought. The discovery of Late Stoicism's ethic of humanity is for them as important as their discovery of nature. They identify it with the true Christian ethic, and contrast it with the scholastic ethic, in which Jesus is expounded according to Aristotle. It is through Late Stoicism that modern times become aware of morality as an independent value. Because Seneca, Epictetus, and Marcus Aurelius speak to such an extent just as Jesus did, they help to spread the conviction that the truly rational ethic and the ethic of the Gospels coincide with one another.

By the time antiquity came to an end, Late Stoicism and Christianity, in spite of the identity of their moral teaching, had torn each other to pieces. In modern times they unite to produce together an ethical outlook on life. Why is it that now possible which before was impossible? Because the chasm which lay between their respective world-views has been bridged. Christianity now treats world- and life-affirmation as valid.

But how could this volte-face of Christianity be brought about? Because of the fact that in spite of its pessimistic world-view it upholds an ethic which, so far as it touches the relation of man to man, is activist. The pessimistic world-view, if it is thought out to a consistent conclusion, must end as in Indian philosophy with a purely world-denying ethic, divorced from action. The unique character, however, of the world-view of Jesus, which is determined by the expectation of the end of the world and the coming of a supernatural kingdom of God, and the directness of his ethical feeling, entail that, in spite of his pessimistic attitude towards the natural world, he proclaims an ethic of active devotion to one's neighbour. This activist ethic is what is wanted to provide the cardinal-point of an evolution from a Christian-pessimistic to a Christian-optimistic philosophy. The modern age, following its instinct, assumes as self-evident that an ethic which deals with the active relations of man to man is pre-supposed to be an ethic which assigns a positive value to action as such, and, further, that such an ethic of action belongs to a world-view which is optimistic and which wills and hopes for a purposive reorganization of relationships.

It is, then, the ethic of active self-devotion taught by Jesus which makes it possible for Christianity, inspired by the spirit of the modern age, to modulate from the pessimistic to the optimistic world-view. This result finds expression in the way the new conception of Christianity, when it has to come to an understanding with the old, rebels against "the Christianity of dogma" under the banner of "the religion of Jesus."

A way is prepared in Erasmus and individual representatives of the Reformation, shyly at first but then more and more clearly, for an interpretation of the teaching of Jesus which corresponds to the spirit of modern times, an interpretation which conceives the teaching as a religion of action in the world. Historically and in actual fact this is a wrong interpretation, for the world-view of Jesus is thoroughly pessimistic so far as concerns the future of the natural world. His religion is not a religion of world-transforming effort, but the religion of awaiting the end of the world. His ethic is characterized by activity only so far as it commands men to practise unbounded devotion to their fellow-men, if they would attain to that inner perfection which is needed for entrance into the supernatural kingdom of God. An ethic of enthusiasm, seemingly focused upon an optimistic world-view, forms part of a pessimistic world-view! That is the magnificent paradox in the teaching of Jesus.

But the modern age was right in overlooking this paradox, and assuming in Jesus an optimistic world-view which corresponded to an ethic of enthusiasm and met with a welcome the spirit of Late Stoicism and that of modern times. For the progress of the spiritual life of Europe this mistake was a necessity. What crises the latter must have gone through, if it had not been able without embarrassment to place the new outlook on the universe under the authority of the great personality of Jesus!

The mistake was such a natural one that till the end of the nineteenth century it was never seriously shaken. When historical criticism, at the beginning of the twentieth century, proclaimed its discovery that Jesus, in spite if his activist ethic, thought and acted under the influence of a pessimistic world-view dominated by the expectation of the end of the world, it aroused indignation. It was accused of degrading Jesus to a mere enthusiast, while after all it was only putting an end to the false modernizing of his personality.[2] What we at the present time have to do is to go through the critical experience of being obliged to think as modern men with a world-view of world- and life-affirmation, and yet let the ethic of Jesus speak to us from out of a pessimistic world-view.

Of this problem, which is disclosing itself to-day, the early period of the modern age suspects nothing. Jesus and the moralists of Late Stoicism together are its authorities for an ethical world- and life-affirmation.

What the Late-Stoic ethic is for the modern age is shown by Erasmus of Rotterdam (1466–1536), Michel de Montaigne (1533–1592), Pierre Charron (1541–1603), Jean Bodin (1530–1596), and Hugo Grotius (1583–1645), and that whether their ideas run predominantly on Christian or on freethinking lines. To the Later Stoics Erasmus owes it that he can understand the simple gospel of Jesus, discovered behind the dogmas of the Church, as the essence of all ethical philosophizing. It is by finding support in them that Montaigne in his *Essays* (1580) is saved from falling into complete ethical scepticism. Because he is inspired by the Later Stoics, Bodin in his work *De la république* (1577), puts forward an ethical ideal of the State to combat the ideas of Machiavelli's *Principe* (1515). Because he draws from the same source, Pierre Charron in his work *De la sagesse* (1601), ventures to assert that ethics are higher than revealed religion, and can maintain themselves in an independent position in face of it without losing anything of their essential nature or of their depth. Because the work of Marcus Aurelius has preceded him, Hugo Grotius is able in his famous work, *De jure belli ac pacis* (1625) to lay so securely the foundations of natural and international law, and thereby to champion the claims of reason and humanity in the domain of jurisprudence.

Other considerations apart, it would have been the first task of the rising power of natural science to restore to currency the

[2] See the writer's books: *Das Messianitats- und Leidensgeheimniss–Eine Skizze des Lebens Jesu* (1901). English version: *The Mystery of the Kingdom of God* (1914 A. & C. Black). *Geschichte der Leben-Jesu Forschung* (1906; new edition, 1922). English version: *The Quest of the Historical Jesus* (1911; 3rd impression, 1922, A. & C. Black).

world-view of Epicurus. Pierre Gassendi (1592–1655) [3] attempts it but fails to accomplish his purpose. By its inward belief in progress the mentality of the modern age is driven in elemental fashion beyond scepticism and sceptical ethics. What is great in Epicurus, namely that in obedience to the deepest demands of truth he tries to think ethically within a nature-philosophy which does not interpret nature as embodying any purpose, can neither be comprehended nor be put before his own age by the philosopher's all too clever modern prophet.

For the weighty questions of absolute truth, that time is by no means ripe. Its capacity is only that of the uncritical. Typical for its spirit is Isaac Newton (1643–1727), who in his investigation of nature is purely empirical, and in his world-view remains simply Christian.

Against the difficulties which crop up for ethics and world- and life-affirmation from a nature-philosophy which works without any presuppositions, the Renaissance and the Post-Renaissance are secure. The belief in progress which arises from the achievements of discovery and invention, and the joy felt in action itself constitute their philosophy of life.

Thanks to belief in progress, new life streams into ethics. The inner relations between ethics and world- and life-affirmation begin to take effect. The elementary impulses to activity which are embodied in the Christian ethic are set free, and belief in progress gives them an aim: the transformation of the circumstances of society and of mankind.

It is not any really deeper ethical thinking that brings on the modern age, but the influence exerted by the belief in progress, which arose out of the achievements of discovery and invention, on the ethic which drew its life from Stoic and Christian thought. The cart is drawn by the belief in progress, and at first ethics have only to run along beside it. But as the cart gets heavier and the road more difficult, so that ethics ought to lend their strength to help, they refuse, because they have no strength of their own. The cart begins to run backward, and carries belief in progress, and ethics with it, down the hill.

The task before philosophy was to change the world- and

3 Gassendi: *De vita, moribus, et doctrina Epicuri* (1647) and *Syntagma philosophiæ Epicuri* (1649).

life-affirmation which arose from enthusiasm over the attainments of discovery and invention into a deeper, inner world- and life-affirmation arising out of thought about the universe and the life of man, and on that same foundation to build up an ethical system. But philosophy could do neither.

About the middle of the nineteenth century, when it has become perfectly clear that we are living with a world- and life-affirmation which has its source merely in our confidence in discovery and invention and not in any profounder thought about the world and life, our fate is sealed. The modern optimistic-ethical world-view, after doing so much for the material development of civilization, has to collapse like a building erected already to a considerable height but on rotten foundations.

Chapter 12

LAYING THE FOUNDATION OF ETHICS IN THE

SEVENTEENTH AND EIGHTEENTH CENTURIES

Hartley, Holbach. Devotion as enlightened egoism.

Hobbes, Locke, Helvetius, Bentham.

Altruism as a natural quality. Hume, Adam Smith.

The English ethic of self-perfecting.

Shaftesbury. An optimistic-ethical nature-philosophy.

THE MODERN AGE FINDS WORLD- AND LIFE-AFFIRMATION SO SELF-evident that it feels no need to give them a sure foundation and deepen them by thought about the world and life. It brushes pessimism aside as reactionary folly, without suspecting how deep down into thought it has sent its roots.

But it does see the necessity of establishing the nature of the ethical. How does it proceed to do this?

That the ethical means action directed to promoting the common good is its firm belief from the first, and it is safe from the fate of ancient thought, that is to say, sticking fast in the mud of resignation while trying to give the ethical a proper foundation. Instead of that it has to answer the question how the unegoistic makes its appearance beside the egoistic, and in what inner relation they stand to each other.

Now begins a process like that which went on after the appearance of Socrates, only the task is proposed this time, not by an individual, but by the spirit of the time. Another attempt is made to consider the ethical problem in isolation, as if it consisted in reflections on the relation of the individual to himself and to society, these having no need to settle their position with regard to ultimate questions of the meaning of the world and of life. The ethical problem seems, too, to be much simpler than it was, because world-affirmation and activity directed toward the general welfare no longer have to be proved, but appear among the hypotheses which are taken for granted.

There are three ways in which the relations between the egoistic and the altruistic can be made clear. Either one assumes that the egoistic in the thought of the individual is automatically converted into the altruistic by consistent meditation. Or one supposes the altruistic to have its beginning in the thought of society and thence to pass over into the convictions of the individual. Or one retires to the position that egoism and altruism are both among the original endowments of human nature. All three explanations are attempted, each with most varied arguments. They are not always carried to a conclusion without intermixture, and with many thinkers there is interplay of one with another.

The attempt to deduce devotion to the common welfare from egoism by psychological considerations is made with the greatest consciousness of the end in view by David Hartley (1705–1757) [1] and Dietrich von Holbach (1723–1789).[2]

Hartley, a theologian who betook himself to the practice of medicine, claims to see in altruism a purposive ennoblement of original selfishness which comes into play under the influence of rational thought. The much-reviled Holbach ascribes its origin to the fact that the individual, if he rightly understands his own interest, will always form his conception of it in connection with the interest of society, and will therefore direct his activities to the latter as well.

Both attempt to erect their building, so far as it goes, with materialistic considerations and then proceed to roof it with idealistic views. But neither with the coarser nor with the finer considerations, nor with both together, can the psychological

---

[1] D. Hartley: *Observations on Man, his Frame, his Duty, and his Expectations* (1749; 6th ed., 1834).

[2] D. von Holbach: *Systéme de la nature ou des lois du monde physique et du monde moral* (1770).

derivation of altruism from egoism produce any convincing result.

The coarser ones do not carry us very far. It is acknowledged, of course, that the prosperity of society depends upon the moral disposition of its members, and that the better the moral condition of society the better is the individual's expectation of prosperity. But it does not follow that the individual becomes more moral the better he understands his own interests. The mutual relation between him and society is not of such a character that he derives benefit from the latter just in proportion as he himself by his moral conduct helps to establish its prosperity. If the majority of its members, with short-sighted egoism, are intent only on their own good, then the man who acts with wider outlook makes sacrifices from which there is no prospect of gain for himself, even if the best happens and they are not lost without benefiting the community. If, on the other hand, through the moral conduct of the majority of its members the condition of society is favourable, the individual profits by it, even if he fails to behave towards it as morality demands. By conduct which disregards both past and future, he will carve for himself an unduly big share of personal prosperity out of the prosperity of the community, milking the cow which the rest provide with fodder. The influence of the individual on the prosperity of the community, and the reaction of social prosperity on that of the individual, do not stand in a simple reciprocal relationship to each other. The consideration, therefore, that egoism, rightly understood, will oblige the individual to resolve on activity which is directed to promoting the common good, is a ship which sails well, but leaks.

The psychological derivation of altruism from egoism must, in some way or other, make an appeal to the self-sacrifice of the individual. This it does by inducing him to consider that in happiness there is a spiritual as well as a material element. Man needs not only external prosperity, but to be respected by others and to be satisfied with himself, and he can have this double experience only when he concerns himself about the prosperity of others. Even Holbach, who tries to be inexorably matter-of-fact, lets these considerations raise their voices.

The attempt is made, therefore, to modulate into the spiritualized conception of happiness above the prolonged bass note of that conception which is derived from ordinary egoism.

The path which this attempt has to follow runs parallel to that which led the successors of Socrates into the abyss of the paradoxical. In order to get from egoism into altruism, and so think out to a conclusion the ethic of the rationally-pleasurable, the Epicureans wished to use the same scale of values for spiritual and material pleasure alike. The only result was that their ethic was transformed into resignation. Now again, in the modern age, and again for the sake of ethics, spiritual happiness is to be regarded as happiness in the same way as is material happiness. Here again the result is a paradox.

Material and spiritual happiness are not so related that the one can find its continuation in the other. If, for the sake of ethics, the second is called in with the first, it does not strengthen the first, but paralyses it. The man who does earnestly try to guide himself by the light of spiritual as well as material happiness, ends by finding that the recognition accorded him by his fellow-men, which at first seemed to make almost the whole of spiritual happiness, becomes more and more meaningless. It is to him a miserable lump of solder which drops down between material and spiritual happiness without being able to unite them. More and more exclusively, he experiences spiritual happiness as the condition in which he is at one with himself and therefore can justifiably accord himself a certain amount of self-approbation.

Spiritual happiness is sufficient unto itself. Either the man is led to resolve on ethical conduct because he expects from it a moulding of the outward circumstances of his being which will bring him profit and pleasure; or he chooses it because he finds his happiness in obeying the inner compulsion to ethical action. In the latter case he has left far behind him all calculations about the interdependence of his morality and his material happiness. The fact that he is a moral man is in itself his happiness, even though it land him in the most disadvantageous situations.

But if spiritual and material happiness can never be welded together, it is useless endeavour to try to depict altruism as an ennobling of egoism.

If the ordinary conception of pleasure, that it may be brought into union with ethics, is submitted to a process of refining, it ends by being refined away. In ancient ethics, in which the refining is done under the influence of an ethical system which is definitely egoistic, it transforms itself into the pleasure of being without pleasure, and allows ethics to end in resignation. In modern ethics, in which the pleasure to be refined is under the influence of altruism, it works itself up into an irrational and immaterialistic enthusiasm. In both cases there is the same paradoxical proceeding, only that in one case it goes in the negative direction, in the other in the positive.

Whenever, then, thought wishes to conceive ethics as springing from pleasure or happiness, it arrives at resignation or enthusiasm, at spiritualized egoistic or at spiritualized expansive conduct.

Where thought is profound there is no way in which natural pleasure can be brought into connection with ethics.

*   *   *

The explanation that altruism is a principle of action which the individual derives from society is to be found expressed in characteristic ways by Thomas Hobbes (1588–1679),[3] John Locke (1632–1704),[4] Adrien Helvetius (1715–1771)[5] and Jeremy Bentham (1748–1832).[6]

Hobbes represents the State as commissioned and empowered by the majority of the individual citizens to employ them to the general advantage. In this way alone, he asserts, is it possible to realize the common good in which the egoism of individuals finds the highest possible degree of prosperity. Left to themselves, men would never be able to get free from their short-sighted egoism, and would, therefore, miss prosperity. Their

---

3 Thomas Hobbes: *Elementa philosophica de cive* (1642); *Leviathan, or the Matter, Form, and Authority of Government* (1651); *De homine.*

4 John Locke: *An Essay concerning Human Understanding* (2 vols., 1690).

5 Adrien Helvetius: *Traité de l'Esprit* (1758).

6 Jeremy Bentham: *An introduction to the Principles of Morals and Legislation* (1780). E. Dumont (1759–1828) of Geneva, an admirer of Bentham who was domiciled in England, reproduced this work in French in a free abbreviation as *Traités de législation civile et pénale* (1802). Frederick Edward Beneke followed this abbreviation when he produced a German translation with the title: *Grundsätze der Civil- und Criminalgesetzgebung* (1830).

only possible course is to join in setting up an authority which will compel them to altruism.

With external means, however, organized society cannot employ the individual in all the activities which are needed for the common good. It must strive to ensure its power over him by means of spiritual conviction as well. Locke takes this need into consideration. According to him it is God and society together who force altruism upon the individual by appealing to his egoism. These two authorities have, that is to say (as our reason enables us to recognize), so ordered the course of things that actions beneficial to society are rewarded, and those injurious to it are punished. God has at his disposal rewards and punishments of endless duration. Society works in two different ways: through the power given to it by the criminal law, and through the law of public opinion which uses praise and blame as spiritual means of compulsion. Man, being guided both by pleasure and its opposite, manages to accommodate himself to those rules which so effectually defend the general good, and thereby becomes moral.

In spite of all their differences on single points, Hobbes and Locke agree in having this external conception of ethics. The essential point of distinction between them is that with Hobbes society alone plies the whip, while with Locke God and society wield it together.

Helvetius, who belonged to a family which had migrated from the Palatinate into France, is more refined and more inward. In his life as farmer-general of taxes and property-owner, he always tried, along with his noble-minded wife, to act with kindness and justice as he explains them in his book. It is clear to him that ethics mean somehow or other enthusiastic action, that is, action which springs from feeling.[7] Society cannot, therefore, force these virtues into the individual; it can only inculcate them, and it does in fact apply all the means and devices which are at its disposal to influence his egoism in their direction. Above all it makes good use of his striving to win recognition and fame. The praise which it pours on that which is "good" in

---

[7] *Translator's Note.*—German "enthusiastisches Handeln." The explanatory periphrasis is added once for all, since "enthusiastic" implies a kind and degree of feeling which is not implied in these philosophical passages.

its own sense of the word is for the mass of men the strongest inducement to work for its interests. Helvetius would perhaps have offered a less external conception of how ethical action is realized, if he had not, with the best intentions, taken so much trouble to depict ethics as a subject which can be taught.

In the view that morality is enthusiastic action to which the individual is roused by society, Bentham agrees entirely with Helvetius, but he develops it with far greater profundity. He turns the ballad into a hymn.

The part played by society in originating morality cannot, according to Bentham, be emphasized too strongly. In vehement words he opposes the view that the human conscience can decide between good and evil. Nothing can be left to subjective feeling. Man is truly moral only when he receives his ethics at the hand of society and executes their commands with ardour.

But if society is to decide about ethics, it must first bring order into its own ethical views, and therefore, says Bentham, must learn to combine clear and definite notions with its presentation of the general good. That done, it must make up its mind to apply this principle with absolute consistency as a foundation for legislation and the establishment of ethical standards, excluding all considerations of a different character. A "moral arithmetic" should be constructed to allow the calculating in correct utility values of all decisions that have to be made.

Dealing in a dry, practical way with all cases of penal legislation, and the establishment of standards by the moral law, Bentham then shows that the principle of the greatest good of the greatest number is applicable in all of them, and guides us safely and accurately in questions of good and evil.

"Moral philosophy, in its general meaning, is the theory underlying the art of so directing the actions of men that there is produced the greatest possible amount of happiness."

It is legislation that decides what moral actions the community can order to be performed. If it is to exert an educative influence it must be completely humane.

"But there are many actions which, though useful to the community, legislation may not command. There are even many injurious actions which it may not forbid, although moral philosophy does so. Legislation is, in a word, a circle with the same centre as moral philosophy, but its circumference is smaller."

Where the resources of the law come to an end, there is nothing that society can do except continually bring to the notice of the individual how greatly he contributes to his own welfare by furthering that of others. Bentham does not make it do this with pedagogic guile as does Helvetius. Society appeals to his feeling for truth. It throws itself at his feet and entreats him for the sake of the general welfare to listen to the voice of reason. Thus the dry way in which Bentham writes about ethics has in it something peculiarly impressive, and explains the powerful influence which this eccentric tenant of the house which looks across St. James's Park has exercised all over the world through the individuals who were inspired by him.

The most influential parts of his work are those in which he intensifies the seriousness of men, and sharpens their outlook, by leading them to reflect, not only on the immediate, but also on the more distant consequences of anything done or left undone, and, further, not only on the material, but on the spiritual, consequences. It is pleasant to note the courage with which this fanatic for utility ventures to represent material blessings as the foundation of those which are spiritual.

Bentham is one of the most powerful moralists who have ever lived, but his mistakes are as great as his insight. The latter is shown in the fact that he conceives morality as a kind of enthusiasm. His mistake is that he thinks he must guarantee the rightness of this enthusiasm by making it nothing higher than a judgment of society which is taken over by the individual.

This compels us to rank Bentham with Hobbes, Locke, and Helvetius, although in other respects he stands high above them. Like them, he makes morality originate outside the individual. Like them, in order to find this explanation of the altruistic, he puts out of action the ethical personality which is in man, and, to compensate for this, raises society to an ethical personality that he may then by a transmission of energy connect individuals with this central power-station. The difference is only that with those other commonplace moralists the individual is a marionette directed by society on ethical principles, whereas in Bentham he carries out with deep conviction the movements suggested to him.

Ethical thought falls from one paradox into another. If, as in antiquity, it thinks out a system in which the activity that must be directed to the common good is not sufficiently represented, it arrives at ethics which are no longer ethics, and ends in resignation. If it assumes and starts from such an activity directed to the common good, it arrives at an ethic in which there is no ethical personality. Strange to say, it is unable to mark out the middle course and let an activity which is directed to the promotion of the common good spring from the ethical personality itself.

*   *   *

The explanations of altruism as an ennobling of egoism which has a spontaneous origin through the activity of reason, or as brought into existence through the influence of society, are obviously unsatisfying both psychologically and ethically. Utilitarianism must therefore necessarily come to admit that altruism is somehow or other given independently in human nature side by side with egoism. It is true that it always appears there as the backward twin-brother who can be reared only with the most careful nursing, and therefore the upholders of the third alternative appeal to the considerations used for the first two. They continually allow the capacity for altruistic feeling to be exposed to the influence of considerations which seem calculated to let egoism flow into altruism. The first two views are taken into service as wet-nurses for the third.

David Hume (1711–1776) [8] and Adam Smith (1723–1790) [9] must be named here.

Hume agrees with the other utilitarians in allowing that the principle of seeking to promote the common good must be

[8] David Hume: *A Treatise of Human Nature: Being an Attempt to introduce the Experimental Method of Reasoning into Moral Subjects* (1740). German translation by Heinrich Jacob (2 vols., 1791): *Inquiry Concerning the Principles of Morals* (1751).

[9] Adam Smith: *The Theory of Moral Sentiments* (1759); *Inquiry into the Nature and Causes of the Wealth of Nations* (1770). German translation of *The Theory of Moral Sentiments* by L. Th. Kosegarten (1791). Adam Smith was Professor of Moral Philosophy at Glasgow.

accepted as the dominant principle of morality. Whether actions are good or bad is decided solely by whether or not they are directed towards the production of general happiness. There is nothing which is in itself ethical or unethical.

To the idea that ethics can have as their object the self-perfecting of the individual, as little weight is given by Hume as by the other utilitarians. Like them, he opposes asceticism and other life-denying demands of Christian ethics, because he cannot discover in them anything profitable for the general welfare.

But what makes men decide to work together for the common good? Consistent utilitarians answer: Reflection about what the common good means. Of this one-sidedness Hume is not guilty, because he does not find it in accord with psychological facts. It is not in high-minded reflection, he asserts, but in direct sympathy that the emotions and actions of benevolence have their source. The virtues which serve the common good have their origin in feeling. We can resolve on acts of love only because there is in us an elementary feeling for the happiness of men, and a dislike of seeing them in misery. We become moral through sympathy.

It would not have been a big step further to explain this sympathy as a form of the egoistic need of happiness, more or less through the assumption that in order to be really happy a man must see happiness around him. But that is not Hume's way. He does not aim at constructive thought but at stating facts, and it is enough for him that direct sympathy with other men be proved to be a principle inherent in human nature. We have to stop somewhere or other, he says, in our search for causes. In every science there are certain general principles beyond which there is no still more general principle for us to discover.

Among the elements which are effective in developing moral feeling, Hume attributes great importance to the love of fame. This keeps us considering ourselves in the light in which we wish to appear in the eyes of others, for the effort to secure the respect of others is the great teacher of virtue. On this point he thinks like Frederick the Great, from whom comes the sentence: "L'amour de la gloire est inné dans les belles âmes: il n'y a qu'à l'animer, il n'y a que l'exciter, et des hommes qui végétaient jusqu'alors, enflammés par ce heureux instinct, vous paraîtront changés en demi-dieux." (*Œuvres de Frédéric le Grand*, vol. ix., p. 98.) [10]

Adam Smith wishes to trace out the idea of sympathy in all its manifestations, and in doing so he discovers that our capacity for sympathy covers more than participation in the weal or woe of others. It brings us, he says, to a community of thought with those who are actively engaged. We feel ourselves directly attracted or repelled by the actions of others and the motives that inspire those actions. Our ethics are the product of these sympathetic experiences. We come in time to take care that an impartial third party can justify and sympathize with the mainspring and the tendency of our actions. Innate sympathy, not only with the actions but also with the experience of others, is thus the beneficent regulator of the behaviour of men to one another. God has implanted this feeling in human nature that it may keep men faithful to work for the common good.

How far this somewhat artificial extension of the notion of sympathy through the doctrine of the impartial third party really means a step forward beyond Hume, we may leave undiscussed.

In his famous work, *An Inquiry into the Nature and Causes of the Wealth of Nations* (1776), Adam Smith founds this prosperity purely upon the entirely free and rational activity of egoism. He says nothing about the part to be played by ethics in economic questions, but leaves economic development to be determined by its own internal laws, confident that, if these are left a free course, the result will be favourable. Adam Smith, the moral philosopher, because he is endowed with a rationalistic optimism, is also the founder of the *laissez-faire* form of economic doctrine, that of the Manchester school. He led industry and commerce in their struggle for liberation from the petty and injurious tutelage of authority. To-day, when economic life among all peoples is again delivered over to the most shortsighted ideas of authorities who never think in terms of economics, we can measure the greatness of his achievement.

---

[10] "The love of fame is innate in noble souls; you have only to arouse it and urge it on, and men who till then merely vegetated, will seem to you, when inflamed by this happy instinct, to be changed into demi-gods."

Like Adam Smith, Bentham is an adherent of the principle of freedom in economic life. At the same time he has an ethical conception of society, and demands from it that in a spirit of progress it shall help to level out as far as possible the differences between rich and poor.

What, then, do Hume and Adam Smith mean for ethics? They introduce the element of empirical psychology. They believe that through the value they give to the significance of sympathy they are giving a natural foundation to utilitarianism, though in reality psychology begins to correct it and to undermine its position. There hovers before the mind of utilitarianism the great conception that ethics are a result of reflection. It thinks to make men moral by keeping their attention fixed on the profound nature of ethics and the necessity of the aims in view.

This conception draws its life from the conviction that thought has been given complete control over the will. The absolute rationality of the ethical is the foundation on which it builds, and if it is not to get quite bewildered about its own nature, it cannot allow itself to recognize, as presuppositions of the ethical, facts which are given it by psychology and cannot be verified independently.

With Hume and Adam Smith, who trace ethics back to something inherent in human nature which resembles instinct, there crops up the problem how ethics can be natural, and at the same time serve as a basis for thought, for that they do form the groundwork of thought must be assumed even by the champions of this psychological utilitarianism. If they were nothing but the exercise of an instinct, they would not be capable of widening and deepening, nor could they be imparted to all and sundry with convincing force. Yet how is it conceivable that thought influences the sympathetic instinct? What have the two in common that the work of one can be carried further by the other?

If Hume and Adam Smith had suspected the far-reaching character of this great problem of ethics which they brought into the field of discussion, they would have had to go on and settle the extent and the depth of this sympathy which they adopted in their scheme, in order to understand how it continues to function in the domain of thought.

But they fail to notice the full importance of what they establish, and believe they have done nothing but give by means of psychology an explanation of altruism which is superior to that commonly approved. The spirit of the time, with its wonderful capacity for holding various ideas side by side, takes possession of their view, and popular utilitarianism now confidently declares that altruism is to be conceived as a rational ennobling of egoism, as a result of the influence of society, and in addition as a manifestation of a natural instinct.

It is, really, only in appearance that the psychological conception of ethics imparts new life to utilitarianism. It is rather a consumption germ which the latter absorbs. The establishment of a natural element in ethics, when the consequences begin to make themselves felt, can only end in its devouring rationalist utilitarianism, as becomes evident in the nineteenth century when biological thought becomes influential in ethics.

The funeral procession of rationalist utilitarianism begins to assemble with Hume and Adam Smith, though it is a long time before the coffin is carried to the cemetery.

*   *   *

Against the utilitarians, who from the content of the moral would derive both its essential nature and the obligation to morality, the "Intellectualists" and the "Intuitionists" enter the lists. The empirical derivation of ethics seems to them to be an endangering of the majesty of the moral. Morality—this is the thought before their minds—is a striving after perfection, and this develops in us because it is implanted in our hearts by nature. Action for the common advantage does not by any means constitute ethics; it is only a manifestation of the struggle for self-perfection.

To this deeper and more comprehensive conception of ethics, however, the Intellectualists and Intuitionists do not give correct expression. For that they are still too much involved in a lifeless and semi-scholastic philosophizing.

Their chief strength lies in their showing up of the weaknesses of the foundation which Hobbes and Locke give to ethics, and to these they principally devote themselves, bringing to their task a great deal that is correct about the directly and absolutely binding character of the moral law. That the meaning of the moral is not to be found merely in the useful character of the actions it inspires, but also in the self-perfecting of the human being which those actions bring about, and, further, that morality presupposes a moral personality, is emphasized by them in many happy turns of expression.

When, however, the task before them is to describe exactly in what way men carry in them the idea of the good as a force which works effectively upon their character, the Intellectualists and the Intuitionists land themselves in a psychologizing which is sometimes ingenious, but often artificial and commonplace. They occupy themselves with logical distinctions instead of investigating in a practical fashion the nature of man. Instead of really developing the problem in answer to the innovators, they work at it with data taken from bygone philosophy. They hark back largely to Plato, and on many points argue consciously or unconsciously, not as philosophers, but as theologians.

They diverge from each other on the details, and attack each other's positions according as they would have the foundations of the ethical more intellectualist, or more sentimental and mystical, or more theological.

The majority of these anti-utilitarians belong to the school of the Cambridge Platonists. We must name here Ralph Cudworth (1617–1688),[11] Henry More (1614–1687),[12] the Rev. Samuel Clarke (1675–1729),[13] Bishop Richard Cumberland (1632–1718),[14] and William Wollaston (1659–1724).[15]

According to Cudworth, the truths of morality are just as evident as these of mathematics. For More the ethical is an intellectual power of the soul meant for the control of natural impulses. Cumberland finds the moral law given in the reason which has been bestowed upon man by God. Clarke, living in the thought world of Isaac Newton, sees it as the spiritual

[11] R. Cudworth: *Intellectual System of the Universe* (1678); *Treatise concerning Eternal and Immutable Morality* (posthumous, 1731).

[12] H. More: *Enchiridium Ethicum* (1667).

[13] S. Clarke: *A Discourse concerning the Unchangeable Obligations of Natural Religion, and the Truth and Certainty of the Christian Revelation* (1706).

[14] R. Cumberland: *De legibus naturæ disquisitio philosophica* (1672).

[15] W. Wollaston: *The Religion of Nature Delineated* (1722).

phenomenon which corresponds to the law of nature. Wollaston defines it as that which is logically right.

When all is said, these thinkers do nothing but amplify the statement that the ethical is ethical. They assert that the utilitarian view of ethics is pitched too low, but they do not succeed in establishing, in contrast to it, a more exalted principle in such a way that a higher and more comprehensive content of ethics can be derived from it. As to content, their ethic does not really differ from that of the utilitarians. Only it lacks the great enthusiastic driving-force which is seen in the latter. To establish a living ethic of self-perfecting is beyond the capacity of the Intellectualists and the Intuitionists.

What is the inner connection between the struggle for self-perfecting and action for the common advantage? This is the weighty question of ethics which crops up in the discussion between the utilitarians and their conservative opponents. At first it remains veiled, and it does not come to clear expression till we reach Kant.

*   *   *

A singular position in the ethical thought of the eighteenth century is held by Anthony Ashley-Cooper, Earl of Shaftesbury (1671–1713).[16] He opposes not only the utilitarians, but the Intellectualists and the Intuitionists as well, and tries to secure a mediating position between them. That the content of ethics is utilitarian he openly admits, but he derives the ethical neither from considerations of usefulness nor from the intellect; he places its origin in feeling. At the same time he emphasizes, as does Adam Smith a few years later, its relationship to the æsthetic.

But the important thing is that he puts forward a living philosophy of nature in combination with ethics. He is convinced that harmony reigns in the universe and that man is meant to experience this harmony in himself. Æsthetic feeling and ethical thinking are for him forms of union with that divine life which

16 *Characteristics of Men, Manners, Opinions, Times* (3 vols., 1711). In the second volume there is included his ethical treatise entitled, *Inquiry concerning Virtue or Merit*, which appeared first, in 1699, independently. It was published in French in 1745 by Denis Diderot.

struggles to find expression in the spiritual being of man as it does in nature.

With Shaftesbury ethics descend from a rocky mountain range into a luxuriant plain. The utilitarians as yet know nothing of a world. Their ethic is restricted to considerations about the relation of the individual to society. The anti-utilitarians have some idea of a world, but not a correct one. They elaborate ethics with a formal theology and a formal philosophizing about the All, but Shaftesbury plants ethical thought in the universe of reality, which he himself contemplates through an idealising optimism, reaching thereby a direct and universal notion of the moral.

A mysticism based on a philosophy of nature begins to spin its magic threads through European thought. The spirit of the Renaissance rules again, this time, however, not like a raging storm, as in Giordano Bruno, but as a gentle breeze. Shaftesbury thinks pantheistically, more pantheistically than he confesses to himself, but his is not a pantheism which throws his age into struggles about world-views, and comes into conflict with theism. It is the harmless pantheism which rules in Hinduism and also in Late Stoicism; pantheism which raises no question of principle, but desires only to be regarded as a vivifying of belief in God.

Shaftesbury also exerts a liberating influence on the spiritual life of his time by according ethics a much freer attitude toward religion than anyone had hitherto ventured to give. Religion, according to him, has not to make decisions about ethics, but on the contrary must prove its own claims to be true by its relation to pure ethical ideas. He even ventures to represent the Christian teaching about rewards and punishment as not consistent with pure ethical considerations. Morality, he says, is pure only when good has been done simply because it is good.

His optimistic-ethical philosophy of nature is offered by Shaftesbury only as a sketch. He throws out his ideas without proving that they are well founded, and without feeling any necessity for thinking them out to a conclusion. He steps with an easy stride across all problems. What a difference between his philosophy of nature and Spinoza's! Yet his meets the needs of the time. He offers what is new to it, and inspires it: ethics bound up with a philosophy of life that is full of vitality.

The belief in progress now clothes itself in a living philosophy which really suits it. This is the process which, thanks to Shaftesbury, began in the first decades of the eighteenth century and went on developing till its end. Hence the appearance of his writings, which were immediately spread abroad through the whole of Europe, is the great event for the spiritual life of the eighteenth century. Voltaire, Diderot, Lessing, Condorcet, Moses Mendelssohn, Wieland, Herder, and Goethe too, are under his influence, and he dominates popular thought completely. Hardly ever has any man had so direct and so powerful an influence on the formation of the world-view of his time as the invalid whose life ended at Naples when he was only forty-two.

Direct continuators of Shaftesbury's ethic are found in Francis Hutcheson (1694–1747) [17] and Bishop Joseph Butler (1692–1752),[18] but they take from it just that fluid indefiniteness which gives it its charm and its strength. Hutcheson, who strongly emphasizes ethics' independence of theology, the relationship of the former to the æsthetic, and their utilitarian content, stands nearer to his teacher than does Butler, who does not go as far in his welcome of utilitarianism, and also opposes, from the Christian standpoint, the optimism of Shaftesbury's world-view.

But Shaftesbury's true successor is J. G. Herder (1744–1803). In his *Ideas on the Philosophy of Human History* (4 vols., 1784–1791), he carries the optimistic-ethical nature-philosophy on into a corresponding philosophy of history.

[17] F. Hutcheson: *An Inquiry into the Original of our Ideas of Beauty and Virtue* (1725); *A System of Moral Philosophy* (1755, posthumous).
[18] Joseph Butler: *Fifteen Sermons upon Human Nature, or Man considered as a Moral Agent* (1726).

Chapter 13

LAYING THE FOUNDATIONS OF CIVILIZATION

IN THE AGE OF RATIONALISM

*The mentality and the achievements of the
ethical belief in progress.*

Obstacles to the reform movement. The French Revolution.

The undermining of the rationalistic world-view.

THANKS TO THE FULLY WORKED OUT OPTIMISTIC-ETHICAL WORLD-view with which the belief in progress is environed in the course of the eighteenth century, these generations prove capable of thinking out the ideals of civilization and advancing towards their realization. The fact that all attempts to give ethics a foundation in reason have proved to be more than unsatisfactory does not move them, if indeed they give the point any consideration at all. By the conviction that they have formed a rational conception of the world which gives it an optimistic-ethical meaning, they surmount all the inner problems of ethics. The alliance which belief-in-progress and ethics have in the course of modern times contracted with one another is sealed by means of their outlook on the world, and now they set to work together. Rational ideals are to be realized.

The ethical and the optimistic come into power, therefore, in the philosophy of the eighteenth century, although they have not yet received any real foundation. Scepticism and materialism range around the fortress like hordes of unconquered enemies, though at first without being dangerous; as a rule they have themselves absorbed no small amount of belief-in-progress and of ethical enthusiasm. Voltaire is an example of the sceptic who stands under the restraint exercised by the prevalent optimistic and ethical thought.

So far as its elements are concerned, the world-view of rationalism hides under the optimistic-ethical monism of Kung-tse (Confucius) and the Later Stoics, but the enthusiasm which supports it is incomparably stronger than any felt by them. The circumstances, too, amid which it appears are far more favourable. So it becomes an elemental and popular force.

In a world-view which springs from a noble faith, but is remarkable also for the extent of its knowledge, the men of the eighteenth century begin to think out ideals of civilization and to realize them in such measure that the greatest epoch in the history of human civilization now dawns.

The characteristic feature of the mentality of this belief in progress which is ever showing itself in works is its magnificent want of respect for reality, whether the past or the present. In all its various forms reality is the imperfect value, which is destined to be replaced by perfection.

The eighteenth century is thoroughly unhistoric. In what is good, as in what is bad, it cuts itself loose from whatever was or is, and is confident of being able to put in its place something that is more valuable, because more ethical or more in accordance with reason. In this conviction the age feels itself so creative that it has no understanding for the creations of original genius. Gothic buildings, early painting, J. S. Bach's music, and the poetry of earlier ages, are regarded by these generations as art which was produced at a time when taste had not yet been purified. Activity which follows rules in accordance with right reason will, they think, introduce a new art which will be superior in every respect to any that has preceded it. Full of this self-confidence, a mediocre musician like Zelter in Berlin works over the scores of Bach's Cantatas. Full of this self-confidence, respectable poetasters re-write the texts of the wonderful old German chorales and replace the originals in the hymn books with their own wretched productions.

That they so naïvely push forward right into the sphere of art the bounds of the creative faculties with which nature endowed them, is a mistake made by these men for which they have often been laughed at. But mockery cannot do them much harm. In those departments of life in which the important matter is the shaping of thought according to ideals given by reason— and such work means for the establishment of civilization very much more than any work accomplished in the promotion of art—they are as creative as any generation ever has been, and as scarcely any will be in the future. They are dismayed by nothing which has to be undertaken in this sphere, and in every department they make the most astonishing advance.

They venture also to deal with religion. That religion should be split up into various antagonistic confessional bodies is to them an offence against reasonable reflection. Only relative, not absolute, authority, they maintain, can be allowed to the belief which is handed down in historical formulas. Finding expression in so many and such varied forms it can, of course, be nothing but a more or less imperfect expression of the ethical religion taught by reason, which must be equally intelligible to all men. The right thing is, therefore, to strive after the religion of reason, and to accept as true only such parts of the various confessions as are in harmony with it.

The churches, naturally, put themselves on the defensive against this spirit, but they are unable in the long run to hold out against the strong general convictions of the age. Protestantism succumbs first, because the elements already within it allow such considerations to find easy access. It carries within itself impulses to rationalism, inherited from Humanism, from Huldreich Zwingli (1484–1531) and from the Italians Lælius (1525–1562) and Faustus Socinus (1539–1604), and these impulses, hitherto suppressed, are now set free.[1]

Catholicism shows itself more capable of resistance. Nothing in its past makes it attuned to the spirit of the age: its strong organization serves as a protection against this. Yet it, too, has to yield considerably, and to allow its doctrines to pass, so far as may be, for a symbolic expression of the religion of reason.

[1] The free-thinking, anti-dogmatic religiousness of Socinianism had been maintained chiefly in Poland, Holland, Hungary, England, and North America. Its closer adherents called themselves also Latitudinarians, the more distant ones Unitarians. The fact that religious rationalism had already existed in a literary form facilitated its appearnce in the eighteenth century.

While utilitarian ethics are on the whole the product of the English spirit, the whole of Europe takes part in establishing the religion of reason. Herbert of Cherbury (1582–1648), John Toland (1669–1722), Anthony Collins (1676–1729), Matthew Tindal (1655–1733), David Hume (1711–1776), Pierre Bayle (1647–1706), Jean-Jacques Rousseau (1712–1778), Voltaire (1694–1778), Denis Diderot (1713–1784), Hermann Samuel Reimarus (1694–1768), Gottfried Wilhelm Leibniz (1646–1716), Christian Wolff (1679–1754), Gotthold Ephraim Lessing (1729–1781), Moses Mendelssohn (1729–1786), and a host of others, whether standing nearer to or further from the Church, and whether or not going further than others in systematic criticism, all bring stones for the erection of the great building in which the piety of illuminated mankind is to live.[2] The researches in the history of religion made by the Germans, like Johann Salomo Semler (1725–1791), Johann David Michaelis (1717–1791), and Johann August Ernesti (1707–1781), provide scientific data which throw light upon the division between eternal truths and the time-conditioned convictions of religion.

The creed of the religion of reason is simply the optimistic-ethical world-view reproduced in a Christian phraseology, that is to say, preserving within it the Christian theism, and the belief in immortality. An all-wise and wholly benevolent Creator has produced the world, and upholds it in corresponding fashion. Man is endowed with free will, and discovers in his reason and his heart the moral law which is meant to lead individuals and mankind to perfection, and to accomplish in the world God's highest purposes. Every man has within him an indestructible soul, which feels his moral life to be the highest happiness, and after death enters a state of pure, spiritual existence.

This belief in God, in virtue, and in immortality was held to have been taught in its purest form in previous ages in the teaching of Jesus. But it was acknowledged that elements of the same beliefs were to be found in all the higher religions.[3]

---

2 Tindal's work bears the title *Christianity as Old as the Creation* (1730). Pierre Bayle's famous *Dictionnaire historique et critique* appeared for the first time in two volumes in 1695.

3 The most impressive, and perhaps the most profound document of the religion of reason is the confession of faith which Rousseau in his novel *Emile* (1762) puts into the mouth of a country minister in Savoy.

If the eighteenth century attained to an optimistic-ethical world-view which was preached so confidently and was so widely accepted, the reason is that it was able to re-interpret Christianity —which had by that time eliminated the world- and life-negation that was originally inherent in it—in that sense. Jesus was to it a teacher who even in his own age and then through all the intervening centuries had been misunderstood, and was now first rightly accepted as a revealer of the religion of reason. Let anyone read a rationalistic Life of Jesus, such as those of Franz Volkmar Reinhard (1753–1812) or Karl Heinrich Venturini (1768–1849).[4] They hold Jesus up to admiration as the champion of enlightenment and of blessings for the common people. This transformation of the historical picture is made easier for them by the fact that the chief component element of the Gospel narrative is ethical teaching, while hardly a hint is given of the late-Jewish pessimistic world-view which it presupposes.

As an immediate result of the obliteration of confessional differences, the middle of the eighteenth century sees the beginning of a period of tolerance in place of the persecution of the unorthodox which had been common only a short time before. The last serious act of confessional intolerance was the expulsion of all evangelicals from the Salzburg district by the Archbishop of that town, Count von Firmian, in the years 1731 and 1732.

About the middle of the century there begins also the movement of opposition to the Jesuits, who were recognized as the enemies of tolerance, and this led to the suppression of the order in 1773 by Pope Clement XIV.[5]

But the religion of reason fought superstition as well as intolerance. In 1704 the philosopher and jurist of Halle, Christian Thomasius (1655–1728), published his essays condemning trial for witchcraft,[6] and about the middle of the century the law courts in most of the States of Europe refused to concern them-

[4] F. V. Reinhard: *Essay concerning the Plan which the Founder of the Christian Religion drew up for the Benefit of Mankind* (1781; 4th ed., 1798). K. H. Venturini: *Natural History of the Great Prophet of Nazareth* (1800–1802). See for an account of them the writer's work: *The Quest of the Historical Jesus* (1906; 4th ed., 1922 (German); 1st English ed., 1910; 3rd, 1922).

[5] Expulsion of the Jesuits from Portugal, 1759; from France, 1764; from Spain and Naples, 1767; from Parma, 1768.

[6] *Short Theses upon the Sin of Witchcraft and the Practice of Trial Therefor.*

selves any longer with the crime of magic. The last death sentence on a witch was passed in 1782 at Glarus, in Switzerland.

About the end of the century it became good form to detest anything which had even a remote connection with superstitious convictions.

Again, the will-to-progress of the eighteenth century makes a clean sweep of nationalist as of religious prejudices. Above and beyond individual nations it points to mankind as the great object towards which ideals are to be directed. Educated people accustom themselves to see in the State not so much an organ of national feeling as a mere organization for legal and economic purposes. Cabinets may carry on war with each other, but in the thought of the common people there grows up a recognition of the brotherhood of nations.

In the sphere of law, too, the will-to-progress acquires strength. The ideas of Hugo Grotius find acceptance. The law of reason is exalted in the convictions of the men of the eighteenth century to a position above all traditional maxims of jurisprudence. It alone is allowed to have permanent authority, and legal decisions have to be in harmony with it. Fundamental principles of law, principles everywhere equally beyond dispute, have to be deduced from human nature. To protect these and thus ensure to every human being a human value with an inviolable measure of freedom of which he can never be robbed, is the first task of the State. The proclamation of "the Rights of Man" by the States of North America and the French Revolution, do no more than give recognition and sanction to what, in the convictions of the time, had already been won.

The first State in which torture was abolished was Prussia, and this was secured by an administrative order of Frederick the Great in 1740. In France a certain amount of torture was practised down to the Revolution—and somewhat later. The thumb-screw was used under the Directory during the examination which the royalist conspirators had to undergo.[7]

Side by side with the fight against absence of law and the existence of inhuman laws, go efforts to adapt law to circum-

[7] See G. Lenôtre: "Les Agents Royalistes sous la Révolution" (*Revue des Deux Mondes*, 1922).

stances. Bentham raises his voice against laws which tolerate usury, against senseless customs duties, and against inhuman methods of colonization.

There dawns an age in which the purposive and the moral are the ruling authorities. Officialdom acquires during these generations familiarity with the notions of duty and honour, which later become natural to it. Without any fuss, far-reaching beneficial reforms are introduced into administration.

The education of mankind in citizenship makes splendid progress. The general good becomes the criterion of excellence both for the commands of rulers and the obedience of their subjects, while at the same time a beginning is made towards securing that everyone shall be educated in a manner corresponding to his human dignity and the needs of his personal welfare. The war against ignorance is begun.

The way is prepared, too, for a more rational method of living. More comfortable houses are built and the land is better cultivated. Even the pulpit uses its influence to promote improvements of this kind. The theory that reason has been given to man to be used consistently and in every department of life plays at this time an important and beneficent part in the preaching of the Gospel, even if the way in which this is done often seems queer. Sermons, for example, frequently treated incidentally of the best methods of manuring, irrigating, and draining the fields. That Jenner's discovery of vaccination was so readily adopted in many districts was due to the enlightenment which was spread abroad by the clergy.

Characteristic of the age of rationalism are the secret societies formed to promote the moral and utilitarian progress of mankind. In 1717 members of the higher ranks of society in London reorganize as "The Order of Freemasons" the brotherhood which in earlier times had been built up by the union in a single body of the members of the mediæval building-lodges, but was now in a state of decay, and to this new organization was assigned the duty of labouring to build up a new humanity. About the middle of the century this order spread all over Europe, and reached the zenith of its success. Princes, officials, and scholars alike joined it in great numbers, and were inspired by it to the achievement of a huge amount of reform.

Similar aims were pursued by the "Order of the Illuminati" (or enlightened) which was founded in Bavaria in 1776, but was suppressed in 1784 by the reactionary Bavarian Government, which was still under the influence of the Jesuits. It is said to have been the intellectual counterpart of the Jesuit order, on the model of whose organization it was formed.

That private societies aiming at the rational and moral perfecting of mankind should work effectively seemed to the men of the eighteenth century so much a matter of course that they assumed them to have existed in earlier times. In a series of rationalist descriptions of the life of Jesus it is assumed that the sect of the Essenes, near the Dead Sea, of which we learn from Josephus, the Jewish writer of the first century A.D., was such an order, and that it was in touch with similar brotherhoods in Egypt and India. Jesus, it is said, was trained by the Essenes, and then helped by them to carry through the *rôle* of the Messiah, in order that with the authority given by a holy yet popular personality he might work to spread true illumination. The famous *Life of Jesus* by Karl Venturini develops this theory in complete detail. According to him, the miracles of Jesus were staged by brothers of this secret association.

At any rate, the fact that the will-to-progress of the eighteenth century created for itself in these private societies organizations which spread throughout Europe, contributed much to its ability to influence the age.

It must be admitted indeed that the men of the rationalistic period were not so great as their achievements. True, they all possessed personality, but it did not reach very deep. It was produced by the enthusiasm which they found in the mentality of the time and shared with many of their contemporaries. The individual acquired personality by taking over a ready-made philosophy which gave him firm standing-ground together with ideals. His own contribution was really nothing more than the capacity for enthusiasm. That is why the men of this age are so remarkably like one another. They all graze side by side in the same nourishing pasture.

Nevertheless, the ideas of the purposive and the ethical have never exercised so much influence over reality as they did among these men of shallow optimism and emotional morale.

No book has been written yet which fully describes their achievements, doing justice to their origin, their character, their number and their significance. We only really comprehend what they accomplished, because we experience the tragic fact that the most valuable part of it is lost to us, while we do not feel in ourselves any ability to reproduce it. They were masters of the facts of life to an extent which we are to-day quite unable to realize.

Only a world-view which accomplishes all that rationalism did has a right to condemn rationalism. The greatness of that philosophy is that its hands are blistered.

*　　*　　*

The great work of reform is never completed, partly because external circumstances arise to check it, but also because the world-view of rationalism becomes convulsed from within. In its confidence in the enlightening power of all that is in accordance with reason, the will-to-progress was inclined to underestimate the resistant power of the traditional, and to aim at carrying through reforms where minds had not been sufficiently prepared for their reception. On these unsuccessful advances followed reaction which permanently injured the work. This was the case in southeastern Europe. Joseph II. of Austria, who was emperor from 1764 to 1790, is the type of the reforming prince. He discontinued the use of torture, opposed the infliction of the death penalty, abolished serfdom, gave the Jews full civic rights, introduced a new method of legislation and a new system of legal administration, took away all class privileges, contended for the equality of all before the law, protected the oppressed, founded schools and hospitals, guaranteed the freedom of the press and freedom of domicile, abolished all State monopolies, and promoted the development of agriculture and industry.

But he was a ruler on the wrong throne. He decreed these reforms and further caused similar shocks, one after another, in countries which, being in spiritual matters still wholly under the dominion of the Catholic Church of that time, were not prepared for them, and moreover in other things as well displayed a specially backward attitude, because they belonged to the zone in which the Europe of that day passed over into Asia.

The Emperor was therefore unable to count upon either any willingness to make sacrifices in the classes which were to give up their privileges, or upon any understanding of his ideas among the common people. In his attempts to organize the monarchy as a unity, and in an effective way for practical purposes, he came into conflict with the nationalities of which it was composed. The reduction in the number of the religious houses, which he undertook from economic considerations, along with the introduction of the freedom of the press and of a system of State education, brought on him the hostility of the Church. Finally, because he is a ruler in the wrong place, this noble reforming emperor dies of a broken heart, while Europe, because the will-to-progress in Austria, owing to unfavorable circumstances, can accomplish nothing even at the time of its greatest strength, is condemned to a period of the deepest misery over the problems of that huge State, which have in this way been rendered insoluble, and over the portion of Asia which continues along the southern bank of the Danube.

In France, too, the wrong men are on the throne. There the spread of the new ideas prepares the way splendidly for reform, but the reforms are not undertaken, because its rulers cannot understand the signs of the times, and allow the State to fall into decay. Consequently the reform movement has to take the road of violence, whereby it slips away from the guidance of the educated, and falls into the hands of the mob, from which it is taken by the powerful genius of Napoleon. Native of an island in which the Europe of that day passed over into Africa, and lacking all but a superficial education, he is uninfluenced by the valuable convictions of his time. Guided solely by the force of his own personality, he decides what is to happen in Europe, and hurls it into wars through which it sinks into misery. Thus from East and from West alike disaster overtakes the work of the will-to-progress.

The French Revolution is a snowstorm falling upon trees in blossom. A transformation which promises great things is in progress, but everywhere silently and slowly. Extraordinarily valuable results are being prepared in the thoughts of men. Provided that circumstances remain even tolerably near the normal, humanity in Europe faces an amazingly beneficial development.

But in place of this there sets in a chaotic period of history in which the will-to-progress has to cease more or less completely from its task, and becomes a bewildered spectator. The first surge of the advance of reforming thought, thought bent with full consciousness of its aims on securing the practical and the ethical, comes to a complete stop.

An experience for which it was in no wise prepared now falls to the lot of the will-to-progress. Up to this time it had always been a more or less worn out reality with which it had had to endeavour to come to terms. In the French Revolution, however, and in the following period, it becomes familiar with a reality which has at its disposal elemental forces. Until now the only factor to be reckoned with had been the force exercised by rational thought. In Napoleon it has to learn to recognize as power a personality with creative genius of its own.

By his reorganization of France, a magnificent work but concerned only with the technical matters of administration, Napoleon creates a new State. His achievement, too, has had the way prepared for it by the work of rationalism, in so far as this upset the equilibrium of the old order and made current the idea of something novel but necessary. But the new State which now comes into existence is not the State which is ethical and in harmony with reason, but merely the State which works well. Its achievements compel our admiration. In the garden which the will-to-progress was laying out in order to plant it with lovely flowers, an individual ploughs for himself a piece of ordinary arable land which at once produces an excellent crop. With the elemental creative forces of reality revealing their power in so imposing a fashion, the noble but unoriginal spirit of the age, with all its higher aims, finds itself in a state of instability from which it never completely recovers. Hegel, who saw Napoleon ride past after the Battle of Jena, tells us that he then saw the World-spirit on horseback. In these words we can hear the expression of the confused spiritual experience of the time.

*　　*　　*

There now sets in a development which works against the spirit of the age. The hitherto unopposed authority of the rational ideal is undermined. Forces of reality which are not guided by it obtain recognition.

While the will-to-progress remains an amazed spectator of events, respect for what is historical revives, though it seemed to have been banished for ever. In religion, in art, and in law, men begin, though at first only quite shyly, to look again with other eyes on the traditional. It is no longer reckoned as merely something which is to be replaced, but men venture to admit to themselves that it conceals within itself original values. The forces of reality, which had been taken by surprise, everywhere act on the defensive, and a guerilla warfare against the will-to-progress begins.

The various religious bodies revoke the abdications which they had made in presence of the religion of reason. The traditional law begins to set itself in opposition to the law laid down by reason. In the atmosphere of passion produced by the Napoleonic wars, the idea of the nation takes on a new character, directing on itself, and beginning to absorb, the universal enthusiasm for ideals. The struggles carried on, no longer by chancelleries but by peoples, are fatal to the ideals of cosmopolitanism and the brotherhood of nations. By this reawakening of national thought a whole series of political problems affecting the whole of Europe are rendered insoluble. Just as the organization of Austria as a unified modern State has now become impossible, so also has the civilizing of Russia, and that it is the destiny of Europe to be ruined on account of territories which are in it but not of it, begins to become apparent.

At the close of the Napoleonic era the whole of Europe is in a condition of misery. Far-seeing ideas of reform can be neither thought out nor worked out; only extemporized palliative measures suit the time. The will-to-progress is therefore unable to recover its former vigour.

It is fatally affected, too, by the fact that everybody with any capacity for independent thought feels himself attracted by this new valuation of reality, and consequently irritated at the one-sided, doctrinaire character of the rationalist way of looking at life.

Nevertheless, the position of the will-to-progress is far from being critical. The first attacks are made by Romanticism and the feeling for reality, but are mere outpost-skirmishes, and for a long time yet the will-to-progress remains master of the field. Bentham remains still the great authority. Alexander II. of Russia, Tsar from 1801 to 1825, instructs the legislative commission which he sets up, to obtain the opinion of the great Englishman on all doubtful points. Madame de Staël expresses the opinion that the fateful period she has lived through will one day be called by posterity not the Napoleonic but the Benthamite age.[8]

The noblest men of the period still live in the unshaken confidence that nothing can delay the speedy and conclusive victory of the purposive and moral. The philosophically minded mathematician and astronomer, the Marquis Marie Jean de Condorcet (1743–1794), though put by the Jacobins upon the list of the proscribed, writes, while living in concealment in Paris in a dismal room in the Rue des Fossoyeurs, his *Historical Sketch of the Progress of the Human Spirit*.[9] Then, betrayed, he wanders about the Clamart quarries, is recognized by the labourers, in spite of his disguise, as an aristocrat, and while confined in the prison of Bourg la Reine, puts an end to his life by poison. The document in which he gave his exposition of the ethical belief in progress concludes with a forward glance at the time, now soon to appear, when reason, having attained a position of permanent sovereignty, will put every human being in possession of the rights which belong to man as man, and will establish purposive and ethical relations in every department of life.

There is one thing, it must be admitted, which Condorcet and those who share his views overlook. Their belief that the final result will be good might be considered justifiable, if the will-to-progress had been endangered only through unfavourable outward circumstances, the revival, that is, of the higher estimation of reality, and the romantic idealizing of the past. But it is far more seriously threatened. The assurance displayed by rationalism rests on the fact that it regards the optimistic-ethical

---

[8] Her dictum is given in the English periodical, *The Atlas*, in its issue of January 27th, 1828.

[9] *Esquisse d'un tableau historique des progrès de l'esprit humain.* It was published in 1795, after the author's death, at the expense of the National Convention.

world-view as proved. But it is not, for it rests, like the world-views of Confucius and the Later Stoics, on a naïve interpretation of the world. All deeper thought, therefore, even if it is not directed against rationalism, or even if it aims at strengthening its position, must in the long run have a disintegrating effect upon it. Hence Kant and Spinoza spell its doom. Kant undermines it by his attempt to provide a deeper foundation for the essence of the ethical. Spinoza, the thinker of the seventeenth century, brings it to confusion when, a hundred years after his death, his nature-philosophy begins to occupy people's attention.

It is about the beginning of the new century, the nineteenth, just when the pressure exerted by material and spiritual circumstances alike begins to make itself felt, that the optimistic-ethical world-view begins to suspect the existence of the serious problems which are arising within it.

Chapter 14

THE OPTIMISTIC-ETHICAL WORLD-VIEW

IN KANT

Kant's ethics, deepened, but lacking content.

Kant's attempt to reach an ethical world-view.

SO FAR AS CONCERNS THE GENERAL TENDENCY OF HIS THOUGHT, Immanuel Kant (1724–1804) lives entirely in the optimistic-ethical world-view of rationalism.[1] He has, however, a feeling that its foundations are not sufficiently deep and firm, and he regards it as his task to give them an altogether securer basis. For this purpose profounder ethics and a less naïve positiveness in assertions about philosophy which touch upon the supra-sensible, seem to him desirable.

Like the English intellectualists and intuitionists, Kant is offended by the idea that the ethics in which the modern age finds satisfaction and its impulse to activity is rooted merely in considerations of the universal advantage of morally good actions. Like them, he feels that ethics is something more than this, and that in the ultimate analysis it has its origin in the compulsion which men experience to strive for self-perfection. But while his predecessors stick fast in the matter provided by semi-scholastic philosophy and theology, he attacks the problem along the lines of pure ethical thought. It follows for him that the fundamental origin and the exalted character of the moral

---

[1] Immanuel Kant: *Kritik der reinen Vernunft* (1781); *Grundlegung zur Metaphysik der Sitten* (1785); *Kritik der praktischen Vernunft* (1788); *Kritik der Urteilskraft* (1790); *Die Religion innerhalb der Grenzen der blossen Vernunft* (1793); *Metaphysik der Sitten* (1797).

can be preserved only if we always consciously make it an end in itself, and never merely a means to an end. Even if moral conduct prove itself to be always advantageous and practical, our motive to it must nevertheless always be a purely inward compulsion. Utilitarian ethics must abdicate before the ethics of immediate and sovereign duty. That is the meaning of the doctrine of the Categorical Imperative.

The English anti-utilitarians had in common with the utilitarians the thought that the moral law was related in essence to empirical natural law. Kant, however, asserts that it has nothing to do with the order of nature, but has its origin in supra-natural impulses. He is the first since Plato to feel, like him, that the ethical is the mysterious fact within us. In powerful language he proves in the *Critique of the Practical Reason* that ethics is a volition which raises us above ourselves, frees us from the natural order of the world of the senses, and attaches us to a higher world-order. That is his great discovery.

In the development of it, however, he falls short of success. Whoever asserts the absoluteness of moral duty, must also give the moral an absolute and completely universal content. He must specify a principle of conduct which shows itself as absolutely binding, and as lying at the foundations of the most varied ethical duties. If he does not succeed in doing this, his work is only a fragment.

When Plato announces that ethics is supra-natural and mysterious, his world-view provides him with a basic principle of the ethical which corresponds to these qualities, and also has a definite content. He is in a position to define ethics as a process of becoming pure and free from the world of sense. This, his own special form of ethics, he develops in the passages where he is consistent with himself. Then, when he cannot complete his argument without active ethics, he has recourse to the popular theory of virtue.

Kant, however, as a child of the modern spirit, cannot let world- and life-negation rank as ethics. Since he can go only a part of the way with Plato, he sees himself faced with the confusing task of letting purposive, activist ethics directed on the empirical world originate in impulses which are not determined by any adaptation to the empirical.

He can find no solution of the problem thus set. In the form which he gives it, it is in fact insoluble. But he never even realises that he has arrived at the problem of finding a basic principle of the moral which is a necessity of thought. He is content with formally characterizing ethical duty as absolutely binding. That duty, unless a content is at once given to it, remains an empty concept, he is unwilling to admit. For the exalted character of his basic principle of the moral, he pays the price of having it devoid of all content.

Beginnings of an attempt to establish a basic moral principle with a content are to be found in his treatise, *Prolegomena to a Metaphysic of Morals* (1785), and again later in *A Metaphysic of Morals* (1797).[2] In the 1785 volume he arrives at the dictum: "Act in such a way that you use human nature both in your own person and in everyone else's always as an end, never merely as a means." But instead of seeing how far the totality of ethical duties can be developed out of this principle, in the 1797 treatise he prefers to set before ethics two ends to be aimed at, the perfecting of oneself and the happiness of others, and to enlarge upon the virtues which promote them.

In his investigation of the ethics which aim at personal perfection, he drives his gallery [3] with sure instinct towards the recognition that all virtues which contribute thereto must be conceived as manifestations of sincerity and or reverence for one's own spiritual being. He does not, however, go the length of comprehending these two as a unity. Just as little does he concern himself to make clear the inner connection between effort directed to self-perfecting and effort directed to the common good, and in that way to dig down to the roots of the ethical as such.

How far Kant is from understanding the problem of finding a basic moral principle which has a definite content can be seen from the fact that he never gets beyond an utterly limited conception of the ethical. He obstinately persists in drawing the boundary of his ethics as narrow as possible, making them concerned with no duties beyond those of man to man. He does

---

[2] "Grundlegung zur Metaphysik der Sitten" (1785). "Metaphysik der Sitten" (1797).

[3] "Treibt den Stollen"—The metaphor is drawn from mining.

not include the relations of man to non-human existence. It is only indirectly that he finds room for the prohibition of cruelty to animals, putting this among the duties of man to himself. By inhuman treatment of animals, he says, sympathy with their sufferings is blunted in us, and thereby "comes a weakening of a natural disposition which is very helpful to our morality in relation to other men, and it gradually dies out."

Again, the vandalism of the destruction of beautiful, natural objects, which are viewed as entirely without feeling, is said to be unethical only because it violates the duty of man to himself by undermining the desire—itself a support to morality—of having something to love without regard to utility.

If the sphere of the ethical is limited to the relations of man to man, then all attempts to reach a basic principle of the moral with an absolutely binding content are rendered hopeless in advance. The absolute demands the universal. If there really is a basic principle for the moral, it must be concerned in some way or other with the relations between man and life as such in all its manifestations.

Kant, then, does not essay the task of developing a system of ethics which corresponds to his deepened conception of the ethical. On the whole he does nothing more than put the current utilitarian ethics under the protectorate of the Categorical Imperative. Behind a magnificent façade he constructs a block of tenements.

His influence on the ethics of his time is twofold. He furthers them by his challenge to profounder reflection on the nature of the ethical and the ethical destiny of man. At the same time he is a danger in that he robs ethics of their simplicity. The strength of the ethics of the age of reason lies in their naïve utilitarian enthusiasm. They directly enlist men in their service by offering them good aims and objects. Kant makes ethics insecure by bringing this directness in question and calling for ethics derived from much less elementary considerations. Profundity is gained at the cost of vitality, because he fails to establish at the same time a basic moral principle with a content, a principle which shall compel acceptance from deep and yet elementary considerations.

Often Kant actually makes it his object to block the natural sources of morality. He will not, for example, allow direct sympathy to be regarded as ethical. The inner feeling for the suffering of another as if it were one's own is not to count as duty in the real sense of the word, but only as a weakness by which the evil in the world is doubled. All help to others must have its source in a reasoned consideration of the duty of contributing to the happiness of mankind.

By taking from ethics their simplicity and directness, Kant also loosens the connection which ethics and the belief in progress had formed with one another, with the result that the two together had proved so productive of good. The disastrous separation between them which later on, in the course of the nineteenth century, became complete, was partly due to him.

He endangers the ethics of his time by wishing to drive out the naïve rationalistic conception of the ethical in favour of a deepened interpretation, without at the same time being in a position to establish for it a basic principle which has been correspondingly deepened, has a definite content of its own, and is directly convincing. He labours at the provision of new foundations without remembering that a house that is not adequately shored up will develop cracks.

* * *

Kant passes by the problem of finding a basic principle of the moral with a definite content, because, while attempting to deepen the concept of the ethical, he pursues an object which lies outside ethics. He wishes to bring ethical idealism into connection with an idealistic representation of the world which has its source in a theory of knowledge. From that source he hopes there will come an ethical philosophy capable of satisfying critical thought.

Why has Kant, with a rigorism which intentionally depreciates ordinary moral experience, ventured forward to the discovery that the moral law has nothing to do with the natural world-order, but is super-sensible? Because he refuses, similarly, to let the world of the senses which is experienced by us in space and time be accepted as anything more than a manifestation of the non-sensible which makes up true reality. The concept of the moral which contains none but inward and spiritual duties is for him the extending ladder which he draws out so as to mount by it to the region of pure Being. He has no feeling of dizziness when, in company with ethics, he climbs above all empirical experience and all empirical aims. He is determined to go right up with ethics, which can never be sufficiently *a priori* for him, because he sets up another ladder of the same length, that of epistemological idealism, and tries to lean one against the other, so that they may give mutual support.

How does it come about that the theoretical assumption that the world of sensible phenomena has a non-sensible world of Being lying behind it, has any importance for philosophy? Because within the notion of absolute duty which man experiences at work within himself there lies a fact of the world-order of that same immaterial world. Hence arises the possibility, thinks Kant, of raising to certainty by means of ethics those great elements in the non-sensible world which are of value for the optimistic-ethical world-view: the ideas of God, of the ethical freedom of the will, and of immortality, which otherwise would always remain merely problematical.

So far as rationalism affirms unhesitatingly from the standpoint of theoretical knowledge the ideas of God, of the ethical freedom of the will (virtue), and of immortality, which make up its optimistic-ethical world-view, it builds upon a foundation which cannot bear the weight of critical thought. Kant wishes, therefore, to erect the optimistic-ethical conception of the universe as a lake-dwelling built upon piles rammed into place by ethics. These three ideas are to be able to claim real existence as necessary postulates of the ethical consciousness.

This plan, however, of thus securing the position of the optimistic-ethical world-view cannot be carried out. It is only the idea of the ethical freedom of the will that can be made a logical demand of the moral consciousness. To establish the ideas of God and immortality as equally "postulates," Kant has to abandon all respectable logic and argue with bold and ever bolder sophisms.

There is no way of uniting epistemological and ethical idealism, however enticing the undertaking looks at first sight. When they are set side by side, the happenings which take place according to a law of causation originating in freedom, and become conscious in man through the moral law, are seen to be identical with the happenings which are universal in the world of things in themselves. There ensues a disastrous confusion of the ethical with the intellectual. If the world of the senses is only a manifestation of an immaterial world, then all the happenings which come about in the space and time sphere of causation produced by necessity are only parallel appearances of the events which are brought about in the intellectual sphere of causation produced by freedom. All happenings, therefore, —human activity just as much as natural happenings—are, according to the point of view, at once immaterial and free, and also natural and necessary. If ethical activity produced by freedom is represented as analogous with the results of epistemological idealism, then either everything that happens in the world, conceived as intellectual happening, is ethical, or there is no such thing as an ethical event. Because he has chosen to put side by side these two things, human activity and natural happening, Kant has to renounce all ability to maintain the difference between them. But the very life of ethics depends on this difference being there and effective.

Epistemological idealism is a dangerous ally for ethical idealism. The world-order of immaterial happening has a supra-ethical character. From the setting side by side of ethical and epistemological idealism there can never result an ethical, but always only a supra-ethical, world-view.

From epistemological idealism, therefore, ethics have nothing to expect, but everything to fear. By its depreciation of the reality of the empirical world ethical philosophy is not helped; but injured.

Ethics have materialist instincts. They want to be concerned with empirical happenings and to transform the circumstances of the empirical world. But if that world is only "appearance," derived from an intellectual world which functions within it or behind it, ethics have nothing on which to act. To wish to influence a self-determined play of appearances has no sense. Ethics can therefore allow validity to the view that the empirical world is mere appearance only with the limitation that activity exerted upon the appearance does at the same time influence the reality lying behind it. But thereby they come into conflict with all epistemological idealism.

Kant is defeated by the same fate which rules in Stoic, Indian, and Chinese monism alike. As soon as thought tries in any way to comprehend ethics in connection with the world-process, it falls at once, consciously or unconsciously, into the supra-ethical manner of regarding it. Fully to shape ethics to an ethical world-view means making them come to terms with nature-philosophy. Ethics are thereupon, as a matter of fact, devoured in one way or another by that philosophy, even if they are verbally saved from such a fate. The coupling of ethical with epistemological idealism is only bringing ethics and nature-philosophy into relation with one another in a roundabout way by which it is hoped to outwit the logic of facts. But this logic cannot be out-witted. The tragical result lies in the ensuing identification of the ethical with the intellectual.

The ethical is not something irrational which becomes ex-plicable when we betake ourselves from the world of appear-ance to the region of immaterial Being that lies behind it. Its spiritual character is of a peculiar kind, and rests upon the fact that the world-process, as such, comes in man into con-tradiction with itself. It follows that the ethical will and ethical freedom of the will are not explicable by any theory of knowl-edge, and cannot, moreover, serve as a support to any such theory.

As a result of conceiving the moral law and empirical obedience to natural law as in absolute opposition to each other, Kant finds himself on the road which leads to a dualistic world-view. Afterwards, however, in order to satisfy the claims of the unitary and optimistic world-view which the spirit of the age prescribes, he manages, with the stratagems which are provided for him by the combination of ethical and epistemological idealism, to work his way back on to the road which leads to the monistic point of view.

Kant is great as an ethical thinker, great too with his theory of knowledge, but as shaper of a world-view he is not in the first rank. By his deepened conception of the nature of the ethical, a conception which lands him in dualistic thought, the problem of the optimistic-ethical conception of life is unfolded in an entirely new way. Difficulties reveal themselves which till then no one could have imagined. But he does not deal with them. He is blinded by his ambition to be the Copernicus of the optimistic-ethical world-view, believing that he can show the difficulties inherent in that view to be misunderstandings which explain themselves away as soon as, by means of his epistemological idealism, actual relations take the place of these which are apparent but inexplicable. In reality he does nothing but replace the naïve optimistic-ethical interpretation of the world which was the basis of action for the rationalists by a fake explanation.

He does not take the trouble to ask himself in what the optimistic ethical world-view really consists, to what final items of knowledge and demands it leads, and how far these are confirmed by experience of the moral law. He takes it over without examination in the formula: "God, Freedom (or Virtue), and Immortality," which was supplied to it by rationalism, and determines to raise it in this naïve form to a certainty!

There is thus in Kant's philosophy the most terrible want of thought interwoven with the deepest thinking. Tremendous new truths, make their appearance in it. But they get only half-way on their journey. The absoluteness of ethical duty is grasped, but its content is not investigated. Experience of the ethical is recognized as the great secret by means of which we comprehend ourselves as "other than the world"; but the dualistic thinking which goes with it is not worked out any further. That the final perceptions of our world-view are assertions of the ethical will is admitted, but the consequences of this supremacy of the will over knowledge are not thought out to a conclusion.

Kant stimulates powerfully the men of his time, but is unable to make secure for them the optimistic-ethical philosophy of life in which they have been living. Although both he and they are content to deceive themselves in the matter, his mission is to deepen it, and . . . to make it become less secure than before.

Chapter 15

NATURE-PHILOSOPHY AND WORLD-VIEW IN

SPINOZA AND LEIBNIZ

*Spinoza's attempt to reach an optimistic-ethical
nature-philosophy.*

*Leibniz's optimistic-ethical world-view side by side
with nature-philosophy.*

JUST WHEN KANT IS BEGINNING TO INFLUENCE MEN'S MINDS, THE
entirely different ideas of a thinker who had now been dead
for a century, Baruch Spinoza (1632–1677),[1] also begin to interest those who are searching for a world-view. The *Critique
of Pure Reason* appears in 1781. In 1785 F. H. Jacobi in his
letters addressed to Moses Mendelssohn, *Concerning the Teaching of Spinoza,* draws attention once more to the philosopher
whom hitherto everyone had attacked without making any
effort to understand him.

Spinoza wants to win ethics from a real nature-philosophy.
He makes no attempt to give an optimistic-ethical interpretation of the universe, or to refashion it with any theory of knowledge. He accepts it just as it is in every respect. His philosophy
is therefore elementary nature-philosophy, but his method of
expounding it is by no means elementary. Acquiescing in the
way Descartes puts the problem and the language he uses, he

---

[1] *Tractatus theologico-politicus* (anonymous, 1670); *Ethica ordine geometrico
demonstrata* (posthumous and anonymous, 1677); German translation by Johann
Lorenz Schmidt, 1744); *Tractatus politicus* (posthumous and anonymous, 1677).
First complete edition of Spinoza's works, 1802–3.

[190]

makes his own thought about the universe proceed "in geometrical fashion" in a series of axioms, definitions, precepts, and proofs. Nature-philosophy is embodied in his philosophizing in a magnificent way, but it is as rigid as an ice-bound landscape.

His chief work—only published after his death, for he dared not publish it himself—he called *Ethics*. The title is confusing, because the nature-philosophy in the work is developed almost as completely as the ethics. It is only when the reader has freed himself of all naïve conceptions in his thought about the universe that he can be permitted, according to Spinoza, to begin upon ethics. The fact that ethics too are broken up into precepts which are given as proved is very prejudicial to their exposition.

In his attempt to found ethics upon nature-philosophy, Spinoza proceeds as follows. Everything that exists, he says, is given in that infinite Being, which may be called either God or Nature. For us, and to us, it presents itself in two forms: as thought (spirit) and as corporeity (matter). Within this divine nature everything, human activity included, is determined by necessity. There is no such thing as doing, there are only happenings. The meaning of human life, therefore, cannot consist in action, but only in coming to an ever clearer understanding of man's relation to the universe. Man becomes happy when, besides belonging to the universe naturally, he also surrenders himself to it consciously and willingly, and loses himself spiritually within it.

Spinoza demands therefore a higher experience of life. With the Stoics and the thinkers of India and China, he belongs to the great family of the monistic and pantheistic nature-philosophers. Like them, he conceives of God merely as the sum-total of nature, and accepts as valid only the notion of God which makes him in this way an independent unity. The attempts, made in the interests of the ethical world-view, to allow God to be at the same time an ethical personality standing outside the universe, are to him an offence against thought. Their only object is of course to obtain with the help of a confessed or unconfessed dualism a starting-point for an optimistic-ethical worldview. They are striving to reach along naïve religious by-roads the goal for which the rationalistic optimistic-ethical interpretation of the universe is making along the direct, but not less naïve, main-road.

The tragic result of monistic thinking in the Stoic, the Indian, and the Chinese philosophies is that nature-philosophy, when consistent, arrives only at resignation, not at ethics. Has Spinoza escaped this fate?

Like Lao-tse, Chwang-tse, Lie-tse, and the Chinese thinkers in general, Spinoza is the representative of an optimistic monism without suspecting that under distant skies in a remote age, he had such great predecessors.[2] His resignation is of a world- and life-affirming character. He conceives of infinite Being not as something devoid of qualities, as do the Indians, but as life with a full content. The self-perfecting, therefore, for which man is to strive is not for him, as it is for them, in any way an anticipation of a state of death, but a living out of life guided by deep reflection. A dignified egoistic world- and life-affirmation speaks through him, as through Chwang-tse.

The efforts of the man who refuses to deceive himself about himself are not directed, therefore, to any sort of action which is recognized as serviceable, but are concerned with maintaining his own Being, and giving it the fullest possible experience of life. Whatever good he does to others he never does for their sakes, but always for his own.

Spinoza rejected the achievement of modern ethics as influenced by Christianity, that is to say, the regarding of altruism as something that belongs to the essence of ethics. He confined himself to the thought that in the last resort all ethical action aims at our own interests, though it may be at our highest spiritual interests. In order to avoid thinking anything which is not a necessity of thought, he went back of his own free will into the captivity in which ancient ethics had their homes.

If he could have let himself go, like Chwang-tse, he would have conducted a campaign against the morality of love and duty. But since he already had as thoroughgoing opponents the authorities, the theologians, whether Jewish or Christian, and almost every philosopher, he had to speak cautiously and offer

---

[2] Lao-tse (born, *circa*: 604 B.C.): *Taoteking;* Chwang-tse (fourth century B.C.): *The True Book of the Southern Flower Land;* Lie-tse (fourth century B.C.): *The True Book of the Primitive Water-spring.*

mankind without attracting notice the philosophy of life which advocates profound and thinking egoism.

Just as God, the totality of universal Being, acts not with any aim or object but from an inner necessity, so also does the man who has attained to insight. He does only what contributes to complete experience of life. Virtue is capacity for self-maintenance at the highest level, and this self-maintenance is attained when reason is the highest motive to action, and efforts after knowledge and freedom from passion take possession of the man and make him free, that is, allow his conduct to be determined by himself alone and on purely inward grounds. The ordinary man is unstable, moved hither and thither in all sorts of ways by outward causes, with no idea of his future fortune or his final fate, like a ship that is tossed about on a stormy sea. Ethics, therefore, consist in living our life more as manifested thought than in corporeal actuality.

Acting with a deep, enlightened egoism and purely from intellectual impulses, a man behaves nobly in every relation of life. In so far as he can, he strives to requite hatred, anger, and contempt with love and noble feeling, because he knows that hatred always arouses repugnance. He seeks at any price to create around him an atmosphere of peace. He never acts deceitfully, but always straight-forwardly. He has no need to feel sympathy. Since he lives entirely under the guidance of reason, he does good whenever the opportunity offers, and therefore does not deliberately need to be roused to noble feeling by any experience of aversion. In fact he avoids sympathy. Again and again he makes it clear to himself that everything that happens is brought about by some necessity in the divine nature and in obedience to eternal laws. Just as he finds nothing in the world which deserves hatred, mockery, and contempt, so he finds in it nothing to evoke sympathy. Man must be ever striving to be virtuous and happy, and if he is conscious of having done good within the limits of what is commanded him, he can with an easy mind leave his fellow-men and the world to their fate. Beyond the possibilities of his own immediate activities, he need have nothing to do with them.

The wise man who practises the higher life-affirmation possesses power. He has power over himself, power over his fellow-men, and power over circumstances. How very similar is the tone of Spinoza's thought to that of Lao-tse, Chwang-tse, and Lie-tse!

Spinoza lived out his own ethics. He passed his life in contented independence until consumption brought it to an early close. He had declined an invitation to be lecturer in philosophy at Heidelberg University. He was strict with himself, but his attitude of resignation was lighted up by a mild trait of deliberate benevolence. The persecutions to which he was exposed failed to embitter him.

Intent though he is on thinking only in accordance with pure nature-philosophy, Spinoza does not concern himself so exclusively with the two natural entities, nature and the individual man, as do many of his Chinese predecessors, but maintains an interest in organized society. He is convinced that it betokens progress when men change from the "natural" stage of society to the "civic." Being formed for living with his fellows, man is freer if he settles by general agreement what belongs to each, and what the relations are to be between himself and society. The State must, therefore, have power to issue general orders as to how people are to live, and to secure respect for its laws by means of penalties.

Spinoza appears to have found no place for genuine devotion to the community. According to him, the perfect human society appears automatically just in proportion as its individual members live according to reason. In contrast, therefore, to his contemporary, Hobbes, he looks for the progress of society, not to the measures taken by the authorities, but to a growth towards perfection in the dispositions of their subjects. The State is to educate its citizens not to submissiveness, but to the right use of freedom. In no way must it do any injury to their sincerity. Therefore it must tolerate all religious views.

Far as Spinoza goes to meet the spirit of the age, there is one point on which he cannot agree with it, namely, that there are ethical aims, aims practical and purposive, to be realized in the world.

Advancing far ahead of his contemporaries, he reaches a universal conception of ethics, and recognizes that from the standpoint of consistent thinking, all moral behaviour can be nothing but an expression of the relation of the individual to the universe. But when ethics have in this way become universal, the next question is how the relation of the individual to the universe is conceivable as producing an effect upon the universe. On the answer to this depends whether genuine activist ethics can be established, or whether the ethical is only so far present as resignation can be explained as ethical.

That is the reef which threatens danger to all nature-philosophy, and whenever a thinker imagines that with clever seamanship and a favourable wind he can sail round it without coming to grief, he is nevertheless finally driven upon it, as by hidden currents, and suffers the same fate as his predecessors. Like Lao-tse and Chwang-tse, like the Indians, the Stoics, and all self-consistent philosophic thinkers before him, Spinoza cannot satisfy the demand of ethics, that the relation of man to the universe shall be conceived of as not merely a spiritual relation, but, at the same time, as active devotion to it in the material world. The opponents of this solitary thinker are instinctively conscious that with the re-establishment of an independent nature-philosophy there appears something which means danger to the optimism and the ethics of their world-view. Hence it is that in the seventeenth and eighteenth centuries everything unites to suppress Spinoza's philosophy.

It is on behalf of optimism that the age is most troubled. The terrible earthquake which in 1755 destroyed Lisbon, set the mass of men asking whether the world is really ruled by a wise and kindly Creator. Voltaire, Kant, and many other thinkers of the age seized on the occurrence as a topic for discussion, partly confessing their perplexity, partly seeking new ways out of the difficulty for their optimism.

* * *

How little optimism and ethics have to expect from a genuine nature-philosophy is shown not only in Spinoza, but also in Gottfried Wilhelm Leibniz (1646–1716).[3] In his *Theodicée* (1710) he tries to be fair to the optimistic world-view. He is helped in this by the fact that his nature-philosophy is much

---

[3] G. W. Leibniz: *Système nouveau de la nature, et de la communication des substances* (1695); *Nouveaux Essais* (1704); *La Monadologie* (1714).

more living and adaptable than Spinoza's. He is also determined to employ every possible device to attach an optimistic meaning to reality. He nevertheless gets no further than a laborious establishment of the conclusion that the actually existing world is the best of all possible worlds.

Moreover, so much of optimism as he rescues is useless for his world-view because it contains no energies which can be directed to ethical action upon the world. When he is consistent with himself he remains, like Spinoza, a prisoner within nature-philosophy. All the difficulties for ethics which Spinoza's deterministic nature-philosophy contains within itself, are to be found also in his. Owing to the fact that he does not put the union of thought (spirit) and extension (matter) far away in the Absolute, but allows it to be realized in countless tiny individualities which in their totality constitute the universe—he calls them monads—his nature-philosophy corresponds to the multiform character of reality much better than does Spinoza's. He anticipates to a considerable extent the modern nature-philosophy which is based on the cell-theory of matter. Yet he, too, remains under the spell of the way the problem is put by Descartes. He does not allow the individualities in which thought and extension are united to enter into living relations with each other, but limits their existence to being merely forces with powers of imagination. Their essential nature consists in being conscious of the universe, more clearly some, more confusedly others, but each independent of the rest.

In Spinoza there is a possibility of reaching a system of ethics, inasmuch as an attempt can be made to give an ethical interpretation to the mystical relation between man and the Absolute. Leibniz bars this path against himself in that he does not recognize such an abstract Absolute as the content of the universe. So it is not the result of chance that he nowhere philosophizes searchingly about ethics. In no way can ethics be deduced from his nature-philosophy.

Instead of admitting this result and unfolding the problem of the relation between ethics and nature-philosophy, he weaves into his philosophy traditional dicta about ethics, and defines the Good as love to God and man.

In nature-philosophy Leibniz is greater than Spinoza, because he deals with living reality more thoroughly. But in the struggle for a correct outlook on the universe, he is far behind him, because Spinoza, a man with a simpler mental endowment, recognizes the reconciliation of ethics and nature-philosophy as the central problem of world-view, and proceeds to tackle the problem.

If Leibniz had remained consistent, he would have ended in atheism, as does the Indian Samkhya philosophy, which similarly makes the world consist of a multiplicity of eternal individualities. Instead of that, in order to preserve a satisfactory conception of life, he introduces into his nature-philosophy a theistic notion of God, and by giving it an optimistic, ethical, and theistic expression, makes it acceptable to the eighteenth century. His philosophy, popularized till it is almost unrecognizable by Christian Wolff (1679–1754), helps to lay the foundations of German rationalism.

But in spite of the treason of which he is thus, though with the best intentions, guilty against nature-philosophy, Leibniz cannot undo the fact that through him thought on the lines of nature-philosophy awoke at that time to activity. Without wishing it, he contributes to making Spinoza an influence.

But for the spirit of the time to let itself be mixed up with nature-philosophy is to step into the dangerous unknown. It therefore resists as long as possible. At last, however, since Kant and Spinoza together are undermining the optimistic-ethical world-view of rationalism which has been built upon the real world and so conveniently furnished, it has to make up its mind to rebuild, and attempt the process of arriving at a conception of optimism and ethics by direct thinking on the essential nature of the world. German speculative philosophy offers its services for the carrying out of this undertaking.

Chapter 16

J. G. FICHTE'S OPTIMISTIC-ETHICAL

WORLD-VIEW

Speculative philosophy and Gnosticism.
Fichte's speculative founding of an ethic and of optimism.
Fichte's mysticism of activity incapable of being
carried through.

THE VISION OF AN OPTIMISTIC-ETHICAL PHILOSOPHY CAST IN ONE mould hovers in front of speculative philosophy, which hopes to discover the meaning of the world by the most direct route. It will have nothing to do with analysing the phenomena of the universe in order to deduce its nature from them. It proceeds deductively, not inductively. In pure abstract thinking it hopes to learn how the real world has evolved out of the notion of Being. It is imaginative nature-philosophy dressed up as logic.

The right to deal with the world in this fashion is derived by speculative thought from the results of epistemological theory, according to which the world as we observe it is more or less our own idea of it. We have, somehow or other, a creative share in its coming into existence. It follows that the logic which is the rule with the finite ego is to be conceived as an emanation of that which holds good with the Absolute. The individual is therefore entitled to disclose in his own thinking the motives and the process of the emanation of the empirical world from the notion of Being. Speculation, or in other words constructive logic, is the key of the secret door to knowledge of the world.

By nature, speculative German philosophy is essentially related to the Græco-Oriental Gnosticism, which in the first centuries of the Christian era advances its views concerning the emergence of the world of the senses from the world of pure Being.[1] The Gnostic systems aim at establishing a philosophy of redemption. They concentrate on the question how the spiritual individualities which are found in the material world arrived there, and how they can return from it into the world of pure Being. Speculative German philosophy on the other hand tries to obtain such a knowledge of the world as shall give a meaning to the activities of the spiritual individualities in the world. Speculative thinking at the beginning of the Christian era is dualistic and pessimistic; at the beginning of the nineteenth century it is monistic and optimistic. In both cases, however, the method of obtaining the world-view is the same.

Among the representatives of the speculative philosophy the most eminent are: Johann Gottlieb Fichte (1762–1814), Friedrich Wilhelm Joseph Schelling (1775–1854), and Georg Wilhelm Friedrich Hegel (1770–1831). It is only Fichte and Hegel, however, who produce world-views with a characteristic stamp of their own. Schelling gets no further than a nature-philosophy, and stands almost completely aside from the struggle for an optimistic-ethical philosophy with which his age is occupied. Kept in a perpetual state of flux, his thinking makes use of all possible standpoints one after another and is now more concerned with natural science, now more akin to Spinoza's, and now to Christian, thought. He never makes a definite, conscious attempt to found a system of ethics.

* * *

Fichte begins as the antipodes of Spinoza.[2] By thinking Kant's

---

[1] The greatest representatives of Gnosticism are Basilides, Valentinus, and Marcion, all three living in the first half of the second century B.C. At the beginning of that century all sorts of Gnostic systems sprang up, as did speculative systems at the beginning of the nineteenth. The two great Christian teachers of Alexandria, Flavius Clemens at the end of the second century A.D., and Origen at the beginning of the third, try to bring the Gnostic speculations into harmony with the doctrine of the Church.

[2] J. G. Fichte: *The Foundations of All Scientific Theories* (1794); *The System of Moral Teaching According to the Principles of Science* (1798); *The Destiny of*

thoughts out to a conclusion he aims at extracting from the universe a confession that it is purely optimistic-ethical.

Kant, according to him, made the mistake of not bringing his two discoveries, epistemological idealism and the ethics of the categorical imperative, into that inward connection with one another in which they really stand.

What is the meaning of the fact that the moral law and the material world both become actual in me? That is the starting-point of Fichte's philosophizing.

Through the categorical imperative, I experience that my particular *ego* is a self-determined will to activity. Correspondingly, every "thing in itself" which I assume to exist behind phenomena as the reality on which they are based, is also a self-determined will to activity. The essential nature, too, of infinite Being can consist of nothing else. The universe is, therefore, the phenomenal form of an infinite, self-determined will to activity.

Why does the absolute *ego* appear as a phenomenon in a world of sense? Why is Being revealed as Becoming? If I understand this, I have comprehended the meaning of the world and of my own life.

Now the absolute *ego,* because it is infinite will to activity, cannot persist in being an *ego.* It establishes a non-*ego* to be a limit to itself in order that it may again and again overcome it, and thereby become conscious of itself as will to activity. This process takes place amid the multiplicity of finite rational beings. In their power of perception the world of the senses becomes actual. To overcome it they recognize as a duty which makes itself mysteriously felt within them and unites them with the world-spirit. This is the meaning of the philosophy of the identity of the *ego* and the non-*ego.*

It is not only, then, that the world exists merely in my idea of it: it is, further, only produced in me in order that I may have something on which my will to fulfilment of duty can

Man (1800); *How to Attain to the Happy Life* (1806); *Addresses to the German Nation* (1808).

A complete edition of J. G. Fichte's works was edited by his son, J. H. Fichte, in 1845 and the following years. A good selection has been published by F. Medicus (1908 to 1912).

exercise itself. The phenomena of becoming and disappearing which I project out of myself exist only that through them I may comprehend myself as an ethical being. In this way epistemological idealism and the categorical imperative, when they unite and one climbs on the shoulders of the other, can look behind the curtain which hides the secret of the world.

Kant protests against the idea that Fichte's system is to be considered the completion of his own philosophy. As a matter of fact, however, Fichte does with ingenious art continue the lines which were begun in the *Critique of Pure Reason* and the *Critique of the Practical Reason,* and think out the ideas of the philosopher of Königsberg to a self-contained world- and life-affirming ethical world-view. He presents them in a generally intelligible form in *The Destiny of Man,* published in 1800. This book is one of the most powerful documents produced by the struggle for an ethical outlook on life.

Fichte gives a content to the abstract, absolute duty of Kant, making it consist in man, as the instrument of the ever-active absolute Ego, assigning to himself the destiny of working with that Ego "to bring the whole world of the senses under the sovereignty of reason."

Since his fundamental moral principle possesses a content, Fichte is able to deduce particular demands from it, but that content is so general and so vague that the code of duty which is drawn out from it has but little vital force. Nothing can really be learnt from this fundamental principle beyond the demand that man shall in every situation of life fulfil the duties which from time to time fall to him as a result of his destined mission to help forward the sovereignty of reason over nature. Fichte therefore distinguishes between the general duties which man, as such, has to fulfil, and the special duties which are incumbent on him because of his natural gifts, his social position, and his profession. These are emphasized as specially important.

By defining ethics as activity which aims at subjecting the material world to reason, Fichte gives a cosmic formulation to the utilitarian ethics of rationalism, and thus supplies a comprehensive and deep foundation for the ethical enthusiasm which was a discovery of his time. Here too he develops what had hovered before the mind of Kant.

At the same time he opposes the representatives of the popular philosophy of the Illumination, and in a polemical pamphlet criticizes very severely Cristoph Friedrich Nicolai. At bottom, however, the only reproach he can level at them is that they wish to go on providing a place for ethics and belief in progress in the naïve world-view arrived at by the healthy human reason, instead of accepting both of them from the philosophy which results from the union of epistemological idealism and the categorical imperative. To persist in imperfect rationalism when the perfect has been made a reality by Kant and himself is, in his opinion, a crime against truth. To him the beginning of wisdom is insight into the paradox that "consciousness of the world of actuality springs from our need of action, not our need of action from our consciousness of the world."

The spirit of Fichte's philosophy is then completely that of rationalism, only that rationalism believes it has found itself with him in the real nature of Being, and now comes forward with still stronger conviction and a still more burning enthusiasm. In Fichte's writings, men are positively whipped up to work for the improvement of the world. With impressive pathos he teaches them to obey the inner voice which urges them on to activity, and indicates to them their definite duty whatever may be the special circumstances of their existence. And he teaches them to recognize that in so doing they are fulfilling the highest, and indeed the only, destiny of their lives.

It is as the result of this inner urge to activity that we long for a better world than the one which we see around us, and belief in that better world is what we live by. Fichte makes confession of unbounded optimism. "All those outbreaks of untamed force before which human power is annihilated, those devastating hurricanes, those earthquakes, those volcanic eruptions, can be nothing else than the last struggles of the wild mass of nature against the uniformly progressive, purposive and life-promoting course to which, in opposition to its own tendencies, it is being compelled." . . . "Nature is to become to us more and more transparent and capable of examination even to its innermost secret; and enlightened human power, armed with its own inventions, is destined to master it without trouble, and then to exploit peacefully its once for all made conquest." [3] Here Fichte gives us the triumphant pæan of the belief in progress which the spirit of the modern age, that lives on the achievements of its knowledge and power, has been composing since the Renaissance. He is as thoroughly convinced as the staunchest rationalist that nature is the buffalo which has remained refractory so long, but will at last be brought beneath the yoke.

That mankind will perfect itself and reach a condition of unbroken peace, is to him as certain as the perfection that nature will one day attain. At present, it is true, we are in a period of arrested progress with temporary setbacks, but when this is past, "and all useful things which have been discovered at one end of the world, get known to and distributed to all men, then mankind, using its powers in complete co-operation and marching forward in step, will raise itself uninterruptedly, without arrest of progress or setback, to a culture of which we can form no conception."

To the State Fichte assigns in his early writings a not very important *rôle*, but in his later works a great one. In *The Foundations of the Law of Nature (Grundlage des Naturrechts)* (1796), it is for him only the maintainer of law and order. In his work *The Complete Commercial State (Der geschlossene Handelsstaat)*, which appeared in 1800, he allows it to organize industry and to take over social duties. In his *Address to the German Nation (Reden an die deutsche Nation,* 1808), he makes it a moral educator and a protector of the virtue of humanity.

The man who, with the help of epistemological idealism, has made his way through to the higher rationalism, is safe from losing his optimism, even though he goes through the cruellest experiences. He has grasped the fact that the material world is only the barrier which the infinitely active will has created on purpose that it may overcome it. This lends him inward independence in the face of all happenings. He has no need to understand them individually. He can let a large proportion of them be put aside as puzzling to his finite spirit. What is essential he knows: that what is real in the world is not matter, but spirit only.

[3] This and the following quotations are from *The Destiny of Man.*

Partaking of the eternally active spirit, man is raised above the world, and is eternal. The sufferings he meets with afflict only nature, "with which he is connected in a marvellous way," but not himself, the being who is exalted above the whole of nature. Of death he has no fear. He does not die for himself, but only for those who survive him. . . . "All death in nature is birth. . . . Nature is throughout nothing but life. It is not death which kills, but the living life which, concealed behind the old one, now begins and proceeds to develop. Death and birth are nothing but the struggle of life with itself in an effort to reveal itself more and more clearly and more and more like its real self." It is in similar words that the Chinese monist, Chwang-tse, announces that life is eternal and the dying of an individual only means that one existence is being re-cast to form another.

*   *   *

Fichte's philosophy of absolute activity is the expression of his own strong ethical personality, which with impetuosity and self-sacrifice takes problems in hand, and uses itself up in the strain involved. But even he is unable to make a genuine combination of epistemological and ethical idealism so as to produce an ethical world-view which is a necessity of thought. The impossibility of the undertaking reveals itself everywhere.

In order to conceive ethics as a part of the normal course of world-happenings, Fichte, like all others who make the same attempt, gives up as hopeless any differentiation between human action and world-happenings. The world-spirit's impulse to activity, he says, experiences itself in man as will to ethical action. But, indeed, the whole world is filled with this will to activity which is forever surging against the limitations it has set up for itself. Everything that happens is only an expression of it. What difference, then, is there between natural and ethical happenings? Between activity in itself and ethical activity? Purposive activity directed with knowledge and intention to the subjection of the world of the senses to reason is ethical, decides Fichte. But what does that mean, when closely examined? It means that the finite spirit becomes moral by entering into and taking seriously the play of the infinite spirit which aims at overcoming its own self-created limitations. Looking in this way at Fichte's thought, we see clearly that with the world-view which results from the combination of ethical and epistemological idealism, ethics have no longer any meaning.

Again, what is the meaning of "bringing the whole of the material world under the sovereignty of reason"? This conception of the ethical is not only too wide, but fantastic. To a limited extent man is able to harness the forces of nature for his service, and with a little stretching of language he can, with Fichte, describe such action as not merely purposive, but also in the widest sense ethical. He has some "influence" on the earth, but none at all upon the universe. That he gives names to the mighty heavenly bodies and can calculate the orbits of many, cannot mean that he brings them under the sovereignty of reason. Upon deep-sea life, too, he exercises no other influence than catching specimens of it and giving them names.

That he may be able to assert that there is such a thing as an ethical purpose in the world, Fichte falsifies its birth certificate, and gives it the categorical imperative for father and epistemological idealism for mother. But this is of no use. The ethical purpose thus produced cannot satisfy ethical thought.

By conceiving the infinite spirit, in which the finite spirit has a share, as will to activity, Fichte tries to make possible a philosophy of ethical world- and life-affirmation. In reality, however, this takes him no further than a more emphatic world- and life-affirmation, into which, with the help of speculative thought, he smuggles the idea of duty, thereupon proclaiming it to be ethical. It fares with him just as with the Chinese nature-philosophers, who similarly exert themselves in vain to produce ethics from world- and life-affirmation.

Absorption in the Absolute by means of action, as in the thought of Fichte, is a prodigious thing, but, like its counterpart, absorption in the Absolute effected by an act of thought, it is not ethical but supra-ethical. The element which is needed by the mysticism of absorption in the Absolute to make it ethical cannot be secured either by enhancing or by depreciating the will to activity.

Fichte's mysticism of activity in which man lets loose his energy in the world is related to the ethics of action, just as

Spinoza's mysticism of knowledge, in which man is absorbed in the world, is related to the ethics of self-perfecting. But it is only very incompletely that either can be developed into real ethics.

The absorption in the Absolute which comes into actuality in an act of thought lies nearer to nature-philosophy than that which completes itself in action. The Brahmans, the Buddha, Lao-tse, Chwang-tse, Spinoza, and the mystics of every age, have experienced the becoming one with the Absolute as a coming-to-rest in it. Fichte's mysticism of activity lies more in the path of dualistic thinking than in that of real nature-philosophy. It is something which has been extorted by enthusiasm, but Fichte is devoted to it, and rightly, because he has a feeling that the interests of the ethics of activity are better guarded by it than by the other. But since he thus once and for all decides for a nature-philosophy, dominated though he is by the ideal of active ethics, he comes more and more to the natural quietist consequences of such a philosophy. He goes through a process of evolution which brings him nearer to Spinoza's world-view. In his *Instruction Concerning the Blessed Life,* which appeared in 1806, six years later than *The Destiny of Man,* it is to him no longer what is ethical which in itself is the highest, but what is religious. The ultimate meaning of life, he now recognizes, is not to act in God, but to be merged in Him. "Self-annihilation is the gateway into the higher life." [4]

He believes, indeed, that he is thereby merely deepening his world-view without diminishing its ethical energy. Right to the end he remains the fiery spirit which consumes itself in activity for promoting the progress of the world. But his thought has bent under the weight of nature-philosophy. Without clearly admitting it to himself, he recognizes that from nature-philosophy there can be drawn only an intellectual, not an ethical, meaning for the world and life. Spinoza observes with a smile how he retires upon the thought beyond which a nature philosophy cannot advance by its own momentum.

Fichte is the first philosopher to declare plainly that no outlook on life is ethical which does not enable man to explain that an enthusiastic active devotion to the universe is grounded

[4] "Anweisung zum seligen Leben."

in the nature of the world and of life. But the road he takes in order to develop this thought leads him astray. Instead of going more deeply into the question how ethical happenings, though coming from the world-spirit, and directed upon the world, are nevertheless different from world-happenings, and investigating the nature of this difference, he employs the trick, which had been made possible by Kant, of declaring, with the help of epistemological idealism, that the ethical world-view is a necessity of thought. Many of his contemporaries believe with him that it has thereby really reached a position of supremacy, and even those who cannot go with him the whole length of the philosophy of the *ego* and non-*ego,* are gripped by the force of the ethical personality which speaks from Fichte's writings.

The direct effect, then, of Fichte's philosophy is that the optimistic, ethical spirit of rationalism maintains its position and becomes stronger and deeper. This enthusiast gives a tremendous impetus to ethics and civilization. But the vessel in which, with a magnificent wind behind him, he starts with his companions on a voyage over the sea of knowledge is leaky. A catastrophe is only a question of time.

Fichte's belief that he has obtained from the nature of the universe the living compulsion to ethical duty and ethical action which he feels within himself, is an illusion. The manner, however, in which he conceives the problem of the optimistic-ethical world-view, and perceives that for its solution ordinary processes afford no help, so that more or less violent methods must be tried in turn, reveals him as a great thinker.

Chapter 17

SCHILLER; GOETHE; SCHLEIERMACHER

Schiller's ethical world-view: Goethe's world-view based on nature-philosophy.

Schleiermacher's attempt at a nature-philosophy.

IT IS A VERY IMPORTANT FACT THAT THE DEEPENED OPTIMISTIC-ethical world-view of Kant and Fichte finds a champion in Friedrich von Schiller (1759–1805), who brings it to the mass of the people with the force added by poetical language. He is himself philosophically gifted, and undertakes to develop it further, for he wishes to broaden the foundations of the ethical by showing its relation to the æsthetic.

In his *Letters Concerning the Æsthetic Education of Mankind* (1795), he works out the idea that art and ethics belong together as far as that in both man maintains with the material world a relation which is free and creative. "The transition from the passive condition of feeling to the active one of thinking and willing comes about in no other way than through an inter-mediate condition of æsthetic freedom. . . . There is no way of making the sentient man rational other than first making him æsthetic." In what way the capacity for freedom which is built up in man by æsthetic practice really disposes him to morality, Schiller does not work out in further detail. His treatise, in spite of all the notice it attracted and deserves, is more rhetorical than substantial. He has not gone to the bottom of the problem of the relations between the æsthetic and the ethical.

In contrast to Schiller, Johann Wolfgang von Goethe (1749–1832), stands in almost as alien an attitude to the philosophy of the deepened rationalism as he does to that of ordinary rationalism. He finds it impossible to share the confidence with which people around him regard optimistic and ethical convictions as well founded. What separates him from Kant and Fichte and Schiller is reverence for the reality of nature. Nature is to him something in herself, not merely something existing for the sake of mankind. He does not require from her that she shall fit herself completely into our optimistic-ethical designs. He does no violence to her either through epistemological and ethical idealism or through presumptuous speculation, but lives in her as a human being who looks at existence with wonder and knows not how to bring her relation to the world-spirit within any formula.

Descartes led modern philosophy astray by cutting the world up into objects which have extension and objects which think, and then refusing to each of them the possibility of influencing the other. Following in his steps, thinkers rack their brains over the problem of these two parallel kinds of existence, and try to comprehend the world in formulas. That the world is life, and that in life lies the riddle of riddles, never enters their minds. Hence they overlook in their philosophizing what is most important. Because Descartes preceded them, the two great spirits who adhere to nature-philosophy, Spinoza and Leibniz, cannot get further than a nature-philosophy which is more or less dead. Being in the line of descent from Descartes, Kant and Fichte renounce all philosophizing over the real world.

Descartes and the ethical belief-in-progress, therefore, agree in a common neglect of nature. Both alike overlook the fact that she is living, and that she exists for her own sake. It is because he cannot join them in this that Goethe dares to confess that he understands nothing about philosophy. His greatness is this: that in a time of abstract and speculative thought he had the courage to remain elemental.

Overwhelmed by the mysterious individual life in nature, he adheres to a magnificently unfinished world-view. With the spirit of an investigator he looks within into everything; in that of an inquirer he looks around upon everything. He wants to think optimistically. Shaftesbury's thoughts exercise their charm upon him also. But in the chorus of optimism which

makes itself heard so loudly around him, he cannot join. World-
and life-affirmation is for him not such a simple thing as it is
for Fichte and Schiller. He strives to reach an ethical conception
of the universe, but admits to himself that he cannot succeed.
So he does not venture to attribute a meaning to nature. To
life, however, he desires to attribute a meaning. He seeks it in
serviceable activity. To give the world-view of activity a place in
nature-philosophy is for him an inner necessity. To the conviction that activity provides the only real satisfaction in life, and
that therein lies the mysterious meaning of existence, he gives
expression in *Faust* as something which he has laboriously gained
during his pilgrimage through existence and to which he will
hold fast, without being able to explain it completely.

Goethe struggles to arrive at a conception of ethical activity,
but cannot reach such a conception because nature-philosophy
is unable to provide him with any criterion of what is ethical.
What that philosophy had to refuse to the Chinese monists and
to Spinoza, it cannot give to him either.

The range of this world-view of Goethe's, conditioned as it
is by reality, remains hidden from his contemporaries. Its incompleteness alienates their sympathies and irritates them. For
knowledge of the world and of life which cannot be reduced to
a system, but sticks fast in facts, they have no understanding.
They hold to their optimism and their ethics.

*   *   *

Daniel Ernst Schleiermacher (1768–1834), stands apart both
from the ordinary and from the deepened rationalism because
he cannot free himself from the influence of Spinoza.[1] His life-
work is directed to preaching the Spinozan nature-philosophy
as being, as far as he can make it so, both ethics and the Christian
religion. Hence he always dresses it up as one or the other.

The accepted ethical code, in Schleiermacher's opinion, makes
man merely run about on the earth as an ethical individual bent
on improving the world. Living in this way, in a constant state

---

[1] D. E. Schleiermacher: *Discourses on Religion for the Educated among its Con-
temners* (1799); *Monologues* (1800); *Outlines of a Critique of Moral Philosophy
down to the Present Day* (1803); *Christian Belief* (1821–23); *Draft of a System of
Moral Philosophy* (posthumous, 1835).

of enthusiasm, he runs the risk of losing himself and becoming unpersonal. He forgets that it is his first duty to be alone with himself, to look within himself, and, instead of being a mere human creature, to become a personality.

This renunciation of rationalism's enthusiasm for activity is to be found in the Monologues, those splendid introspective meditations meant for the first New Year's Day of the nineteenth century. One seems to hear in them Lao-tse and Chwang-tse criticising the moralism and the fanaticism for progress of Confucius.

According to Schleiermacher man's first task is to realize his oneness with the Infinite and in the Infinite to see the universe. Only what results from this as action is really significant, and has importance for morality.

Spinoza's ethics consisted in keeping oneself at the highest level and living rather a life of thought than a life of corporeal existence. Schleiermacher's ethics have the same objective, except that he seeks to combine with it a more comprehensive interest in the world than is to be found in Spinoza. He is helped in this direction by his belief that progress is immanent.

We have, he says, no other perfecting to bring about in things than that which is inherent in them. Ethics, therefore, are not a setting up of laws, but the recognition and description of the tendencies working for perfection which appear in the world, together with behaviour in the same sense. The moral law is not distinct from the law of nature and pursues no different aims. It is only the law of nature arriving in man at the consciousness of itself.

So Schleiermacher's task was not, as was Fichte's, the bringing of the universe under the sovereignty of reason; it consisted solely in supporting the oneness of nature and reason in the sphere of human action, which is ever striving to realize itself within that universe. "All ethical knowledge is the expression of the ever-beginning but never completed efforts of reason to become nature." Ethics are a contemplative "science." They revolve around the two poles of natural science and human history.

The ethics which result from this fundamental conception, like those of Lao-tse and Chwang-tse, are so toned down that there is no longer any real power in them. However completely Schleiermacher may try to conceal this fact by the wonderful way he presents his theme, it plays only a subordinate *rôle*. What gives a meaning to human existence is something which is independent of deeds; it is the oneness with the Infinite which is experienced in feeling.

In clever dialectic, but not in reality, Schleiermacher's ethics surpass Spinoza's. His philosophy is the same as that of Spinoza, only enriched by his belief in the immanence of progress. Hence his ethics glow with somewhat more brilliant colours.

Thus do a living nature-philosophy in Goethe and a Spinozan nature-philosophy in Schleiermacher undermine the ground on which stand the men of the now beginning nineteenth century, whose thinking is so enthusiastically optimistic-ethical. The crowd pays no attention to their dangerous proceedings. It gazes at the fireworks of Kant and Fichte, while Schiller recites his poetry. And now there begin to rise bursts of rockets which throw a peculiarly brilliant light. The past-master in the art of firework display, Hegel, has come into action.

Chapter 18

HEGEL'S SUPRA-ETHICAL OPTIMISTIC

WORLD-VIEW

Ethics in Hegel's nature-philosophy, and in his philosophy of history.

Hegel's supra-ethical world-view. His belief in progress.

IN HIS SPECULATIVE PHILOSOPHY FICHTE'S FIRST AND CHIEF interest was ethical. Hegel, a profounder and more objective thinker, aims at truth before everything.[1] While availing himself of any helpful considerations provided by facts, he endeavours to discover the meaning of Being. So he cannot join Fichte in the violent procedure, suggested by his ethics, of giving the world the categorical imperative for father and epistemological idealism for mother. Before going so far as to write out a birth-certificate for the world, he undertakes some essential investigations. He studies the laws which govern events, as they are revealed in history. He then lays these as the foundation for the constructive operations which are to explain the origin of the world from the notion of Being. His philosophy, therefore, is a philosophy of history become cosmic. The building, so far as one can measure it externally, is solidly constructed. That is why it is still convincing even where its lines lose themselves in infinity.

What, then, does Hegel discover to be the principle under-

[1] Friedrich Hegel *Phenomenology of the Spirit* (1807); *The Science of Logic* (3 vols., 1812–26); *Encyclopædia of the Philosophical Sciences* (1817); *The Philosophy of Law* (1821); *The Philosophy of History* (posthumous, 1840). Complete edition of his works in eighteen volumes, prepared by his pupils, 1832–45.

[213]

lying the course of events in history? He discovers that every process of becoming advances with natural progress, and that this progress realizes itself in the occurrence of a consecutive series of contradictions which invariably issue in reconciliation! In thoughts as in facts, every thesis evokes an antithesis. Then these unite in a synthesis which preserves what is valuable in both of them. Every synthesis that is reached becomes again a thesis for a new antithesis. From these there results again a new synthesis, and so on forever.

With the aid of this scheme, Hegel can expound the course of history. From it he is, at the same time, able to develop the basic principles of logic. Hence he is sure that with it also it must be possible to make intelligible how the conceptual world which can be logically developed out of the notion of Being passes over into being the world of reality. He carries this fancy through to its conclusion in such magnificent fashion, that even we, who are proof against its charm, can understand how it was possible to become intoxicated with it.

While Fichte seeks to give an ethical meaning to the expansion of pure Being into the world of reality, Hegel from the very outset takes his stand upon the assertion that in its ultimate analysis the meaning of the world can only be found in the realm of the spirit. The Absolute has no other object in bringing a world into existence than to become conscious of itself. It is infinitely creative spirit, but not, as in Fichte's thought, with the object of endless activity, but with that of returning into itself by the road of its own creations.

In nature the Absolute comprehends itself only very dimly. It is first in man that it really experiences itself, and that in three ascending stages. In the man who is concerned only with himself and nature it is still subjective spirit. In the communal spirit of men who co-operate for the legal and ethical organization of human society, it expands to objective spirit and at the same time, on a basis of concepts provided within this spirit, shows itself capable of being creative. In art, in religion, and in philosophy it becomes conscious of itself as absolute spirit, existing in and for itself, and having overcome the contradictions of subject and object, thought and being. In art it contemplates itself as such; in religious devotion it presents itself as such; in philosophy, which is pure thought, it comprehends itself as such. With the world represented as thought, the Absolute experiences itself.

Before the destiny to which Spinoza submits with a smile, against which Fichte and Schleiermacher rebel, Hegel bows in courageous reverence for truth. His world-view is supra-ethical mysticism. The ethical is to him only a phase in the development of the immaterial. Civilization he conceives not as ethical, but only as intellectual.

For proof that the ethical is nothing in itself, but only a phenomenon of the intellectual, Hegel appeals to French usage. "The moral," he says, "must be taken in the wider sense in which it signifies not the morally good alone. 'Le moral' in French is the antithesis of the physical, and means the spiritual, the intellectual, or the non-material in general." [2]

The notion of the ethical with which Hegel works is extraordinarily wide. It consists in "the will having for its objects not subjective, that is to say, selfish, interests, but a universal content." [3] It is the business of thought to define this universal content in particular instances.

If Hegel had fully explored the fact that the individual will comes to a point where it assigns itself universal objects, and had felt this fact to be the mystery that it is, he could not have passed as lightly as he does over the ethical problem. He would have had to admit to himself that the spiritual element which manifests itself in it is unique in character, and cannot be included in any higher form of spirituality, or classified under any other at all. The problem of the mutual relationship between the spiritual and the moral would have been clearly posed.

But Hegel is so anxious to find some sort of shelter for his speculative optimistic world-view that he estimates the birth of the ethical in man not by and for itself, but simply as a phenomenon of the rise of the supra-individual spirit. Instead of directing his thought to the question of how the individual spirit in each several person can be at the same time supra-individual and conscious of its oneness with the Absolute, Hegel sets out to make intelligible the higher experience of the indi-

[2] *The Encyclopædia,* Part III. (1845 ed.), p. 386.
[3] *The Encyclopædia of Philosophical Sciences,* Part III. (1845 ed.), p. 359.

vidual by means of the mutual relation between it and the universal spirit of the collective body to which it belongs. He says it is presumption for the individual spirit as such to seek, as it does in Indian thought, to comprehend its relation to the Absolute. Becoming one with the Absolute is an experience of the universal spirit of collective humanity when it has reached its loftiest height. Only when it stands in connection with this, as a river with the waters of a lake through which it has flowed, can the individual spirit obtain experience of the Absolute. This is the fatal turning towards the general and supra-personal at which the Hegelian philosophy becomes superficial.

Ethics, then, for Hegel have at bottom only the significance that they make possible the growth of a society in the collective spirit of which the absolute spirit can come to a consciousness of itself. Man becomes moral by submitting voluntarily to the demands which society recognizes as expedient with a view to the creation of the higher life of the spirit.

Hegel has no ethics for the individual. The deep problems of ethical self-perfecting and of the relations between man and man do not concern him. When he does discuss ethics, he at once turns to the family, society, and the State.

With Bentham ethics complete law. Hegel works the two in together. It is significant that he wrote no treatise on ethics. All that he does publish about ethics is to be found in his philosophy of law.

His first concern is to show that the State, correctly conceived, is not merely a legal, but a legal-ethical entity. Fichte had made it the ethical educator of the individual. For Hegel it is the essential element in all moral happenings, "the self-conscious moral substance," as he expresses it. What is most valuable in the moral is realized in it and through it. This overvaluing of the State is a natural consequence of his low valuation of the spiritual significance of individuality as such.

*   *   *

Hegel can have nothing to do with Fichte's idea—an idea which he found impossible to develop to a conclusion—of giving ethics a cosmic foundation in such a way that their content might be the bringing of the world under the sovereignty of reason. His feeling for reality debars him from anything so fantastic. But his complete abandonment of the cosmic conception of ethics is disastrous. Instead of allowing ethics and nature-philosophy to try conclusions together in his speculative thought, he makes a sacrifice of ethics from the start. He refuses them the liberty (which they enjoyed with Spinoza, Fichte, and Schleiermacher), of trying to be understood as the relation of the individual to the universe. They are forbidden, further, to try (as they can do with the Chinese monists), to get accepted as part of the meaning of the universe. They are restricted to being a standard for the regulation of the relations between individuals and society. They may not be active as a formative idea in the creation of a world-view upon a foundation of nature-philosophy. They are simply built into the edifice as an already shaped and dressed stone.

In consequence of Hegel's allowing ethics no significance beyond that of a preparatory motive to realizing the spiritual meaning of the world, his teaching becomes remarkably analogous to the Brahmanic. Hegel and the Brahmans are akin because, as consistent thinkers, they venture to admit that thought about the world and the Absolute which lies behind it can reach only an intellectual, not an ethical, meaning in the union of the finite spirit with the infinite, and therefore value ethics only as a preparatory motive thereto. With the Brahmans ethics prepare the individual for the intellectual act in which he experiences the Absolute in himself and in death passes into that Absolute. With Hegel they help in the formation of society, in whose communal spirit the Absolute first becomes capable of experiencing itself.

It is only a relative difference between Hegel and the Brahmans that the latter make their intellectualist mysticism individualist and world- and life-denying, while Hegel develops his as world- and life-affirming, and makes the intellectual act take place only when a society has produced the requisite spirituality. The inner similarity in character of the two world-views is not affected thereby. One is the complement of the other. Both give value to ethics only as a phase of intellectuality.

With Hegel, as with the Brahmans, a place is found for ethics, but this is not shown to be necessary. For the realization of the consciousness of oneness with the Absolute the decisive element for the Brahmans is, in the last resort, only a sufficient advance in world- and life-denial, and depth of meditation. With Hegel, society, which has to create the spirituality in which the absolute spirit experiences itself in the finite, could come into existence just as well by means of law alone, as by means of ethics and law together. His ethics are, in truth, only a species of law.

With the Brahmans ethics are a colouring which their world- and life-negation takes on for a certain distance; with Hegel they are a similar mode of manifestation of world- and life-affirmation. Hegel's world-view is in itself supra-ethical mysticism of world- and life-affirmation, just as that of the Brahmans is supra-ethical mysticism of world- and life-negation.

That his philosophy is this and nothing else, Hegel admits in the fit of brutal frankness under the influence of which he wrote on June 25th, 1820, the famous Preface to his *Philosophy of Law*. Our task, he there explains, is not to re-fashion reality in accordance with ideals which have arisen in our spirit, but only to listen to the way in which the real world affirms itself, and us within itself, in its own immanent impulse to progress. "What is rational is real, and what is real is rational." We must recognize the eternal which is present under the form of the temporal and transient and is developing within this, and thereby become reconciled with reality. It is not for philosophy to set up ideas about what is to be. Its task is to understand what is. It does not bring forth any new age, but is only "its own age comprehended in thought." It always arrives too late to teach us what the world ought to be, and begins to speak only when reality has completed its process of construction. "Minerva's owl does not begin its flight till darkness is closing in." Sincere recognition of reality will create beneficent peace in our hearts.

Rationalism is ethical belief in progress combined with ethical will-to-progress. It was as such that Kant and Fichte had undertaken to deepen it. After passing through Hegel's mind it is only a belief in progress—belief in immanent progress. It is this alone that this powerful speculative thinker believes himself able to place upon a cosmic foundation. Here he is in contact with Schleiermacher. On the whole, and reduced to the simplest possible expression, his world-view and Schleiermacher's lie not very far apart. The secret feud in which the two thinkers lived with one another had in reality no objective justification.

The extent of the strategical retreat on which Hegel starts remains hidden from his contemporaries. They rejoice unreservedly at the magnificent energy which his system displays, and the more ingenuously because he himself only once, in the Preface to his *Philosophy of Law,* expresses himself freely about the final results of his thinking. The fact that with him the moon of ethics is obscured does not evoke the excitement that might normally have been expected, because, in compensation, he makes the sun of the cosmically founded belief in progress shine all the brighter. Being still under the influences of rationalism, the men of that time are so accustomed to regard ethics and belief in progress as organically connected that they look on the strengthening of optimism effected by Hegel as being also a strengthening of ethics.

Hegel's formal assumption that progress comes about through a succession of antitheses which are always finally reconciled in valuable syntheses has kept optimism alive through most critical times right on to the present day. He is the creator of that confident feeling for reality with which Europe staggered into the second half of the nineteenth century without becoming aware that ethics have at some point or other been left behind. And that being so, he is able to hold his optimistic philosophy of history, from which springs his world-view, only because he lives in a period when a general temper which works with ethical energies of extraordinary strength is carrying humanity forward in an extraordinary way. Whence comes the progress which he experiences all around him, the great philosophic historian does not recognize. He explains what is ethical in origin as due to natural forces.

In Hegel's philosophy the connection between ethics and belief in progress, on which the spiritual energy of modern times has always rested, is broken, and with the separation both are ruined. Ethics languish, and the belief in progress, now left to itself, becomes spiritless and powerless because it is now only a belief in immanent progress, and no longer a belief in progress brought about by enthusiasm. With Hegel originates the spirit which borrows its ideals empirically from reality and believes in the progress of humanity more than it labours to promote it. He stands on the bridge of an ocean liner and explains to the passengers the wonders of the machinery in the vessel that is carrying them, and the mysteries of the calculation of its course. But he gives no thought to the necessary maintenance of the fires under the boilers. Hence the speed gradually diminishes until the vessel comes at last to a standstill. It no longer obeys the helm, and becomes a plaything of the gales.

Chapter 19

THE LATER UTILITARIANISM. BIOLOGICAL

AND SOCIOLOGICAL ETHICS

Beneke, Feuerbach, Laas, Auguste Comte, John Stuart Mill.
Darwin and Spencer.
The weak points in biological and sociological utilitarianism.
Sociological ethics and socialism. Mechanical belief
in progress.

THE FACT THAT SPECULATIVE PHILOSOPHY ALSO IS UNABLE TO establish the truth of the optimistic-ethical world-view upon a basis of nature-philosophy is not felt with all its weight in the intellectual life of Europe. In that philosophy we have a form of thought which flames out like a flash of lightning and vanishes as quickly, but it is confined to Germany. The rest of Europe takes hardly any notice of Fichte and Hegel, just as, indeed, it paid scarcely any attention to Kant. It does not understand that these adventurous advances in the struggle for the optimistic-ethical world-view have been undertaken by leaders who see clearly that the battle is not to be won on the usual lines. The universal conviction is, of course, that the victory was won long before, and can no longer be disputed. It is only later that people in France and England see what Kant, Fichte, and Hegel were aiming at and what their significance was in the struggle for a world-view.

For the intellectual life of Europe, then, the philosophy of rationalism still stands upright at a time when it has, in truth, already collapsed. Generally speaking a generation lives, of course, less by the world-view that has been produced within it than by that of the previous age. The light of a star is still visible to us when it has long ceased to exist. There is hardly anything in the world that clings so toughly to life as does a world-view.

It never becomes clear, then, to popular utilitarian ethics that in the course of the first half of the nineteenth century they are being gradually robbed of their philosophy of life by new modes of thought, those of historical science, romanticism, nature-philosophy, and natural science. Certain that they are still in favour with the healthy human reason, they remain unmoved at their post, and still do a considerable amount of work. Whenever, too, they consider their future prospects, they assume that if they should ever have to give up all connection with rationalism, they will be able to come to terms with positivism, the philosophy which has been sobered by the exact sciences. As a matter of fact, rationalism does merge imperceptibly into a kind of popular positivism. The optimistic-ethical interpretation of the universe is still relied on, but less unreservedly and less enthusiastically than before. In this weakened form rationalism is maintained till the end of the nineteenth century, and even later, always working to produce the temper that desires civilization, whether independently or accompanied by popular religiousness.

While, then, Kant, Fichte, and Schleiermacher are struggling with the ethical problem, Bentham supplies the world with a system of ethics. The periodical entitled *The Utilitarian* (*L'Utilitaire*) is started in Paris in 1829 to propagate his views. In England the *Westminster Review* works for him. In 1830 Friedrich Eduard Beneke's translation of his *Principles of Civil and Criminal Legislation* paves a way for him in Germany. At his death—which occurred in 1832, a year after Hegel's—Bentham could take to the grave with him the conviction that, thanks to him, ethics which provided enlightenment both for the reason and for the heart had proved victorious everywhere.

All the earlier methods followed to establish utilitarianism continue at work in the nineteenth century. Friedrich Eduard

Beneke (1798–1854),[1] the translator of Bentham, and Ludwig Andreas Feuerbach (1804–1872) [2] take up with confidence the attempts of David Hartley and Dietrich von Holbach to derive the unegoistic directly from the egoistic, and try hard to complete them in a deepened psychology. Beneke believes he can show how through the continuous influence of reason on the feelings of pleasure and non-pleasure, there develops in man a capacity for moral judgment which holds up before him as the highest goal for his activity the universal perfecting of human society. Feuerbach derives altruism from the possession by man of an impulse to think himself into the personality of others and to put himself in their place. Thereby, he says, his impulse to seek happiness loses its original independence, and suffers if the happiness of others is spoilt. At last, under the influence of habit, man forgets altogether that his helpful behaviour was originally meant to satisfy the impulse to seek his own happiness, and he conceives his own care for the welfare of his fellows as duty.

Ernst Laas (1837–1885),[3] repeats the view that ethics consist primarily in the individual's acceptance of the rules laid down by society, an acceptance which from being a matter of habit becomes at last unconscious and automatic.

In general, however, the mainstay of the utilitarianism of the nineteenth century is the assumption, first made by David Hume and Adam Smith, that from the very beginning the non-egoistic is given in human nature side by side with the egoistic.

Auguste Comte (1798–1857) [4] in his *Physiology of Society* praises as the greatest achievement of his time the then commencing recognition of the fundamental social tendency in

[1] F. E. Beneke: *Prolegomena to a Physiology of Morals* (1822); *The Natural System of Practical Philosophy* (3 vols., 1837–40). By his appearance as a champion of utilitarianism and his consequent attitude of hostility to Kant, Beneke drew upon himself the enmity of Hegel, and was compelled in 1822 to stop the course of lectures which he was giving as a *Privat-dozent* at Berlin University. After Hegel's death he filled a professorship at Berlin.

[2] L. A. Feuerbach: *What is Christianity?* (1841); *Divinity, Freedom, and Immortality from the Standpoint of Anthropology* (1866).

[3] Ernst Laas: *Idealism and Positivism* (3 vols., 1879–84).

[4] *The Physiology of Society* is the fourth volume of Comte's *Course of Positive Philosophy* (6 vols., 1830–42).

human nature. In his opinion the future of mankind depends on intelligence working correctly and perseveringly on this endowment and so rendering man's natural benevolence capable of achieving the noblest and most beneficial objects. If devotion to the universal good remains active in the multitude of individuals so as to provide the necessary complement to their natural egoism there will arise from the rational state of tension between the two a society which is ever drawing nearer to perfection in its economic and social relations.

A great defender and developer of utilitarianism in England was John Stuart Mill (1806–1873),[5] who thus followed in the footsteps of his father, James Mill (1773–1836).

*   *   *

Utilitarian ethics receive unexpected help from natural science. Biology declares itself able to explain by reference to its origin the altruism which thinkers had decided to accept as inherent in man by the side of the egoistic, but not further derivable from it. The unegoistic, so it teaches, does as a matter of fact grow out of the egoistic, only it does not issue from it afresh on every occasion as a result of conscious reflection by the individual. The change has taken place in the species by a long and slow process and is now revealed as an acquired faculty. The conviction that the welfare of the individual is best secured if the whole body of individuals is also active in promoting the common good has been established by experience in the struggle for existence. Action on this principle has thus become a characteristic of individuals which develops more and more in the course of generations. We possess this devotion to others as descendants of herds which maintained themselves in the struggle for existence while others succumbed, because the social impulses were developed in them the most strongly and the most universally.

This thought is developed by Charles Darwin (1869–1882)[6]

---

[5] John Stuart Mill: *Principles of Political Economy* (2 vols., 1848); *Utilitarianism* (1861). There is a German translation of his works by Th. Gomperz (12 vols., 1869–86). It was J. S. Mill who introduced into philosophy the word "utilitarian" as the descriptive title of this particular school of ethics.
[6] Charles Darwin: *The Descent of Man and Selection in Relation to Sex* (1871).

in his *Descent of Man,* and by Herbert Spencer (1820–1903) [7] in his *Principles of Ethics.* Each of these thinkers refers to the other.

Altruism therefore is now regarded as natural and at the same time as something which has come into existence through reflection, whilst the relation subsisting between it and egoism is understood as having obviously become rational. On this judgment is founded at the same time the conviction that the co-operation of these two impulses, as it developed in the past, will also be perfected in the future. More and more will these two impulses show clearly their mutual dependence on each other. From sporadic altruism, developing in the animal kingdom for the production and maintenance of new generations, we have advanced to a settled altruism which serves to maintain the family and society. To bring this to completion must now be our aim. We shall succeed if the compromise between egoism and altruism continues to grow better adjusted and more purposive. We must advance to the view which at first seems to be a paradox that (to use Spencer's language) the general prosperity can be reached mainly through an adequate struggle on the part of all individuals for their own prosperity, and that of individuals, on the other hand, partly through their struggle for the general prosperity.

Comte's *Physiology of Society* is thus given a foundation in natural science by Darwin and Spencer.

Utilitarianism now continues on its way full of satisfaction at having found itself accepted by modern biology and in the history of evolution as natural. But it has not thereby become either fresher or more capable. It advances more and more slowly. Its breath fails. What is the matter with it? Its ethical energy leaves it because it has conceived itself to be natural. The fatal fact that ethics cease to be ethics in proportion as they are brought into harmony with natural happenings, is fulfilled not only when ethics are developed from nature-philosophy but also when they are explained by biology.

Ethics consist in this: that natural happenings in man are seen, on the basis of conscious reflection, to carry within them

[7] Herbert Spencer: *Social Statistics* (1851); *The Data of Ethics* (1879); *The Principles of Ethics* (1892).

an inner contradiction. The more this contradiction is removed into the sphere of that which goes back to instinct, the weaker do ethics become.

Assuredly the origin of ethics is that something which is contained as instinct in our will-to-live is absorbed by conscious reflection and further developed. The great question is, however, what this last and most original element in the instinct of solidarity is,—this element which by thinking is developed far beyond everything instinctive—and in what way this development is accomplished. By proclaiming developed herd-mentality to be ethics, Darwin and Spencer show that they have not gone to the root of the problem of the relation between instinct and reflection in ethics. If nature wishes to have a perfect herd, she does not appeal to ethics, but gives the individuals, as in the ant- or the bee-kingdom, instincts by the force of which they are wholly merged in the society.

But ethics are the putting into practice of the principle of solidarity on a basis of free reflection, and this practice, moreover, directs itself not only to individuals of the same species, but to everything living in general. The ethics of Darwin and Spencer are a failure from the first, because they are too narrow and do not leave the irrational its rights. The social impulse which they put in the place of the sympathy which is assumed by Hume and Adam Smith is set at a lower pitch than the latter, and is correspondingly less calculated to explain real ethics.

The transition from egoism to altruism is then equally impracticable if one transfers the proceeding from the individual to the species. The fact that the process is thereby prolonged allows numerous series of most delicate transitions to be taken into account and their results summed up as inheritance of acquired characters. Nevertheless, that does not explain truly ethical altruism. The fruits of ethics are hung upon the bush of social impulse, but the bush itself did not bear them.

*   *   *

The strength of utilitarianism lies in its simplicity. Bentham and Adam Smith still show this quality. They have society in their minds as the sum of a number of individuals, not as an organized body. Their efforts are directed to inducing human beings to do as much good as they can to each other.

With John Stuart Mill this simplicity disappears. It occurs to him, and then in still stronger measure to Spencer and the others, that the ethics of the conduct of an individual to his fellows cannot be carried out as a matter of reasoning. Hence, they conclude, "scientific ethics" has to do only with the relations between individuals and organized society as such.

Bentham's simple utilitarianism puts before the individual an estimate of the manifold ways in which society needs his devotion, if it is to see all its members prosperous, and, further, it appeals to his enthusiasm. The utilitarianism which has become biological and sociological tries to reckon up for the individual the correct balance between egoism and altruism. It endeavours to be social-science transformed into sentiment.

Adam Smith keeps ethics and sociology still apart in such a way that he is not a sociologist when he speaks as a moralist, and not a moralist when he puts forward sociological theories. Now, however, the two points of view are worked in together, and indeed in such a way that ethics are merged in sociology.

The ethics of simple utilitarianism are concerned with actions due to enthusiasm, the biologico-sociological ethics with the conscientious employment of the complicated machinery of organized society. In the former an occasional piece of ineffective action means at worst a waste of power, in the latter a disturbance of the organism. Hence thorough-going utilitarianism comes to a depreciatory estimate of the morality of the individual which springs from ethical convictions in a single person and does not think biologically and sociologically.

The later utilitarians regard it as an established fact that in the sphere of individual ethics there are no more discoveries to make. They look on ethics as an uninteresting hinterland, to advance into which is not worth while. They therefore confine themselves to the fertile coast land of social ethics, perceiving, no doubt, that the streams which water this lower ground come from the hinterland of individual ethics. But instead of following them up to their sources their only care is to make the lower ground safe from occasional inundations which may be caused by them. They therefore lead the streams into such deep-lying channels that the land becomes arid.

Scientific ethics undertake the impossible, namely to regulate altruism from outside. They try to drive watermills without any head of water, and to shoot with a bow which is but half-bent.

How tortured are Spencer's disquisitions on absolute and relative ethics! For the natural, ethical point of view absolute ethics consist in a man experiencing directly in himself an absolute ethical "must." Because absolute ethics think of devotion without limits and would lead straight to self-sacrifice which would in some way or other suspend life and activity, they have to come to an understanding with reality and decide what measure of self-sacrifice is to be made, and how far that minimum of compromise can be allowed which is necessary to ensure a continuation of life and activity. In this origin from absolute ethics of applied, relative ethics, the scientific, biological point of view cannot acquiesce. Spencer transforms the conception of absolute ethics and turns it into the conduct of the perfect man in the perfect society. We have no need, he says, to picture to ourselves the ideal man except "as he would exist in ideal social surroundings." "According to the evolution hypothesis the two mutually condition each other, and only where both are to be found, is such ideal action also possible."

This form of ethics is then objective in origin. It is determined by the relation in which society and the individual stand to one another in their mutual state of imperfection. Into the place of the living conception of absolute ethics there steps a fiction. For the ethics of sociological utilitarianism provide for man only relative standards, subject to changes of time and circumstances. That means that they can only feebly rouse his will to the ethical. They even reduce him to a state of confusion because they take from him the elementary conviction that he has to exert himself to the utmost without regard to what the given situation is like, and must contend with circumstances from an inward compulsion, even without the certainty of any result at all.

Spencer is more biologist than moralist. A code of ethics is to him merely the setting in which the principle of utility comes to us after it has been worked up in the brain-cells together with the experiences it has produced, and after it has been passed on by heredity. Thus he gives up all the inward forces by which ethics live. The urge to attain to a perfecting of the personality which has to be reached through morality, and the longing for a spiritual bliss which is to be experienced within its bounds, are deprived of their functions.

The ethics of Jesus and of the religious thinkers of India completely withdraw from society to the individual. The utilitarianism which has become scientific ethics gives up individual ethics in order that social ethics alone may have currency. In the one case ethics can survive because they keep possession of the mother-country, and have sacrificed only its foreign possessions. In the other they strive to exert their authority in the foreign possessions while the mother-country belongs to them no more. Individual ethics without social ethics are imperfect, but they can be very profound and full of vitality. Social ethics without individual ethics are like a limb with a tourniquet round it, into which life no longer flows. They become so impoverished that they really cease to be ethics at all.

The reduction to impotence of scientific, biological ethics is seen not only in the fact that in the end all ethical standards become merely relative, but also in the fact that ethics can no longer uphold the duty of humanity as is necessary.

A sinister uniformity prevails in the evolution of ethics. The ethics of antiquity began to teach humanity after it had lost in the Later Stoicism its interest in organized society as it found it existing in the ancient State. Modern utilitarianism, again, loses its sensitiveness to the duty of humanity in proportion to the consistency with which it develops into the ethics of organized society. It cannot be otherwise. The essence of humanity consists in individuals never allowing themselves to think impersonally in terms of expediency as does society, or to sacrifice individual existences in order to attain their object. The outlook which seeks the welfare of organized society cannot do otherwise than compromise with the sacrifice of individuals or groups of individuals. In Bentham, with whom utilitarianism is still simple and concerns itself with the conduct of individuals to the multitude of other individuals, the idea of humanity has not been tampered with. Biological, sociological utilitarianism is obliged to abandon it as sentimentality which cannot be maintained in the face of matter-of-fact ethical reflection. Thus sociological ethics contribute not a little to the disappearance from the modern mind of any shrinking from inhumanity. They allow individuals to adopt the mentality of society instead of keeping them in a state of tension with regard to it.

Society cannot exist without sacrifice. The ethics which spring from individuals try to distribute this in such a way that through the devotion of individuals as many sacrifices as possible are voluntary, and that the individuals who are most severely hit are relieved of their burden by others in so far as is possible. This is the doctrine of self-sacrifice. The sociological morality which no longer reaches back to individual ethics can only decree that the progress of society advances according to inexorable laws at the price of the freedom and prosperity of individuals and groups of individuals. This is the doctrine of being sacrificed by others.

If followed out consistently, biological and sociological utilitarianism arrives finally, even if with hesitation, at the conviction that in reality it no longer has for its object the greatest possible happiness of the greatest possible number. To this object, formulated by Bentham, it must now assign, as being sentimental, a place behind one which corresponds more exactly to reality. What is to be realized in the ever more complete development of the reciprocal relations between the individual and society is not, if one dares to admit it, an increase in the welfare either of the individual or of society but . . . the enhancing and perfecting of life as such. However much it may struggle against it, utilitarianism, as soon as it has become biological and sociological, undergoes a change in its ethical character, and enters the service of supra-ethical aims. Spencer still fights to keep it in the path of a natural ethical feeling.

Developed utilitarianism, directed to the enhancing and perfecting of life, can no longer regard the claims of humanity as absolutely binding, but must make up its mind in certain cases to go outside them. Biology has become its master.

If it be granted that progress in the welfare of society depends on the application of the conclusions of biology and scientific sociology, it is not as a matter of course necessary to leave to the good pleasure of the individual the corresponding conduct which is to be ethical. It can be imposed upon him, if by economic measures and measures of organization the relation between the individual and society is determined in such a way that it automatically functions as is most expedient. Thus by the side of social ethics socialism makes its appearance. Henri de Saint-Simon (1760–1825),[8] Charles Fourier (1772–1837),[9] and P. J. Proudhon (1809–1865),[10] in France, Robert Owen the mill-owner (1771–1858),[11] in England, and Ferdinand Lassalle (1825–1864),[12] and others in Germany, prelude its appearance. Karl Marx (1818–1883)[13] and Friedrich Engels (1820–1895) put forward in *Das Kapital* its consistent programme, demanding the abolition of private property and the State-regulation both of labour and of the reward of labour.

Das Kapital is a doctrinaire book which works with definitions and tables, but never goes very deeply into questions of life and the conditions of life. The great influence it exerts rests on the fact that it preaches belief in a progress which is inherent in events and works itself out in them automatically. It undertakes to unveil the mechanism of history, and to show how the succession of different methods of social organization—slavery, feudalism, and bourgeois wage-system—tend towards the final replacement of private production by State-communistic production as the logical crown of the whole of evolution. Through Marx, Hegel's belief in inherent progress becomes, if with a

---

[8] Henri de Saint-Simon: *L'Organisateur* (1819–20); *Catéchisme des Industriels* (1823–24).

[9] Charles Fourier: *Le nouveau monde industriel et sociétaire* (1829).

[10] P. J. Proudhon: *Qu'est-ce que la Propriété?* (1840).

[11] Robert Owen: *A New View of Society* (1813); and *Book of the New Moral World* (7 parts, 1836–49).

[12] Ferdinand Lassalle: *Das System der erworbenen Rechte* (2 vols., 1861); *Offenes Antwortschreiben an das Centralkomitee zur Berufung eines allgemeinen deutschen Arbeiterkongresses* (1863).

[13] Karl Marx: *Manifesto of the Communist Party* (1848, in collaboration with Friedrich Engels); *Capital* (vol. i., 1867; the second and third volumes were published in 1884 and 1894 by Friedrich Engels).

somewhat different interpretation, the conviction of the masses. His optimistic feeling for reality takes the helm.

Through the rise of socialism ethical utilitarianism loses in importance. The hopes of the masses begin to centre no longer on what can be accomplished in the world by an ethical temper which is steadily growing stronger and working ever more and more effectively in social matters, but on what is reached when free course is secured for the laws of progress which are assumed to be inherent in things.

It is true that ethical utilitarianism is still maintained among the educated as an influential disposition to reform. In competition with socialism there even begins a vigorous movement which stirs individuals, society, and the State, alike, into effective action against social distress. One of its leaders is Friedrich Albert Lange (1828–1875), the author of *The History of Materialism* (1866). In his work *The Labour Question in its Significance for the Present and the Future* (1866) he discusses the social tasks of the time and the measures that will be effective for their accomplishment, and appeals for ethical idealism, without which, he says, nothing profitable can be accomplished.[14]

Christianity too supports the movement. In 1864 Bishop Ketteler, of Mainz, comes forward, demanding in his book *The Labour Question and Christianity* the creation of a Christian-social temper.[15]

In England it is the clergymen, Frederick Denison Maurice (1805–1872) and Charles Kingsley (1819–1875), who bid Christendom adopt a social way of thinking. Kingsley's famous sermon *The Message of the Church to Working Men* was preached on the evening of Sunday, June 22nd, 1851, to working men who had come to London to see the first International Exhibition. On account of the excitement it caused, the Bishop of London inhibited him from preaching.[16]

[14] The same spirit pervades the work of the national economist, Gustav Schmoller of Berlin: *Concerning Some Questions of Law and National Economy* (1875). Schmoller was the leader of the so-called "Socialists of the Chair" (Kathedersozialisten).

[15] The first to set before Christendom its duty to take part in the solution of the social question is Félicité de Lamennais (1782–1854) in his *Paroles d'un croyant* (1833). This book was condemned by the Pope in 1834.

[16] The English public was made familiar with working-class misery by Kingsley's novel *Yeast* (which appeared in 1848 in *Fraser's Magazine*, and in 1851 was

In Russia, Count Leo Tolstoi (1828–1910) [17] let loose the force of the ethical thinking of Jesus. He did not, like others, interpret his words as teaching a social idealism focused on the service of systematic purposive effort, but made them the commands to the absolute, uncalculating devotion which their author meant them to be. In his *Confessions,* which in the eighties were read throughout the world, the lava of primitive Christianity is poured into the Christianity of modern times.

The social-ethical movement produced the greatest results in Germany, because in that country the State welcomed it in the person of the Hohenzollerns. In 1883 and 1884 the Reichstag, in spite of the disapproving attitude of the Social Democratic Party, passed laws for the protection of the worker which may be considered to be models of their kind.

In the bosom of socialism itself thoughtful spirits like Eduard Bernstein (b. 1850),[18] and others, came to see that even the most effective measures taken for the social organization of society cannot succeed unless there is a strong ethical idealism behind them as their driving force. This was a return to the spirit of Lassalle.

There exists, then, an active social ethical disposition. Nevertheless it is only a trickling stream of water in a big river-bed. That the reforms called for under the guidance of ethics can be realized is no longer a general conviction, as it was in the age of rationalism. The ethical temper which would work for the future of mankind becomes less and less appreciated. In the victory, so fateful for the development of civilized mankind, won by Marxian State-socialism over the social ideas of Lassalle

---

printed as a book), and by two articles of Henry Mayhew's in the *Morning Chronicle* (December 14th and 18th, 1849).

That Christian Socialism made its appearance first in England and France is connected with the fact that the industry which creates social problems developed earliest in these countries.

[17] Leo Tolstoi: *My Confessions;* German translation as *Worin besteht mein Glaube* (1884); French as *Ma Réligion* (1884); English as *Christ's Christianity* (1885). See also *What then shall we do?* (German, 1886). The fact that Tolstoi's ethical Christianity associates itself with contempt for civilization brings it near to primitive Christianity. But the all-important question, how the power of the ethical thoughts of Jesus are to work in the temper and the circumstances of modern times, it does not answer. Tolstoi is a great stimulator but no guide.

[18] Eduard Bernstein: *The Presuppositions of Socialism, and the Tasks of Social Democracy* (1899).

(which allow much more natural play to the forces of reality), we see an expression of the fact that in the mentality of the masses the belief-in-progress has been emancipated from ethics and has become mechanistic. Confusion in the conception of civilization and ruin of the civilized way of thinking are the consequence of this disastrous separation. The spirit of the modern age renounces thereby the very thing which had really constituted its strength.

How remarkable are the vicissitudes undergone by ethics! Utilitarianism refuses all contact with nature-philosophy. It wishes to be a form of ethics which is concerned only with the practical, but it does not on that account escape its fate, which is to be wrecked upon nature-philosophy. In its attempt to secure a basis for itself and to think itself out completely, it changes into biological-sociological utilitarianism. Next it loses its ethical character. Without becoming aware of it, it has, of course, at the same time become involved with nature and natural happenings, and has given cosmic problems a place within itself. Although it pretends to be only the practical ethics of human society, it has become a product of nature. It has been no good removing all the distaffs: the Sleeping Beauty pricks her finger nevertheless. No ethics can avoid trying conclusions with nature-philosophy.

Chapter 20

SCHOPENHAUER AND NIETZSCHE

Schopenhauer. An ethic of world- and life-denial.

Absorption of ethics in world- and life-denial.

Nietzsche's criticism of current ethics.

Nietzsche's ethic of higher life-affirmation.

AS BAD LUCK WILL HAVE IT, THE TWO MOST IMPORTANT ETHICAL thinkers of the second half of the nineteenth century, Schopenhauer and Nietzsche, do not help the age in the search for what it needs, namely, a system of social ethics which is also true ethics. Concerned only with individualist ethics from which no social ethics can be developed, they offer incitements which, however valuable in themselves, cannot arrest the demoralization in the general outlook on life which is in progress.

Common to both is the fact that they are elemental moralists. They pursue no abstract cosmic speculations. Ethics are for them an experience of the will-to-live. They are therefore, from their very core, cosmic.

In Schopenhauer the will-to-live tries to become ethical by turning to world- and life-negation; in Nietzsche by devoting itself to a deepened world- and life-affirmation.

From the standpoint of their own elemental ethics, these two thinkers, who stand in such deep contrast to each other, rise as judges of what they find accepted as ethics in their time.

Arthur Schopenhauer (1788–1860) begins to publish at the beginning of the century. His *The World as Will and Idea* appears in 1819.[1] But he first obtains a hearing about 1860 when speculative philosophy had definitely gone bankrupt, and the unsatisfactory nature of the ethics of popular utilitarianism, as also of that of Kant's successors, was generally acknowledged.

The most important among the earlier of these is Johann Friedrich Herbart (1776–1841). His importance lies in the department of psychological investigation. It is on a psychological foundation that he tries to establish ethics in his *General Practical Philosophy* (1808). He traces morality back to five direct and ultimate judgments, which cannot be derived from anything beyond themselves, and may be compared with æsthetic judgments. They are: the ideas of inward freedom, of perfection, of benevolence, of right, and of equity. By submitting itself to this mode of outlook, which starts from pure intuition and is confirmed as correct for human beings by the course of their experience, the will becomes ethical.

Instead, therefore, of seeking one basic principle for morality, Herbart accepts several ethical ideas which appear side by side. This anæmic ethical theory possesses no convincing power. But in his teaching about society and the State Herbart does produce something of solid value.

Among the earlier successors of Kant there belongs also Immanuel Hermann Fichte (1797–1879) a son of J. G. Fichte, the so-called Younger Fichte, with his *System of Ethics* (2 vols., 1850–1853), which in its time enjoyed considerable repute.

Schopenhauer is the first representative in Western thought of a consistent world- and life-denying system of ethics. The incentive came to him from the philosophy of India, which early in the nineteenth century began to be known in Europe.[2] For the exposition of his world-view he starts, like Fichte, from Kant's epistemological idealism. Like Fichte he defines the essence of things in themselves, which is to be accepted as underlying all phenomena, to be Will, not, however, like Fichte,

1 What Schopenhauer wrote after this, his chief work, which was printed when he was thirty, are only appendices and popular explanations of it: *Concerning the Will in Nature* (1836), *The Two Fundamental Problems of Ethics* (1840), *Parerga and Paralipomena* (2 vols., 1851).

2 In 1802–1804 Anquetil Duperron (1731–1805) published in two volumes, with a Latin translation, the *Oupnek'hat*, a collection of fifty Upanishads which he had brought back from India in a Persian text.

as will to action, but more directly and more correctly, as will-to-live. The world, he says, I can understand only by analogy with myself. Myself, looked at from outside, I conceive as a physical phenomenon in space and time, but looked at from within, as will-to-live. Everything, accordingly, which meets me in the world of phenomena is a manifestation of the will-to-live.

What is the meaning, then, of the world-process? Simply that countless individualities which are rooted in the universal will-to-live are continually seeking satisfaction, which is never gratified, in aims which they set before themselves in obedience to an inward impulse. Again and again they experience the disappointment that pleasure longed for, not pleasure attained, is real pleasure; they have continually to struggle against hindrances; their won will-to-live continually comes into conflict with other wills-to-live. The world is meaningless and all existence is suffering. The knowledge of this is attained by the will-to-live in the highest living creatures, who are gifted with the power of remaining always conscious that the totality of what is around them, outside themselves, is merely a world of appearances. Surveying in this way the totality of existence, the will is in a position to reach clarity of thought about itself and about existence.

That it must effect something worth while in the world is the obsession with which the will-to-live has befooled itself in European philosophy. When it has attained to knowledge of itself, it knows that optimistic world-affirmation is of no benefit to it. It can only hurry it on from unrest to unrest, from disappointment to disappointment. What it must try to do is to step out from the terrible game in which, bedazzled, it is taking part, and settle itself to rest in world- and life-negation.

For Spinoza the meaning of the world-process is that supreme individualities arise, who find their experience within the Absolute; for Fichte that the urge to activity of the Absolute comprehends itself in supreme individualities as ethical; for Hegel that the Absolute in supreme individualities arrives at adequate consciousness of itself; for Schopenhauer that in supreme individualities the Absolute attains to knowledge of itself, and finds deliverance from the blind urge to life-affirmation which is within it. The meaning of the world-process, therefore, is always found in this: that the Finite and the Infinite blend their experiences in one another. Spinoza, Fichte, and Hegel—and this is the weakness of their world-view—cannot make it properly intelligible how far this experience in the Finite has really a meaning for the Absolute. In Schopenhauer, however, it has such a meaning. In man the universal will-to-live begins to turn from the path of unrest and suffering into the path of peace.

The transition from Being to nothingness is introduced. This nothingness is nothingness, it is true, only for the will-to-live, which is still filled with an urge to life-affirmation and with its conception of the world. What it is in itself, this Nirvana of the Buddhists, cannot be defined by our conceptions, which come to us through our senses.

That Schopenhauer develops his pessimistic-ethical, as Fichte his optimistic-ethical, world-view, with the material provided by epistemological idealism has not the importance that he himself attributes to this fact. Indian predecessors have made this connection easier for him. In itself, pessimism can be developed just as well without epistemological idealism. The drama of the tragical experience of the will-to-live remains the same whatever the scenery and costumes with which it is played.

Although, therefore, it makes its appearance in the dress of Kant's theory of knowledge, Schopenhauer's philosophy is elemental nature-philosophy.

What then is the ethical content of his system?

Like the philosophy of the Indians it appears in a three-fold shape: as ethics of resignation, as ethics of universal pity, and as ethics of world-renunciation.

About resignation Schopenhauer speaks in forcible words. In language which rises to the level of poetry, he describes how the man who is intent on his own self-perfecting does not meet the destinies of his existence in childish resistance to what is hard, but feels them as incitements to become free from the world. In the disagreeable circumstances which poison his existence, and in the misfortune which threatens to crush him, he suddenly feels himself lifted out of everything on which he sets value, and brought to the triumphant feeling that nothing can any longer do him harm. The field of resignation, which the philosophical ethics of modern times had allowed to lie fallow for generations, is replanted by Schopenhauer.

Ethics are pity. All life is suffering. The will-to-live which has attained to knowledge is therefore seized with deep pity for all creatures. It experiences not only the woe of mankind, but that of all creatures with it. What is called in ordinary ethics "love" is in its real essence pity. In his overpowering feeling of pity the will-to-live is diverted from itself. Its purification begins.

How anxious Kant and Hegel and others are in their ethics to deprive direct pity of its rights, because it does not suit their theories! Schopenhauer takes the gag out of its mouth and bids it speak. Those who, like Fichte, Schleiermacher, and others, base ethics on a laboriously thought out world-scheme, expect man to run every time to the topmost attic of his reflections to fetch down his motives to moral action. According to the sociological utilitarians he should always first sit down and calculate what is ethical. Schopenhauer bids him do something never yet heard of in philosophical ethics—listen to his own heart. The elemental ethical which by the others has been pushed into the corner, can now, thanks to him, take its proper place again.

The others, in order not to get embarrassed with their theories, have to limit ethics exclusively to the conduct of man to man. They anxiously insist that pity for animals is not ethical in itself, but has importance only in view of the kindly disposition which must be maintained among men. Schopenhauer tears down these fences, and teaches love to the most insignificant being in creation.

The artificial and curious pleas, too, which the rest produce to put man into an ethical relation to organized society disappear in Schopenhauer. Fichte's and Hegel's ethical overvaluation of the State makes him smile. He himself is left free from the necessity of dragging into ethics worldly things which refuse to be fitted in. He can allow the conviction that ethics consist in being different from the world to flame up in dazzling clearness. He is pledged to no concessions, since he does not, like the others, represent a morality which has a purposive aim in the world. Because his philosophy is world- and life-denying he can be an elemental moralist when others have to renounce being that. Nor does he need, like them, to sever all connection with Jesus and religious ethics. He can appeal as often as he likes to the fact that his philosophy only establishes what has always been accepted by the piety of Christianity and of the Indians as the essential element in the moral. It is well known that Schopenhauer judged Christianity to have the Indian spirit, and to be probably, in some way or other, of Indian origin.[3]

Elemental morality now once more obtains its right place in a thinking conception of the universe, and this explains the enthusiasm which Schopenhauer arouses when he at last gets known. That it was possible to ignore for nearly forty years the very significant matter which he gave to the world remains one of the most remarkable facts in the history of European thought. The optimistic world-view passed at that time for so self-evident that the man who laid hands upon it, even in the directly illuminating thoughts upon ethics to which Schopenhauer gave utterance, could not obtain a hearing. At a later period also many attach themselves to Schopenhauer only because of his ethical maxims with their natural and attractive appeal, and refuse to accept his consistent world-view of world- and life-negation. It is a right feeling which guides them.

*   *   *

Schopenhauer's outlook on the universe, like that of the Brahmans, because it reveals itself as consistent world- and life-denial, is in the last resort not ethical but supra-ethical. Even though through several chapters of his ethics he can speak in more elemental fashion than Spinoza, Fichte, Schleiermacher, and Hegel, he is nevertheless in reality no more ethical than they are. He ends, as they do, in the frozen sea of the supra-ethical point of view, only at the South Pole instead of at the North. The price which he pays for being able to outbid them in elemental ethics is his philosophy of world- and life-negation. But the price is a ruinous one.

With Schopenhauer, as with the Indians, ethics are only a phase of world- and life-negation. They are nothing in them-

[3] *The World as Will and Idea*, vol. ii., chap. xli.

selves but merely what they are in the frame provided by that world-view. And everywhere there peeps through his ethically tinted world- and life-negation world- and life-negation as such. Like a ghostly sun in the sky it devours ethics, just as the real sun devours a mass of clouds from which men are vainly hoping to get a refreshing shower of rain.

On the assumption of world- and life-negation all ethical action is illusory. Schopenhauer's pity is merely deliberative. Of pity which brings help he can have no real knowledge any more than can the Indian thinkers. Like all will-to-action in the world, such pity has no sense. It has no power to lighten the misery of the rest of creation, since that misery lies in the will-to-live, which is irretrievably full of suffering. The one thing, therefore, that pity can do is to enlighten the will-to-live everywhere about the delusion in which it is held captive, and bring it to the apathy and peace offered by world- and life-negation. Schopenhauer's pity, like that of the Brahmans and the Buddha, is at bottom merely theoretical. It can use as its own the words of the religion of love, but it stands at a far lower level. As is the case with the thinkers of India, the ideal of inactivity obstructs the way to the real ethics of love.

The ethics also of self-perfecting are present in Schopenhauer more in word than in reality. The attainment of inward freedom from the world is really ethical only if the personality is thereby enabled to work as a more direct force in the world, but this thought is not to be found either in Schopenhauer or in the Indians. World- and life-negation is with them an end in itself, and it continues to assert itself when its ethical character has ceased. Higher than ethics, says Schopenhauer, stands asceticism. Everything which helps to deaden the will-to-live, is to him significant. Men and women who renounce love and the hope of offspring so that there may be less life in the world, are to him in the right. Those who deliberately choose religious suicide, and after employing every conceivable device for deadening the will-to-live allow the lamp of life to be extinguished, as the Brahmans do, by withholding all nourishment from the body, these similarly act as truly enlightened men. Only suicide as the outcome of despair is to be rejected. That is, of course, not a result of the true life-denial, but is, on the contrary, the act of a life-affirming will, which is simply discontented with the conditions in which it finds itself.[4]

With Schopenhauer, then, ethics reach only so far as world- and life-negation has willed and so far as that is in a position to be declared ethical. They are only an introduction to and a preparation for, liberation from the world. It is, at bottom, by an intellectual act that the suspension of the will-to-live is consummated. If I have won my way through to understanding that the whole phenomenal world is delusion and misery, and that my will-to-live has no need to take the world or itself seriously, then I am saved. How far and to what extent I then take part in the game of life with the consciousness that I am but a player, has no importance.

Schopenhauer does not think out the pessimistic world-view in the great and calm manner of the wise men of India. He behaves under its influence like a nervous and sickly European. While they, on the basis of the liberating knowledge they have reached, advance with majestic gait from the ethical to the supra-ethical, and leave good and evil behind them, as things over which they have equally triumphed, he reveals himself as a miserable Western sceptic.[5] Incapable of living out the world-view which he preaches, he clings to life as to money, appreciates the pleasures of the table as well as those of love, and has more contempt than pity for mankind. As though to justify himself in this, in *The World as Will and Idea*, where he has just been speaking about the deadening of the will-to-live, he rebels against the notion that anyone who teaches a saintly course of life must also live like a saint. "It is indeed," so runs the famous passage, "a strange demand to make of a moralist that he shall recommend no other virtue than those which he himself possesses. To sum up in a series of conceptions the whole essence of the world, in abstract terms, in general terms, and with clearness, and to offer it thus as a reflected copy in permanent rational conceptions which are always ready to hand: that and nothing else is philosophy."[6]

[4] *The World as Will and Idea*, vol. i., chap. lxix.

[5] That the man who has won through to complete world- and life-negation remains holy even if he commits actions which according to accepted ideas are unethical, is taught by the Bhagavadgita as well as by the Upanishads.

[6] *The World as Will and Idea*, vol. i., chap. lxviii.

With these sentences Schopenhauer's philosophy commits suicide. Hegel has a right to say that philosophy is only reflective, not imperative, thinking, for his own philosophy does not claim to be anything more. But *The World as Will and Idea* protests with illuminating language and in a tone of urgent entreaty against the will-to-live. It ought therefore to be the life-creed of the author.

The fact that Schopenhauer can for a moment so far forget himself as to express himself sceptically about ethics has its own deep-reaching explanation. It belongs to the essence of world- and life-negation, which he wishes to proclaim as ethics, that it cannot be thought out consistently to a conclusion, and cannot be consistently put into practice. Even with the Brahmans and the Buddha it keeps itself alive by inadmissible concessions to world- and life-affirmation. But with Schopenhauer it goes so far in that direction that he can no longer make any attempt to bring theory and practice into harmony, but must resolutely live in an atmosphere of mendacity.

He does succeed in making the ethical radiance which world- and life-negation can assume flash up in brilliant colours. But of really producing ethics from world- and life-negation he is as little capable as the Indians.

* * *

Friedrich Nietzsche (1844–1900) in the early period of his activity is under the spell of Schopenhauer.[7] One of his *Old-fashioned Reflections* bears the title: "Schopenhauer as Educator." Later on he goes through a development which leads him to recognize as the ideal a scientifically deepened Positivism and Utilitarianism. He is his real self first when, starting with *Joyous Science,* he tries to establish his world-view of the higher life-affirmation, and thereby becomes anti-Schopenhauer, anti-Christian, and anti-Utilitarian.

His criticism of current philosophical and religious ethics is passionate and malicious. But it goes deep. He casts at them

[7] Friedrich Nietzsche: *Old-fashioned Reflections* (4 parts, 1873–1876); *Human and All too Human* (3 vols., 1878–1880); *Joyous Science* (1882); *Thus spake Zarathustra* (4 parts, 1883–1885); *Beyond Good and Evil* (1886); *On the Genealogy of Morality* (1887); *The Will to Power* (posthumous, 1906).

two reproaches: that they have made a pact with unveracity, and that they do not allow a human being to become a personality. In this he says only what had long been due. Sceptics had already made public many such complaints. But he speaks as one who is searching for the truth, and concerned about the spiritual future of mankind, thus giving such complaints a new tone and a wider range. Whereas the current philosophy believed that it had in the main solved the ethical problem, and was united with biological and sociological utilitarianism in the conviction that in the department of individual ethics there were no more discoveries to be made, Nietzsche overthrows the whole game, and shows that all ethics rest upon the morals of the individual. The question about the essential nature of good and evil which was generally accepted as settled, he puts forward again in elemental fashion. The truth that ethics in their real nature are a process of self-perfecting shines out in his works, as in Kant's, although in a different light. Hence his place is in the first rank of the ethical thinkers of mankind. Those who were torn from their false certainty when his impassioned writings descended on the lowlands of the thought of the outgoing nineteenth century, as the south wind sweeps down from the high mountains in spring, can never forget the gratitude they owe to this upheaver of thought, with his preaching of veracity and personality.

According to Nietzsche, accepted ethics are deficient in veracity, because the conceptions of good and evil which they put into circulation do not spring out of man's reflection on the meaning of his life, but have been invented in order to keep individuals useful to the majority. The weak proclaim that sympathy and love are good, because that is to their advantage. Thus led astray, all men try to force themselves to the opinion that they fulfil the highest destiny of their existence by self-sacrifice and the devotion of their lives to others. But this opinion never becomes a real inward conviction. They live out their lives without any thought of their own as to what makes life valuable. They join the crowd in praising the morality of humility and self-sacrifice as the true morality, but they do not really believe in it. They feel self-assertion to be what is natural, and act accordingly without admitting the fact to themselves. They do not question the general ethical prestige of humility and self-sacrifice; they help to maintain it, from fear that individuals stronger than themselves might become dangerous to them, if this method of taming men were abandoned.

Current morality, then, is something with which mankind as a whole is deceived by means of traditional views, and with which individuals deceive themselves.

With indignant statements like these, Nietzsche is so far in the right, that the ethics of humility and self-sacrifice do as a matter of principle avoid engaging in a clear and practical discussion with reality. They exist by leaving quite undetermined the degree of life-denial involved. In theory they proclaim life-negation; in practice, however, they allow a life-affirmation which has thereby become unnatural and sickly to prevail. Stripped of all its passion, then, Nietzsche's criticism means that only that system of ethics deserves to be accepted which springs from independent reflection on the meaning of life, and arrives at a straightforward understanding with reality.

Individual morality comes before social morality. Not what it means for society, but what it means for the perfecting of the individual, is the first question which has to be put. Does it allow a man to become a personality or not? It is here, says Nietzsche, that current ethics fail. They do not allow men to grow straight up, but train them like stunted trees on espaliers. They put humility and self-surrender before men as the content of perfection, but for the ethical which consists in man being one with himself and thoroughly sincere, it has no understanding.

What does "noble" mean? shouts Nietzsche with harsh words to his age as being the ethical question which has been forgotten. Those who, when the question re-echoed everywhere, were touched by the truth which was stirring, and the anxiety which was quivering within it, have received from that solitary thinker all that he had to give to the world.

If life-negation brings with it so much that is unnatural and fraught with doubt, it cannot be ethics. Ethics, then, must consist of a higher life-affirmation.

But what is higher life-affirmation? Fichte and the speculative philosophers in general make it consist in this: that the will of man conceives itself within the infinite will, and in consequence of this no longer belongs to the universe in merely natural fashion, but to it surrenders itself consciously and willingly as an energy which acts in intelligent harmony with the infinite will. Nietzsche sees clearly that in this way they have not arrived at any convincing idea of the content of the higher life-affirmation, but are moving in the region of the abstract. He himself means to remain at all costs elemental, and he therefore avoids philosophizing about the universe, showing himself thereby to be a true moralist like Socrates. He jeers at those who, not content with belittling mankind, proceed further to profane the reality of the world by declaring that it exists merely in the human imagination. It is only on the essential nature of the will-to-live and the way to use it most completely in experience, that he wishes to reflect.

His original belief was that he could conceive the higher life-affirmation as the development to a higher spirituality of the will-to-live. But when he attempted to develop this idea in the course of his study, it took on another form. Higher spirituality means, of course, the repressing of natural impulses and natural claims on life, and is thereby in some way or other connected with life-negation. Higher life-affirmation, therefore, can only consist in the entire content of the will-to-live being raised to its highest conceivable power. Man fulfils the meaning of his life by affirming with the clearest consciousness of himself everything that is within him—even his impulses to secure power and pleasure.

But Nietzsche cannot get rid of the antagonism between the spiritual and the natural. Just in proportion as he emphasizes the natural does the spiritual shrink back. Gradually, under the visible influence of the mental disease which is threatening him, his ideal man becomes the "superman," who asserts himself triumphantly against all fate, and seeks his own ends without any consideration for the rest of mankind.

From the very outset Nietzsche is condemned, in his thinking out of what life-affirmation means, to arrive at the higher form of it by a more or less meaningless living out of life to the full.

He wants to listen to the highest efforts of the will-to-live without putting it in any relation to the universe. But the higher life-affirmation can be a living thing only when life-affirmation tries to understand itself in world-affirmation. Life-affirmation in itself, in whichever direction it turns, can only become enhanced life-affirmation never a higher form of it. Unable to follow any fixed course, it careers wildly in circles like a ship with its tiller firmly lashed.

Nietzsche, however, instinctively shrinks from fitting life-affirmation into world-affirmation, and bringing it by that method to development into a higher and ethical life-affirmation. Life-affirmation within world-affirmation means self-devotion to the world, but with that there follows somehow or other life-negation within the life-affirmation. But it is just this interplay of the two that Nietzsche wants to get rid of, because it is there that ordinary ethics come to grief. . . .

He was not the first to put forward in Western thought the theory of living one's own life to the full. Greek sophists and others after them anticipated him in this. There is a great difference, however, between him and his predecessors. They are for living a full life because it brings them enjoyment. He, on the other hand, brings to the theory the much deeper thought that by living one's own life victoriously to the full, life itself is honoured, and that by the enhancement of life the meaning of existence is realized. Men of genius and strong individuality, therefore, should be intent only on allowing the greatness that is in them to have free play.[8]

Nietzsche's true predecessors are unknown to him. They have their home, like those of Spinoza, in China. In that country life-affirmation made the attempt to come to clear ideas about itself. In Lao-tse and his pupils it is still naïvely ethical. In Chwang-tse it becomes cheerful resignation; in Lie-tse the will to secret power over things; in Yang-tse it ends in an all-round living

---

[8] Max Stirner (1806–1856), whose real name was Kaspar Schmidt, has recently been regarded as a predecessor of Nietzsche's on account of his book, *The Individual and His Property* (1845), in which he supports the theory of merciless egoism. But he is not. He has provided no deep philosophical background for his anarchistic egoism. He speaks as a mere logician, and does not rise above the level of the Greek sophists. A religious reverence for life, such as Nietzsche feels, is not to be found in him.

of life to the full. Nietzsche is a synthesis, appearing in European mentality, of Lie-tse and Yang-tse. It is only we Europeans who are capable of producing the philosophy of brutality.

Zarathustra is for him the symbol of the thoughts which are forming within him: Zarathustra the hero of veracity who dares to value natural life as a good thing, and Zarathustra the genius who is far removed from the Jewish-Christian mode of thought.

At bottom Nietzsche is no more unethical than Schopenhauer. He is misled by the ethical element which there is in life-affirmation into giving the status of ethics to life-affirmation as such. Thereby he falls into the absurdities which follow from an exclusive affirmation of life, just as Schopenhauer falls into those of an exclusive denial of life. Nietzsche's will-to-power should cause no more offence than Schopenhauer's will-to-self-annihilation, as it is explained in the passages in his works which deal with asceticism. It is interesting to note that neither of the two men lives in accordance with his view of life. Schopenhauer is no ascetic but a *bon vivant,* and Nietzsche does not lord it over his fellow men but lives in seclusion.

Life-affirmation and life-negation are both for a certain distance ethical; pursued to a conclusion they become unethical. This result, which was reached by the optimistic thought of China and the pessimistic thought of India, makes its appearance in Europe in Nietzsche and Schopenhauer because they are the only thinkers in this continent who philosophize in elemental fashion about the will-to-live, and venture to follow the paths of one-sidedness. Each completing the other, they pronounce sentence on the ethics of European philosophy by bringing into daylight again the elemental ethical thoughts contained in life-negation as in life-affirmation, thoughts which philosophy was keeping buried. Arriving as they do at the non-ethical by thinking out to a conclusion, one of them life-negation, the other life-affirmation, they corroborate together the statement that the ethical consists neither of life-negation nor of life-affirmation, but is a mysterious combination of the two.

Chapter 21

THE ISSUE OF THE WESTERN STRUGGLE

FOR A WORLD-VIEW

Academic thinkers: Sidgwick, Stephen, Alexander, Wundt,
Paulsen, Höffding.

The ethic of self-perfecting, Kant's successors:
Cohen, Herrmann.

The ethic of self-perfecting: Martineau, Green, Bradley,
Laurie, Seth, and Royce.

Nature-philosophy and ethics. Fouillée, Guyau, Lange, Stern.

Nature-philosophy and ethics in Eduard von Hartmann.

Nature-philosophy and ethics in Bergson, Chamberlain,
Keyserling, Haeckel.

The death-agony of the optimistic-ethical world-view.

THE ATTEMPTS OF SPECULATIVE PHILOSOPHY TO FIND A FOUNDA-
tion for ethics in knowledge of the nature of the world have
come to grief. Ethics based on science and sociology are seen
to be powerless. Schopenhauer and Nietzsche, although they
bring back into general consideration some elementary questions of ethics, are unable, nevertheless, to establish an ethical
system that can give satisfaction.

In the later decades of the nineteenth century, therefore, ethics find themselves in an unenviable position. But they remain of good courage being confident that they have at their disposal a sufficiency of "scientifically" recognized results to guarantee an assured existence.

This conviction is produced by a series of inter-related works —chiefly academic manuals of ethics. Their authors are of the opinion that ethics can be built, like the arch of a bridge, upon two piers. One of their piers is the natural ethical character of man; the other they find in those needs of society which influence the mental outlook of individuals. They consider their task to be the bringing into actual existence of the arch (the possibility of completing which they take for granted), building it with the solid material of modern psychology, biology, and sociology, and dividing the load in the best calculated way between the two piers. Fundamentally they do nothing beyond restoring with new means the standpoint of Hume.

The following writers try to carry through this adjustment of the morality which starts from the standpoint of ethical personality and that which starts from the standpoint of society: Henry Sidgwick (1838–1900),[1] Leslie Stephen (1832–1904),[2] Samuel Alexander (b. 1859),[3] Wilhelm Wundt (b. 1832),[4] Friedrich Paulsen (1846–1908),[5] Friedrich Jodl (b. 1849),[6] Georg von Gizyki (1851–1895),[7] Harald Höffding (b. 1843),[8] and others. Of these ethical writers who, in spite of the variety of experience they bring to bear on the subject, are essentially

[1] H. Sidgwick: *The Method of Ethics* (1874). (German translation by C. Bauer, 1909.)

[2] Leslie Stephen: *The Science of Ethics* (1882).

[3] S. Alexander: *Moral Order and Progress: An Analysis of Ethical Conceptions* (1889).

[4] Wm. Wundt: *Ethics: An Examination of the Facts and Laws of the Moral Life* (1887).

[5] Friedrich Paulsen: *A System of Ethics* (1889).

[6] Friedrich Jodl: *A History of Ethics as Philosophical Science* (2 vols., 2nd ed., 1906 and 1912).

[7] Georg von Gizyki: *Moral Philosophy, expounded so as to be intelligible to all* (1888).

[8] Harald Höffding (a Dane): *Ethics* (1887). (German translation, 1888.)

Georg Simmel (1858–1918) adopts a critical attitude towards modern "scientific" ethics in his *Introduction to Moral Science* (1892).

related to one another, the most original is Leslie Stephen, the scientifically soundest is Wilhelm Wundt, the most ethical is Harald Höffding.

Höffding makes the ethical originate partly out of a consideration which limits the sovereignty of the present moment. "An action (he says) is good which preserves the totality of life and gives fulness and life to its content; an action is bad which has a more or less decided tendency to break into and narrow the totality of life and its content." Supporting this consideration come also instincts of sympathy, which make us feel pleasure in the pleasure of others, and pain in their pain. The aim of ethics is general prosperity.

Of these ethical writers some put the chief emphasis on the ethical disposition of the individual, while others hold that ethics are constituted chiefly by their content, which aims at the good of society. What is common to them all is that they try to combine the ethics of ethical personality and the ethics of utilitarianism without having inquired into their higher unity. That is why the chapters in which they touch on the problem of the basic principle of the moral are always the least clear and the least living part of their works. One is conscious of how happy they feel when they have waded through this swamp, and can launch out into consideration of the different ethical standpoints which have emerged in history, or can face questions on single points in ethical practice. And when they handle practical questions, it is obvious that they are not in possession of any serviceable basic principle of the moral. Their coming to terms with reality is a mere groping here and there. The considerations on the strength of which they decide are set out now in this sense, now in that. Hence these ethical writers frequently offer very interesting discussions on ethical problems, but the conception of the moral never gets from them any real explanation or any deepening. The criterion of a real code of ethics is whether it allows their full rights to the problems of personal morality and of the relation of man to man, problems with which we are concerned every day and every hour, and by means of which we must become ethical personalities. These academical works do not do this. Therefore, although they may arrive at results which deserve attention, they are not capable of giving effective ethical impulses to the thought of their time.

*   *   *

This mediating form of ethics is not left uncriticized. In Germany inheritors of the Kantian spirit like Hermann Cohen (b. 1842) [9] and Wilhelm Herrmann (1846–1922) [10] oppose it, and in English-speaking countries successors of the Intuitionists like James Martineau (1805–1900),[11] F. H. Bradley (b. 1846),[12] T. H. Green (1836–1882),[13] Simon Laurie (1829–1909),[14] and James Seth (b. 1860).[15]

In spite of wide differences in detail, these thinkers agree in refusing to derive ethics either from the ethical disposition of man or from the claims of society. They represent ethics as produced entirely through the ethical personality. To become ethical personalities, they say, we step out of ourselves and work for the good of the community.

Cohen and Herrmann attempt to reach ethics which will form a consistent unity by using logic to put a content into the empty categorical imperative of Kant. They wish to make good what he missed in his *Grundlegung zur Metaphysik der Sitten* (Foundations for a Metaphysic of Morals) and in his *Metaphysik der Sitten* (A Metaphysic of Morals). Cohen finds the origin of ethics in the pure Will thinking out the idea of one's fellow-man and the idea of the associating of men to form a state, his ethical *ego* being brought into existence by this logical operation. The morality thus attained consists in honesty, modesty, loyalty, justice, and humanity, and culminates in the representation of the State as the highest creation of the moral

9 H. Cohen: *Kant's Foundation given to Ethics* (1877); *Ethics of the Pure Will* (1904).

10 W. Herrmann: *Ethics* (1901).

In France Charles Renouvier (1838–1903) tries, in his *Science of the Moral* (1869), to restore the Kantian system of ethics.

11 James Martineau: *Types of Ethical Theory* (2 vols., 1885).

12 F. H. Bradley: *Ethical Studies* (1876).

13 T. H. Green: *Prolegomena to Ethics* (posthumous, 1883).

14 Simon Laurie: *Ethica, or the Ethics of Reason* (1885). (A French translation by Georges Remack, 1902.)

15 James Seth: *Study of Ethical Principles* (3rd ed., 1894).

spirit. But that it is only the offspring of mental ability is betrayed by the whole story of its appearance. The "pure will" is an abstraction with which nothing can be set in motion.

Instead of obtaining ethics by deduction, using abstract logical methods, Wilhelm Herrmann opens the backdoor of experience. He does indeed make ethics consist in "the bowing of the individual before the power of a something which is universally valid in thought," but that content of ethics which is a necessity of thought we are to reach by seeing ourselves in each other as if in a mirror, and deciding what kind of conduct makes us mutually "reliable." The thought of the unconditional claim originates, therefore, spontaneously in us, but awakes to the fact that it is determined by its content "through experience of human intercourse, and in relations of mutual trust."

Herrmann did not complete this system of philosophic ethics. He sketched it as an introduction to a not less artificial theological system. His conception is allied to Adam Smith's theory of the impartial third party.[16]

* * *

Martineau, Green, Bradley, Laurie, and Seth try to reach ethics which can form a consistent unity by making the whole of ethics originate in the need for self-perfecting. Of these, Martineau goes more on the lines of the eighteenth century Cambridge Platonists. Ethics consist for him in thinking ourselves into the ideal of perfection which God gave us with our life, and letting ourselves be determined by it. T. H. Green, F. H. Bradley, Simon Laurie, and James Seth show more or less the influence of J. G. Fichte. The ethical is with them founded on the fact that man wishes to live out his life in the deepest way as an effective personality, and thereby attain to true union with the infinite spirit. This thought is expounded best by T. H. Green. He is also led at the same time to the relation between civilization and ethics, and determines that all the achievements of human activity, especially the political and social perfecting of society, are nothing in themselves, and have a real meaning only so far as they render attainable by individuals a more thorough perfection of heart. A spiritualized

[16] See page 160.

conception of civilization is therefore now struggling for acceptance. On American soil Josiah Royce (1855–1916) [17] was a representative of this ethic of self-perfecting.

In the effort to conceive of ethics as a whole as concerned with self-perfecting, that is to say, with conduct which springs from inward necessity, these thinkers express thoughts which are full of vitality. To be energetically occupied with the basic principle of the moral, even though it leads in the direction of the universal and apparently abstract, always brings with it results which are of practical value, even if the solution of the problem itself is not thereby advanced beyond a certain point.

These thinkers go so far on these lines as to understand ethics to be higher life-affirmation, consisting in our co-operation with the activity which the world-spirit wills for us. They represent the mysticism of activity taught by J. G. Fichte, but without its speculative foundation.

They leave unsolved, however, indeed they do not even put, the question, how the higher life-affirmation comes to give itself a content which stands in contradiction to the course of nature. They conceive of higher life-affirmation as altruism, that is to say as life-affirmation within which life-negation is active. But how does this paradox come about? How far is this direction of the will, which contradicts the natural will-to-live, a necessity of thought? Why must man become different from the world in order to exist and work in the world in true harmony with the world-spirit? And what meaning has this conduct of his for the happenings which take place in the universe?

*   *   *

The thought of Alfred Fouillée (1838–1913) [18] and Jean Marie Guyau (1854–1888) [19] also circles round the conception of ethics as higher life-affirmation. They too conceive of the ethical as self-devotion, that is to say, as life-affirmation within

---

17 Josiah Royce: *The Spirit of Modern Philosophy* (1892); *Religious Aspects of Philosophy* (4th ed., 1892).

18 A. Fouillée: *Critique des systèmes de morale contemporaine* (1883): *Evolutionisme des idées-forces* (1890; German translation, 1908); *La morale des idées-forces* (1907).

19 Jean Marie Guyau: *La morale anglaise contemporaine* (1879); *Esquisse d'une morale sans obligation ni sanction* (1885); *L'irréligion de l'avenir* (1886). A German version of his works appeared in 6 vols. in 1912.

which life-negation is present, but they dig deeper than the English and American representatives of the ethics of self-perfecting in that they seek to conceive of ethics within a nature-philosophy. Hence questions come to be discussed which these had left unnoticed. The problems of the basic principle of the moral and that of the optimistic-ethical world-view are once more opened up and, for the first time, in a comprehensive and elemental way.

Fouillée philosophizes in a noble way about the will-to-live. The ideas directed towards ethical ideals which come into our minds, like all our ideas in general, are, he says, not simply thoughts, but the expression of forces which press within us towards making existence full and complete.[20] Speaking generally, we must in this matter clearly understand that the evolution which in the course of the world produces and maintains existence is the work of representative forces (*idées-forces*), and is therefore to be explained in the last analysis as psychic. It reaches its highest point in man's ideas, which will their ends with clear consciousness. In this highest being, man, reality gets so far as to produce ideals which go out beyond reality, and by their means is led on beyond itself. Ethics are therefore a result of the evolution of the world. The idea of self-perfecting through self-devotion, which we experience as the mysterious element within us, is after all a natural manifestation of the will-to-live. The *ego* which has reached the farthest height of willing and representing enlarges itself by over-lapping other human existences. Self-devotion is, therefore, not a surrender of the self, but a manifestation of its expansion.[21] The man who analyses himself more deeply learns by experience that the highest life-affirmation comes about, not by the natural will-to-live simply rising into will-to-power, but by its "expanding." "Act towards others as if you became conscious of them at the same time as you become conscious of yourself."[22]

[20] "Toute idée enveloppe un élément impulsif; nulle idée n'est un état simplement représentatif." (Every idea contains an element of impulse; no idea is merely a condition of re-presenting something in thought.)

[21] . . . "notre conscience de nous-même tendant à sa plénitude par son expansion en autrui." (. . . our consciousness of ourselves, which presses on to its full growth by expanding into others.)

[22] "Agis envers les autres comme si tu avais conscience des autres en même temps que de toi."

Jean Marie Guyau, a pupil and friend of Fouillée, in his *"Esquisse d'une morale sans obligation ni sanction,"* tries to develop the thought of this ethical life-affirmation through expansion. Ordinary morality, he says, stands helpless before this insoluble cleft between the *ego* and other men, but living nature makes no stop at that point. The individual life is expansive because it is life. As in the physical sphere it carries within itself the impulse to produce fresh life like itself, so in the spiritual sphere also it wishes to widen its own existence by linking it on to other life like itself. Life is not only the intake of food, but also production and fruitfulness; real living consists not only in receiving, but in a giving out of oneself as well. Man is an organism which imparts itself to others; its perfection consists in the most complete imparting of itself. In this philosophizing, then, Hume's notion of sympathy is given more profound expression.

Fouillée and Guyau, both of them invalids, lived together at Nice and Mentone. Trying in one another's company to realize the ethical higher life-affirmation, they take their exercise on the very shore on which Nietzsche that same year thought out his heightened life-affirmation of *Beyond Good and Evil.* He knows their works, as they know his, but they remain personally unknown to each other.[23]

Fouillée and Guyau, because they think deeply, are led to nature-philosophy by their philosophizing about the way in which the will-to-live is to become ethical. They wish to conceive ethics, within a world- and life-affirming nature-philosophy, as a deepening of life-affirmation, and also as a necessity of thought. In this matter they join the procession of the Chinese monists. That which these, like Spinoza and Fichte, attempted and failed to do, they attempt again in the confidence that their nature-philosophy will be fairer to the conception of living existence than was that of the others.

Navigating the rushing stream of heightened life-affirmation, they try with mighty efforts at the oars to reach the bank of the ethical. They believe that they will be able to land there

23 Fouillée reveals his attitude towards Nietzsche in a work entitled *Nietzsche and Immoralism.* Notes on the works of Fouillée and Guyau have been preserved by Nietzsche.

... but the waves carry them past it, like all those who attempted the journey before them.

They fail to show convincingly that life-affirmation in its highest form, by a paradox which lies in the nature of things, becomes ethical altruism. This proposition by which they would change the world-view from natural to ethical, is truth only for the thought which dares to make the same leap because it sees no possibility otherwise of reaching land from the drifting boat.

The ethics of Fouillée and Guyau, then, are an enthusiastic conception of life to which man pulls himself up when coming to terms with reality, in order to assert and exert himself in the universe in accordance with a higher value which he feels he embodies.

So Fouillée and Guyau are elemental moralists like Schopenhauer and Nietzsche. They are not, however, like the latter, making a voyage with their rudder tightly lashed in the circle of world- and life-negation or world-negation and life-affirmation; they hold on their course with sure perception towards the mysterious union of world-affirmation, life-affirmation, and life-negation which constitutes ethical life-affirmation. . . . But this course takes them out over the boundless ocean. They never reach land.

In order to understand themselves as a direction of the will-to-live which is a necessity of thought, and to think themselves out to an ethical world-view, ethics must come to terms with nature-philosophy. We find them, then, attempting—as did the Rationalists, and Kant and the speculative philosophers—to read into the world, in simple or in detailed thought, an optimistic-ethical meaning, or at least, as with Spinoza, to give an ethical character in some way or other to the relation of the individual to the universe. These two men also, Fouillée and Guyau, wrestle with nature-philosophy in order from it to justify ethics and an ethical world-view as not without meaning. At the same time, however, they dare—and this is the new element which appears in them—to look straight in the face the possibility that it will perhaps be impossible to carry their undertaking through. What will then become of ethics and world-view? Although they really ought to collapse, they do nevertheless remain standing—so Fouillée and Guyau judge.

Whether the idea of the good can ultimately claim any objective validity cannot be asserted with complete certainty, says Fouillée in his *Morale des Idées-forces*. Man must finally be content to force himself to acceptance of the ethically expansive life-affirmation, merely because he feels it to be the only thing which is capable of making life valuable. Out of love for the ideal he triumphs over all doubt, and sacrifices himself to it, untroubled about whether or no anything results from his doing so.

Guyau's *"Esquisse d'une morale sans obligation ni sanction"* ends in similar thoughts. An inner force, he says, works upon us and drives us forward. Do we go forward alone, or will the idea eventually win for itself some influence upon nature? . . . Anyhow let us go forward! . . . "Perhaps the earth, perhaps mankind, will one day reach some as yet unknown goal which they themselves have created. There is no hand leading us, no eye watching on our behalf; the rudder was broken long ago, or rather there never was one at all; it has to be provided. That is a big task, and it is our task." . . . Ethical men are crossing the ocean of events on a rudderless and mastless derelict, hoping nevertheless that they will some day and somewhere reach land.

In these sentences there is announced from afar the disappearance of the optimistic-ethical interpretation of the world. Because they dare to abandon this, and proclaim in principle the sovereign independence of ethics, Fouillée and Guyau belong among the greatest thinkers who have had a share in shaping our conception of the universe.

They do not, however, follow to the end the path on which they have stumbled. While they make ethics independent of whether their activity can or cannot prove itself legitimate as significant and effective in the totality of world-happenings, they assume the existence of a conflict between world-view and life-view, which philosophy down to their day had actually not noticed. But they do not investigate its nature, and do not show how it is that life-view can venture to assert itself in opposition to world-view, and even to exalt itself as the more important. They are content to prophesy that ethics and ethical world-view will grow green again as mighty oases, fed by subterranean springs, even if the sand-storms of scepticism should have turned into a desert the broad territory of the optimistic-ethical knowledge of the world, in which we once wished to make our home. At bottom, however, they hope that nothing like this will happen. Their confidence that a nature-philosophy which deals in the proper way with the nature of Being will after all finally reach ethics and an ethical world-view, is not completely overthrown.

Since they at first claim only a hypothetical validity for their new outlook, and do not develop it as a matter of principle, Fouillée and Guyau do not exercise upon the thought of the end of the nineteenth century and the beginning of the twentieth the influence which they deserve to have. Their age indeed, was not ready for that renunciation of knowledge for which their writings were preparing the way.

A forerunner of their ethic is to be found in that which Friedrich Albert Lange sketches as his own at the end of his *History of Materialism* (1866). Ethics, he says, are an imaginative creation on which we determine, because we carry an ideal within ourselves. We rise above the actual because we find no satisfaction in it. We are ethical because our life thereby obtains a definite character such as we long for. . . . Ethics mean becoming free from the world.

Lange also, then, has already reached the view that from direct philosophizing about the world and life an ethical outlook on the universe results, not as a necessity of thought, but as a necessity for life. But like the two French thinkers he just throws out the thought instead of following it into all its presuppositions and consequences.

A peculiar supplement which completes the ethics of Fouillée, Guyau, and Lange, without actually going back to them, is provided by the Berlin physician, Wilhelm Stern, in an inquiry, which has attracted far too little notice, into the evolutionary origin of ethics.[24] The essential nature of the moral, he says, is the impulse to the maintenance of life by the repelling of all injurious attacks upon it, an impulse through which the individual being experiences a feeling of relationship to all other animate beings in face of nature's injurious attacks upon them.

24 Wilhelm Stern, *Foundation of Ethics as a Positive Science* (Berlin, 1897).

How has this mentality arisen in us? Through the fact that animate beings of the most varied kinds have been obliged through countless generations to fight side by side for existence against the forces of nature, and in their common distress have ceased to be hostile to one another, so that they might attempt a common resistance to the annihilation which threatened them, or perish in a common ruin. This experience, which began with their first and lowest stage of existence and has become through thousands of millions of generations more and more pronounced, has given its special character to the psychology of all living beings. All ethics are an affirmation of life, the character of which is determined by perception of the dangers to existence which living beings experience in common.

How much deeper does Wilhelm Stern go than did Darwin! According to Darwin, experience of the never-ceasing, universal danger to existence produces in the end nothing but the herd-instinct, which holds together creatures of the same species. According to Stern, there is developed by the same experience a kind of solidarity with everything that lives. The barriers fall. Man experiences sympathy with animals, as they experience it, only less completely, with him. Ethics are not merely something peculiar to man, but, in a less developed form, are to be seen also in the animal world as such. Self-devotion is an experience of the deepened impulse to self-preservation. In the active as well as in the passive meaning of the word the whole animate creation is to be included within the basic principle of the moral.

The fundamental commandment of ethics, then, is that we cause no suffering to any living creature, not even the lowest, unless it is to effect some necessary protection for ourselves, and that we be ready to undertake, whenever we can, positive action for the benefit of other creatures.

In Fouillée, Guyau, and Lange ethics try to come to terms with nature-philosophy, but without any advance towards becoming cosmic. They fall into the anachronism of regarding themselves still, even at that date, as nothing beyond the regulating of the disposition of man towards his fellow-men, instead of expanding so as to comprehend the conduct of man towards every living creature and towards Being in general. In Stern this obvious, further step is taken.

Only a system of ethics that has become universal and cosmic is capable of taking in hand the investigation of the basic principle of the moral; only such a system can really attempt to come to terms in intelligible fashion with nature-philosophy.

* * *

Eduard von Hartmann (1842–1906) [25] also endeavours to include ethics in nature-philosophy. His *Philosophy of the Unconscious* is largely in line with the thoughts of Fouillée, but in the matter of an outlook on the universe he takes a different course. Instead of allowing ethics, when coming to terms with nature-philosophy, to experience freedom from this, he compels their adjustment to such a philosophy. And his nature-philosophy is pessimistic. It confesses to being unable to discover in what happens in the world any principle which contains a meaning. Therefore, so Hartmann concludes, as do the Indians and Schopenhauer, the world-process is something which must come to a standstill. Everything that exists must gradually enter on the blessed condition of willlessness. Ethics are the state of mind which brings this development into action.

In language obscure enough, at the end of his *Phenomenology of the Moral Consciousness,* von Hartmann formulates his pessimistic-ethical philosophy as follows: "Existence in the world of matter is the incarnation of the Godhead; the world-process is the history of the passion of the incarnate God, and at the same time the way to the redemption of Him who is crucified in the flesh; but morality is co-operation for the shortening of this road of suffering and redemption."

Then, however, instead of unfolding what this ethic is, and how it is to come into force, he undertakes to show that all ethical standpoints which have ever made their appearance at all in history have their own justification. He wants to house them all within an evolution which necessarily leads to pessimistic ethics.

25 Eduard von Hartmann: *Philosophy of the Unconscious* (1879); *Phenomenology of the Moral Consciousness* (1789).

Every moral principle which shows itself in history, von Hartmann asserts, changes when it searches for the completion which lies nearest to it. It lives itself out, and then makes way for the higher moral principle which logically issues from it. That is how the ethical consciousness in individuals and in mankind works itself up from one moral principle to another till it reaches the highest knowledge. From the primitive moral principle of aiming at individual pleasure it travels past the authoritarian, the æsthetic, the sentimental, and the intellectual moral systems, which are one and all subjective, to the objective morality of care for the general happiness. But still beyond this it is led to the evolutionary moral principle of the development of civilization, and here it learns to think on supra-moral lines. It grasps the notion that for moral consideration there is still something higher than the prosperity of individuals and of society, namely "contest and struggle for the maintenance and enhancing of civilization." This, according to usual ideas, unethical conception of ethics has to be developed completely, so that it may then be resolved into the ethics of world- and life-negation.

By this insight into the logic of the course of ethical evolution, von Hartmann is saved from protesting, as would an ordinary ethical thinker, against the unethical civilization-ethics of the close of the nineteenth century. He knows, on the contrary, that he is helping the cause of rightly understood ethical progress, if he treats that form of ethics with respect as a necessary phenomenon, and urges that it be allowed to live itself out with the utmost completeness. Accordingly he asserts that we have learnt to see through the ethic which aims at making men and peoples happy as being a piece of sentimentality, and ought now to make up our minds to deal seriously with the supra-ethical ethic of the enhancement of life and civilization. We must learn to regard as good whatever is necessary for the development of civilization, and we are no longer at liberty to condemn war in the name of ethics. "The principle of the development of civilization compels us to recognize all these protests as unsound, since wars are the chief means of carrying on the struggle between races, that is to say, the process of natural selection within mankind, and preparation for the effective waging of war has

formed one of the most important means of education and training for mankind in every phase of the development of civilization, as it will also be, so far as we can see, in the future." [26]
Economic misery too, and the conflicts which arise from it, are
seen by the ethical spirit which looks further ahead to subserve
a higher objective. The sufferings under the wage system, which
are far greater than those under slavery, are necessary for the
course of civilization. The struggle which they evoke calls
forces into being and has an educative effect. The course of
civilization needs a favoured minority to serve as bearers of its
ideas. Beneficence and charity to the poor must therefore be
practised with moderation. The need which spurs men on to
active work must not be banished from the world.

Another element in the course of civilization is the taking
into possession of the whole earth by the race with the highest
civilization, which must therefore increase its numbers as much
as possible. In order to make the female population zealous
about the task which thus falls to them, women must be raised
intellectually. This is done by inculcating as much as possible
patriotism and national feeling, by arousing their historical
sense, and by filling them with enthusiasm for the principle
of civilization which underlies evolution. "To effect this object,
the history of civilization must be made the foundation of all
instruction in the upper classes of girls' schools." [27]

It is desirable, therefore, to make efforts to secure the "improvement of the human type," and the attainment of an
enhancement of civilization in which "the world-spirit becomes
in increasing measure conscious of itself."

In his nature-philosophy and his philosophy of history, then,
Eduard von Hartmann reaches a supra-ethical conception of
life in which Hegel and Nietzsche drink to brotherhood, and
the principles of inhumanity and relativity, which underlie
biologico-sociological ethics, sit at table with garlands on their
heads.

How and when the supra-ethical ethics of enhanced world-
and life-affirmation pass over into the highest ethics of world-
and life-negation, and in what way this highest system of ethics,

[26] *Phenomenology*, p. 670.
[27] *Idem*, p. 700.

in which we function as redeemers of the absolute, is to be carried out in practice, von Hartmann is unable to make clear. The abstruse modulations with which, in the last chapters of his work, he tries to get from one to the other provide us with ample proof of the unnatural character of the undertaking. To produce a philosophy with Hegel for body and Schopenhauer for head, is an absurdity. By his resolve to attempt it, von Hartmann admits his inability to make enhanced life-affirmation become in a natural way ethical.

Eduard von Hartmann prefers to the profession of moralist that of philosopher of the history of morals. Instead of serving the world with an ethical system of morals, he makes it happy with the discovery of the principle of inherent progress in the history of morals, and thus helps to befool completely the thought of his age, which is living its life in an unethical and unspiritual optimism.

From the history of ethics nothing is to be gained except a certain amount of clearness about the problem of ethics. Anyone who discovers in it principles which promise automatic progress in the ethical development of mankind, has mendaciously read these principles into the facts as a result of his miserably faulty construction of that history.

*   *   *

Henri Bergson (b. 1860) [28] renounces altogether the attempt to bring together nature-philosophy and ethics. Houston Stewart Chamberlain (b. 1855) [29] and Count Hermann Keyserling (b. 1880) [30] make the attempt but without reaching any result.

In his philosophizing about nature, Bergson does not go beyond the *rôle* of the observing subject. He analyses in a masterly

---

[28] Henri Bergson: *Sur les données immédiates de la conscience* (1888). (English translation by F. L. Pogson, 1910: *Time and Freewill: An Essay on the Immediate Data of Consciousness*.) *Matière et memoire. Essai sur la relation du corps et de l'esprit* (1896). (English translation by N. M. Paul and W. S. Palmer: *Matter and Memory*, 1911.) *L'évolution créatrice* (1907). (English translation by A. Mitchell: *Creative Evolution*, 1911.)

[29] H. S. Chamberlain: *The Foundations of the Nineteenth Century* (1899). (14th German edition, 1922.) *Immanuel Kant* (1905); *Goethe* (1912).

[30] Count Hermann Keyserling: *The Structure of the World* (1906); *A Philosopher's Travel-Diary* (2 vols., 1919); *Philosophy as Art* (1920).

way the nature of the process of knowledge. His investigations into the origin of our conception of time and of the actions of our consciousness which are bound up with it, have taught us how to comprehend the course of nature in its living reality. Leading us on beyond the science which consists in external affirming and calculating, Bergson shows that the true knowledge of Being comes to us through a sort of intuition. Philosophizing means experiencing our consciousness as an emanation of the creative impulse which rules in the world. Bergson's nature-philosophy has therefore a close inward connection with that of Fouillée, but he does not find it necessary, as Fouillée does, to produce from it a world- and life-view. He limits himself to depicting it from the standpoint of the problem of the theory of knowledge. He does not attempt any analysis of the ethical consciousness. Year after year we have waited for him to complete his work, as he no doubt himself intended, with an attempt at producing an ethic based on nature-philosophy. But he has contented himself with developing in ever-new forms his theories about our inner knowledge of the real. He never comes to the recognition that all deepening of our knowledge of the world acquires its real significance only so far as it teaches us to understand what we ought to aim at in life. He lets the waves of events roll past us, as if we were seated on an island in the stream, whereas we are in reality obliged to exert ourselves in it as swimmers.

During the war the German cinema theatres were crammed. People went to see the pictures in order to forget their hunger. Bergson's philosophy brings before us as living events the world which Kant depicted in motionless wall-pictures. But to satisfy the hunger of to-day for ethics he does nothing. He has no world-view to offer us in which we can find a life-view. A quietistic, sceptical mood overshadows his philosophy.

Houston Stewart Chamberlain tries to find a world-view which is based on nature-philosophy and is at the same time ethical. His work entitled *Immanuel Kant* (1905), which is really a journey through the problems raised by philosophy and the attempts to solve them, ends in the thought that, if we wish to reach a real civilization, we have to combine Goethe's nature-philosophy, which conceives becoming as an eternal being, with

Kant's judgment about the nature of duty. But he finds himself unable to develop such a world-view to completion.

Stimulated by Chamberlain, Hermann Keyserling goes far beyond Bergson in the aims of his thinking. He wants to reach clear ideas not only about knowledge of the world, but also about life and work in the world. From the pinnacle, however, to which he mounts, he sees only the fields of wisdom; those of ethics are veiled in mist. The highest idea, so he declares at the conclusion of his work, *The Structure of the World,* is that of truth. We want to know, because knowledge, "whether it visibly serves life at present or not, already implies in itself a purposive reaction to the outer world." In correct knowledge the human spirit enters into reciprocal relations with the universe. Life carries within itself its own purposive character.

Keyserling finds it quite in order that the outlook on life of great men should be superior to ordinary moral standards. One must not reproach Leonardo da Vinci for working as willingly in the service of the French king, Francis I., as he had done previously in that of the Sforzas whom Francis expelled. "Almost every great spirit is a complete egoist." If anyone has experience of life in its full extent and depth and living force, and works in reciprocity with the universe, interest in the human race is a kind of specialization which is no longer incumbent on him.

In the Preface to the second edition of *The Structure of the World* (1920), Keyserling admits that he has not reached a decision about the ethical problem. In his *Philosophy as Art* (1920), he declares it to be the foremost duty of our time to "make the wise man a possible type, to draw him out by education, and give him all necessary publicity and scope for his activities."

The wise man is the one man who is capable of veracity, the man who lets all the tones of life sound within him, and seeks to be in tune with the fundamental key-note which is given in him. He has no universally valid conception of the universe to impart to others. Not even for himself has he a conception that is definite and final; he has only one which is liable to constant alteration for the better. He himself is unalterable only in this, that he wants to live his life in its entirety and in the most vital co-operation with the universe, and at the same time ever strives to be himself. Sincere and emphatic life-affirmation is therefore the last word of this philosophizing about the world and life. . . .

Thus does nature-philosophy admit that it cannot produce ethics.

With the lesser spirits self-deception goes further. The ordinary scientific monism, the greatness of which consists in its being an elemental movement towards veracity in an age which is weary of veracity, is still convinced that from its insight into the essential nature of life, into the development of lower life into higher, and into the inner connection of the individual life with the life of the universe, it can somehow or other arrive at ethics. But it is significant that its representatives take altogether different roads in the search for ethics. An incredible absence of thought and of plan reigns in the ethical philosophizing of the ordinary scientific nature-philosophy. Many of its representatives have before their mind's eye a conception of the moral as a becoming one with the universe, a conception which is related to that of the Stoics and Spinoza. Others, influenced by Nietzsche, entertain the thought that true ethics are an enhanced and aristocratic life-affirmation, and have nothing to do with the claims of the "democratic" social ethics.[31] Others again, like Johannes Unold in his work *Monism and Its Ideals* (1908), try to bring together nature-philosophy and ethics in such a way as to let them conceive of the human activity which is directed to social ends as the final result of the development of the organic world. There are also scientific nature-philosophers who are content to put together out of what is commonly regarded as moral a system of ethics which is universally accepted, and to exalt it, so far as they can, into a product of nature-philosophy. In Ernst Haeckel's (1834–1919) work *The Riddle of the Universe* (1899), an ethic of that character is built on to the palace of nature-philosophy like a kitchen. It is maintained that the basic principle of monistic ethical theory is the equal justification of egoism and altruism, and

[31] Thus Otto Braun in his essay "Monism and Ethics" in the volume entitled *Monism Expounded in Contributions from its Representatives* (edited by Arthur Drews; vol. i., 1908). The poverty of this form of ethics is clearly revealed when the editor tries to indicate its content.

supplies the equilibrium between them. Both are laws of nature. Egoism serves the preservation of the individual, altruism that of the species. That "golden rule of morality" is said to be of equal significance with the rule which Jesus and other ethical thinkers before him are said to have proclaimed in the demand that we shall love our neighbour as ourselves. Spencer and water is poured out under a Christian label.

*   *   *

An inexorable development of thought, then, brings it about that the philosophy of the end of the nineteenth century and the beginning of the twentieth, either advances to a supraethical world-view, or lives among ethical ruins. What happens in the great German speculative philosophy of the beginning of the nineteenth century is a prelude to the *dénouement* of the drama. In that philosophy an ethical world-view tries to find a foundation in speculative nature-philosophy, and in doing so becomes, as stands confessed in Hegel, supra-ethical. Later, ethics are believed capable of providing a "scientific" conception of themselves, thanks to the results reached by psychology, biology, and sociology, but in proportion as they effect this, their energy decreases. Later still, when, through the growth of science and the inward changes in thought, a nature-philosophy which is in harmony with scientific observation of nature becomes the only possible philosophy, ethics once more have to make a real attempt to find a basis in a nature-philosophy which is directed upon the universe. There is nothing, however, but the enhancement and perfecting of life which nature-philosophy can give as the meaning of life. Hence ethics must struggle to conceive the enhancement and perfecting of life as something which comes to pass within the field of ethical ideas, and it is this for which, without ever attaining its goal, the most modern thought is striving, on lines of development which are often apparently irreconcilable.

Whenever an ethic really relies in any way upon nature-philosophy for the production of the convincing, ethical world-view for which the age is longing, it gets wrecked upon it in one way or another. Either it actually attempts to give itself out to be somehow a natural enhancement of life, and thereby so alters its character that it ceases to be really and truly ethics. Or it abdicates; perhaps, as with Keyserling, leaving the field free to supra-ethical world-view; perhaps, as with Bergson, leaving nature-philosophy and ethical questions with it, to rest in peace.

Thus the sun of ethics becomes darkened for our generation. Nature-philosophy pushes itself forward like a wall of cloud. Just as an inundation overwhelms pastures and fields with its water-borne *débris,* so do the supra-ethical and the unethical ways of thinking break in upon our mentality. They bring about the most terrible devastations without anyone having any clear idea of what the catastrophe means, or indeed being conscious of anything wrong beyond that the spirit of the time is rendering all ethical standards powerless.

Everywhere there grows up an unethical conception of civilization. The masses reconcile themselves in an incomprehensible way to the theory of the relativity of all ethical standards and to thoughts of inhumanity. Freed from any obligation to the exercise of ethical will, the belief in progress suffers a process of externalization which increases from year to year, becoming finally nothing better than a wooden façade which conceals the pessimism behind it. That we have lapsed into pessimism is betrayed by the fact that the demand for the spiritual advance of society and mankind is no longer seriously made among us. We have now resigned ourselves, as if no explanation of it were needed, to the fate of being obliged to smile at the high-flying hopes of previous generations. There is no longer to be found among us the true world- and life-affirmation which reaches down to the depths of the spiritual nature of man. Unavowed pessimism has been consuming us for decades.

Delivered over to events in an attitude of mind which is powerless because it is entirely without any true and ethical ideals of progress, we are experiencing the collapse of material and spiritual civilization alike.

By its belief in an optimistic-ethical philosophy the modern age became capable of a mighty advance towards civilization. But as its thought has not been able to show this philosophy to be founded in the nature of things, we have sunk, consciously and unconsciously, into a condition in which we have no world-view at all, a condition of pessimism, too, and of absence of all ethical conviction, so that we are on the point of complete ruin.

The bankruptcy of the optimistic-ethical philosophy was announced beforehand as little as was the financial bankruptcy of the ruined states of Europe. But just as the latter was gradually revealed, by the constantly diminishing value of the paper-money that was issued, as having actually come about, so is the former being gradually revealed by the constantly diminishing power among us of the true and profound ideals of civilization.

Chapter 22

THE NEW WAY

Why the optimistic-ethical world-view cannot be carried through to the logical conclusion.

Life-view independent of world-view.

THE GREATNESS OF EUROPEAN PHILOSOPHY CONSISTS IN ITS HAVING chosen the optimistic-ethical world-view; its weakness in its having again and again imagined that it was putting that conception on a firm foundation, instead of making clear to itself the difficulties of doing so. The task before our generation is to strive with deepened thought to reach a truer and more valuable world-view, and thus bring to an end our living on and on without any philosophy of life at all.

Our age is striking out unmeaningly in every direction like a fallen horse in the traces. It is trying with external measures and new organization to solve the difficult problems with which it has to deal, but all in vain. The horse cannot get on its feet again till it is unharnessed and allowed to get its head up. Our world will not get upon its feet again till it lets the truth come home to it that salvation is not to be found in active measures but in new ways of thinking.

But new ways of thinking can arise only if a true and valuable conception of life casts its spell upon individuals.

The one serviceable world-view is the optimistic-ethical. Its renewal is a duty incumbent on us. Can we prove it to be true?

In the struggle of the thinkers who for centuries exerted themselves to demonstrate the truth of optimistic-ethical philosophy, and kept surrendering themselves comfortably to the

[271]

illusion, always very soon shattered, that they had succeeded, the problem with which we are concerned reveals itself in outlines which become clearer and clearer. We are now in a position to reckon up why these or those paths, apparently so full of promise, have led to nothing, and can lead to nothing. By the insight into the problem thus won we shall be kept off impassable roads and forced to follow the only track which is practicable.

The most general result of the attempts made up to the present is this: that the optimistic-ethical interpretation of the world, by which it was hoped to put the optimistic-ethical world-view on a firm foundation, cannot be developed to a conclusion. Yet how logical and natural it seems to tune the meaning of life and the meaning of the world to the same key! How invitingly the path opens out to explaining our own existence from the nature and significance of the universe! It rises so naturally to the crest of the foothills that one can only believe it leads up to the highest point of knowledge. But high up in the ascent it breaks off with chasms ahead.

The consideration that the meaning of human life must be conceivable within the meaning of the universe is so obvious to thought, that it never lets itself be led from its path by the failure, one after another, of all attempts in that direction. It merely concludes that it has not tackled the problem in the right way. It therefore has resort to the whisperings of the theory of knowledge, and undertakes to depreciate the reality of the world in order to deal with it more successfully. In Kant, in the speculative philosophy, and in much "spiritualistic" popular philosophy which has been current almost down to our own day, it preserved its hope of reaching the goal by some sort of combination of epistemological with ethical idealism. Hence the philosophy of academic manuals declaims against the ingenuous thinking which tries to reach a world-view without first having been baptized by Kant with fire and the holy spirit. But this too is a vain proceeding. The crafty and fraudulent attempts to form a conception of the world with an optimistic-ethical meaning meet with no better success than the naïve ones. What our thinking tries to proclaim as knowledge is never anything but an unjustifiable interpretation of the world.

Against the admission of this, thought guards itself with the courage of despair, because it fears it will find itself in that case with no idea of what to do in face of the problem of life. What meaning can we give to human existence, if we must renounce all pretence of knowing the meaning of the world? Nevertheless there remains only one thing for thought to do, and that is to adapt itself to facts.

The hopelessness of the attempt to find the meaning of life within the meaning of the universe is shown first of all by the fact that in the course of nature there is no purposiveness to be seen in which the activities of men, and of mankind as a whole, could in any way intervene. On one of the smaller among the millions of heavenly bodies there have lived for a short space of time human beings. For how long will they continue so to live? Any lowering or raising of the temperature of the earth, any change in the inclination of the axis of their planet, a rise in the level of the ocean, or a change in the composition of the atmosphere, can put an end to their existence. Or the earth itself may fall, as so many other heavenly bodies have fallen, a victim to some cosmic catastrophe. We are entirely ignorant of what significance we have for the earth. How much less then may we presume to try to attribute to the infinite universe a meaning which has us for its object, or which can be explained in terms of our existence!

It is not, however, merely the huge disproportion between the universe and man which makes it impossible for us to give the aims and objects of mankind a logical place in those of the universe. Any such attempt is made useless beforehand by the fact that we fail to succeed in discovering any general purposiveness in the course of nature. Whatever we do find of purposiveness in the world is never anything but an isolated instance.

In the production and maintenance of some definite form of life, nature does sometimes act purposively in a magnificent way. But in no way does she ever seem intent on uniting these instances of purposiveness which are directed to single objects into a collective purpose. She never undertakes to let life coalesce with life to form a collective life. She is wonderfully creative force, and at the same time senselessly destructive force. We face her absolutely perplexed. What is full of meaning within the meaningless, the meaningless within what is full of meaning: that is the essential nature of the universe.

*   *   *

European thought has tried to ignore these elemental certainties. It can do so no longer, and it is of no use to try. The facts have silently produced their consequences. While the optimistic-ethical world-view is still current among us as a dogma, we no longer possess the ethical world- and life-affirmation which should result from it. Perplexity and pessimism have taken possession of us without our admitting the fact.

There remains, therefore, nothing for us to do but confess that we understand nothing of the world, and are surrounded by complete enigmas. Our knowledge is becoming sceptical.

Just as thought has hitherto allowed world-view and life-view to be mutually dependent on each other, so have we in consequence fallen a prey to a sceptical conception of life. But is it really the case that life-view is towed along by world-view, and when the latter can no longer be kept afloat must sink with it into the depths? Necessity bids us cut the tow-rope and try to let life-view continue its voyage independently.

This manœuvre is not so unexpected as it seems. While people still acted as though their life-view were taken from their world-view, the relationship between the two was really just the opposite, for their world-view was formed from their life-view. What they put forward as their view of the world was an interpretation of the world in the light of their life-view.

The life-view held by European thought being optimistic-ethical, the same character was attributed to world-view in defiance of facts. Wishful thinking, without admitting it, overpowered knowledge. Life-view prompted and world-view recited. So the belief that life-view was derived from world-view was only a fiction.

In Kant this overpowering of knowledge, which till then had been but naïvely practised, was worked out systematically. His doctrine of the "Postulates of the Practical Reason" means just this: that the will claims for itself the decisive word in the last pronouncements of the world-view. Only Kant manages to arrange the matter so cleverly that the will never forces its supremacy on knowledge, but receives it from the latter as a free gift, and then makes use of it in carefully chosen parliamentary phrases. It proceeds as if it had been invoked by the theoretical reason to provide possible truths with the reality belonging to truths which are necessities of thought.

In Fichte the will dictates its world-view to knowledge without any regard for the arts of diplomacy.

From the middle of the nineteenth century onward, there can be discerned in natural science a tendency no longer to claim that philosophy must be accommodated to scientifically established facts. The valuable convictions of the traditional world-view are to hold good, even if they cannot be brought into harmony with the accepted knowledge of the world. After the publication of Du Bois-Raymond's (1818–1896) lectures "On the Limits of Our Knowledge of Nature" (1872) with a certain school of natural science it begins to be considered almost a part of good manners to declare oneself incompetent in questions of world-view. There grows up gradually what one may call a modern doctrine of the two-fold nature of truth. To this movement expression is given by the "Keplerbund," which was founded in 1907 by representatives of natural science, and goes so far as to declare acceptable to natural science the valuable pronouncements of the current philosophy of life, even when given in formulas provided by ecclesiastical authority. This new doctrine of the two-fold nature of truth is brought to philosophical expression by the theory of the solidity of "value-judgments." By means of this theory Albrecht Ritschl (1822–1889) and his imitators try to uphold the validity of a religious, side by side with a scientific, conception of life. Almost the whole religious world, in so far as it tries to remain a thinking body, grasps at such expedients. Next, in William James's (1842–1910) philosophy of Pragmatism the will admits in half-naïve, half-cynical fashion that all the knowledge professed by its world-view has been produced by itself.

That the valuable assertions of philosophy are to be traced back to the will which has been determined by valuable convictions is therefore a fact, and since Kant's day a fact that has been admitted in the most varied directions. The shock given to the feeling for veracity, which accompanies this no longer naïve but half-conscious and insidiously employed interpretation of the world, plays a fatal part in the mentality of our time.

But why go on with this dirty business? Why keep knowledge in subservience to the will by means of a kind of infamous secret police? Any world-view deduced therefrom must ever be a miserable thing. Let us allow will and knowledge to come together in a relation honourable to both.

In what has hitherto been called world-view there are two things united: view of the world and life-view. So long as it was possible to cherish the illusion that the two were harmonious and each completed the other, there was nothing to be said against this combination. Now, however, when the divergence can no longer be concealed, the wider conception of world-view which includes life-view organically within itself, must be given up. It is no longer permissible to go on either naïvely believing that we get our conception of life from our conception of the world, or furtively elevating in some way or other our conception of life into a conception of the world. We are standing at a turning-point of thought. Critical action which clears away all prevailing *naïvetés* and dishonesties has become necessary. We must make up our minds to leave our conceptions of life and of the world mutually independent of each other, and see that a straightforward understanding between the two is reached. We have to admit that because our conception of life is made up of convictions which are given in our will-to-live but are not confirmed by knowledge of the world, we have allowed it to go beyond the varied knowledge which makes up our conception of the world.

This renunciation of world-view in the old sense, that is of a unitary world-view which is complete in itself, means a painful experience for our thought. We come hereby to a dualism against which we at every moment instinctively rebel. But we must surrender to facts. Our will to live has to accommodate itself to the inconceivable truth that it is unable with its own valuable convictions to discover itself again in the manifold will-to-live which is seen manifested in the world. We wanted to form a philosophy of life for ourselves out of items of knowledge gathered from the world. But it is our destiny to live by means of convictions which an inward necessity makes a part of our thought.

In the old rationalism reason undertook to investigate the world. In the new it has to take as its task the attaining to clarity about the will-to-live which is in us. Thus we return to an elemental philosophizing which is once more busied with questions of world- and life-view as they directly affect men, and seeks to give a safe foundation to, and to keep alive, the valuable ideas which we find in ourselves. It is in a conception of life which is dependent on itself alone, and seeks to come in a straightforward way to an understanding with world-knowledge, that we hope to find once more power to attain to ethical world- and life-affirmation.

Chapter 23

THE FOUNDATIONS OF OPTIMISM SECURED

FROM THE WILL-TO-LIVE

The pessimistic result of knowledge.
The world- and life-affirmation of the will-to-live.

THERE ARE TWO THINGS WHICH THOUGHT HAS TO DO FOR US; IT must lead us from the naïve to a deepened world- and life-affirmation, and must let us go on from mere ethical impulses to an ethic which is a necessity of thought.

Deepened world- and life-affirmation consists in this: that we have the will to maintain our own life and every kind of existence that we can in any way influence, and to bring them to their highest value. It demands from us that we think out all ideals of the material and spiritual perfecting of individual men, of society, and of mankind as a whole, and let ourselves be determined by them to steady activity and constant hope. It does not allow us to withdraw into ourselves, but orders us to bring to bear a living, and so far as possible an active, interest on everything which happens around us. To endure a state of unrest through our relation to the world, when by withdrawing into ourselves we might enjoy rest: that is the burden which deeper world- and life-affirmation lays upon us.

We begin our life-course in an unsophisticated world- and life-affirmation. The will-to-live which is in us gives us that as natural. But later, when thought awakes, questions crop up which make a problem of what has hitherto been a matter of course. What meaning will you give your life? What do you mean to do in the world? When, along with these questions, we begin trying to reconcile knowledge and will-to-live, facts get in the way with confusing suggestions. Life attracts us, they say, with a thousand expectations, and fulfils hardly one of them. And the fulfilled expectation is almost a disappointment, for only anticipated pleasure is really pleasure; in pleasure which is fulfilled its opposite is already stirring. Unrest, disappointment and pain are our lot in the short span of time which lies between our entrance on life and our departure from it. What is spiritual is in a dreadful state of dependence on our bodily nature. Our existence is at the mercy of meaningless happenings and can be brought to an end by them at any moment. The will-to-live gives me an impulse to action, but the action is just as if I wanted to plough the sea, and sow in the furrows. What did those who worked before me effect? What significance in the endless chain of world-happenings have their efforts had? With all its illusive promises, the will-to-live only means to mislead me into prolonging my existence, and allowing to enter on existence other beings to whom the same miserable lot has been assigned as to myself, so that the game may go on and on without end.

The discoveries in the field of knowledge which the will-to-live encounters when it begins to think, are therefore altogether pessimistic. It is not by accident that all religious world-views, except the Chinese, have a more or less pessimistic tone and bid man expect nothing from his existence here.

Who will prevent us from making use of the freedom we are allowed, and casting existence from us? Every thinking human being makes acquaintance with this thought. We let it take a deeper hold of us than we suspect from one another, as indeed we are all more oppressed by the riddles of existence than we allow others to notice.

What determines us, so long as we are comparatively in our right mind, to reject the thought of putting an end to our existence? An instinctive feeling of repulsion from such a deed. The will-to-live is stronger than the pessimistic facts of knowledge. An instinctive reverence for life is within us, for we are will-to-live. . . .

Even the consistently pessimistic thought of Brahmanism makes to the will-to-live the concession that voluntary death may only come about when the individual has put behind him a considerable portion of life. The Buddha goes still further. He rejects any violent exit from existence and demands only that we mortify the will-to-live within us.

All pessimism, then, is inconsistent. It does not push open the door to freedom, but makes concessions to the obvious fact of existence. In Indian thought, with its pessimistic tendency, there is an attempt to make these concessions as small as possible, and to maintain the impossible fiction that merely bare life is being lived, with complete abstinence from any share in the happenings which are taking place here, there, and everywhere about it. With us the concessions are larger, since the conflict between the will-to-live and pessimistic recognition of facts is to a certain extent damped down and obscured by the optimistic outlook on the world which prevails in the general mode of thought. There arises an unthinking will-to-live which lives out its life trying to snatch possession of as much happiness as possible, and wishes to do something active without having made clear to itself what its intentions really are.

Whether somewhat more or somewhat less of world- and life-affirmation is retained matters little. Whenever the deepened world- and life-affirmation is not fully reached, there remains only a depreciated will-to-live, which is not equal to the tasks of life.

Thought usually deprives the will-to-live of the force lent it by its freedom from pre-conceptions, without being able to induce it to adopt a practice of reflection in which it would find new and higher force. Thus it still possesses energy enough to continue in life, but not enough to overcome pessimism. The stream becomes a swamp.

That is the experience which determines the character of men's existence, without their confessing it to themselves. They nourish themselves scantily on a little bit of happiness and many vain thoughts, which life puts in their manger. It is only by the pressure of necessity, exerted by elementary duties which throng upon them, that they are kept on the path of life.

Often their will-to-live is changed into a kind of intoxication. Spring sunshine, trees in flower, passing clouds, fields of waving corn provoke it. A will-to-live which announces itself in many forms in magnificent phenomena all around them, carries their own will-to-live along with it. Full of delight, they want to take part in the mighty symphony which they hear. They find the world beautiful. . . . But the transport passes. Horrid discords allow them once more to hear only noise, where they thought they perceived music. The beauty of nature is darkened by the suffering they discover everywhere within it. Now they see once more that they are drifting like shipwrecked men over a waste of waters, only that their boat is at one moment raised aloft on mountainous waves and the next sinks into the valleys between them, and that now sunbeams, and now heavy clouds, rest upon the heaving billows.

Now they would like to persuade themselves that there is land in the direction in which they are drifting. Their will-to-live befools their thinking, so that it makes efforts to see the world as it would like to see it. It compels it also to hand them a chart which confirms their hopes of land. Once more they bend to the oars, till once again their arms drop with fatigue, and their gaze wanders, disappointed, from billow to billow.

That is the voyage of the will-to-live which has abjured thought.

Is there, then, nothing that the will-to-live can do but drift along without thought, or sink in pessimistic knowledge? Yes, there is. It must indeed voyage across this boundless sea; but it can hoist sails, and steer a definite course.

*　　*　　*

The will-to-live which tries to know the world is a shipwrecked castaway; the will-to-live which gets to know itself is a bold mariner.

The will-to-live is not restricted to maintaining its existence on what the ever unsatisfying knowledge of the world offers it; it can feed on the life-forces which it finds in itself. The knowledge which I acquire from my will-to-live is richer than that which I win by observation of the world. There are given in it values and incitements bearing on my relation to the world and to life which find no justification in my reflection upon the world and existence. Why then tune down one's will-to-live to the pitch of one's knowledge of the world, or undertake the meaningless task of tuning up one's knowledge of the world to the higher pitch of one's will-to-live? The right and obvious course is to let the ideas which are given in our will-to-live be accepted as the higher and decisive kind of knowledge.

My knowledge of the world is a knowledge from outside, and remains for ever incomplete. The knowledge derived from my will-to-live is direct, and takes me back to the mysterious movements of life as it is in itself.

The highest knowledge, then, is to know that I must be true to the will-to-live. It is this knowledge that hands me the compass for the voyage I have to make in the night without the aid of a chart. To live out one's life in the direction of its course, to raise it to higher power, and to ennoble it, is natural. Every depreciation of the will-to-live is an act of insincerity towards myself, or a symptom of unhealthiness.

The essential nature of the will-to-live is determination to live itself to the full. It carries within it the impulse to realize itself in the highest possible perfection. In the flowering tree, in the strange forms of the medusa, in the blade of grass, in the crystal; everywhere it strives to reach the perfection with which it is endowed. In everything that exists there is at work an imaginative force, which is determined by ideals. In us beings who can move about freely and are capable of pre-considered, purposive activity, the craving for perfection is given in such a way that we aim at raising to their highest material and spiritual value both ourselves and every existing thing which is open to our influence.

How this striving originated within us, and how it has developed, we do not know, but it is given with our existence. We must act upon it, if we would not be unfaithful to the mysterious will-to-live which is within us.

When the will-to-live arrives at the critical point where its early unsophisticated world- and life-affirmation must be changed into a reflective philosophy, it is the part of thought to assist it by holding it to the thinking out of all the ideas which are given within it and to the surrender of itself to them. That the will-to-live within us becomes true to itself and remains so; that it experiences no degeneration but develops itself to complete vitality; that is what decides the fate of our existence.

When it comes to clearness about itself, the will-to-live knows that it is dependent on itself alone. Its destiny is to attain to freedom from the world. Its knowledge of the world can show that its striving to raise to their highest value its own life and every living thing which can be influenced by it must remain problematic when regarded in relation to the universe. This fact will not disturb it. Its world- and life-affirmation carries its meaning in itself. It follows from an inward necessity, and is sufficient for itself. By its means my existence joins in pursuing the aims of the mysterious universal will of which I am a manifestation. In my deepened world- and life-affirmation, I manifest reverence for life. With consciousness and with volition I devote myself to Being. I become of service to the ideas which it thinks out in me; I become imaginative force like that which works mysteriously in nature, and thus I give my existence a meaning from within outwards.

Reverence for life means to be in the grasp of the infinite, inexplicable, forward-urging Will in which all Being is grounded. It raises us above all knowledge of things and lets us become like a tree which is safe against drought, because it is planted among running streams. All living piety flows from reverence for life and the compulsion towards ideals which is given in it. In reverence for life lies piety in its most elemental and deepest form, in which it has not yet become involved with, or has abandoned the hope of, any explanation of the world. It is piety which comes from inward necessity, and therefore asks no questions about ends to be pursued.

The will-to-live, too, which has become reflective and has penetrated to deeper world- and life-affirmation, tries to secure happiness and success, for as will-to-live it is will to the realizing of ideals. But it does not live on happiness and success. What portion of these it obtains is a strengthening of itself which it thankfully accepts, though it is resolved on action, even if happiness and success should be denied it. It sows as one who does not count on living to reap the harvest.

The will-to-live is not a flame which burns only when events provide suitable fuel; it blazes up, and that with the purest light, when it is forced to feed on what it derives from itself. Then, too, when events seem to leave no future for it but suffering, it still holds out as an active will. In deep reverence for life it makes the existence which according to usual ideas is no longer in any way worth living, precious, because even in such an existence it experiences its own freedom from the world. Quiet and peace radiate from a being like that upon others, and cause them also to be touched by the secret that we must all, whether active or passive, preserve our freedom in order truly to live.

True resignation is not a becoming weary of the world, but the quiet triumph which the will-to-live celebrates at the hour of its greatest need over the circumstances of life. It flourishes only in the soil of deep world- and life-affirmation.

In this way our life is a coming to an understanding between our will-to-live and the world, along with which we have continually to be on our guard against allowing any deterioration in our will-to-live. The struggle between optimism and pessimism is never fought to a finish within us. We are ever wandering on slipping rubble above the abyss of pessimism. When that which we experience in our own existence, or learn from the history of mankind, falls oppressively upon our will-to-live and robs us of our freshness and our power of deliberation, we may lose hold, and be carried away with the moving boulders into the depths beneath. But knowing that what awaits us below is death, we work our way up to the path again. . . .

Or it may perhaps be that pessimism comes over us, like the bliss of complete rest over those who, tired out, sit down in the snow. No longer to be obliged to hope for and aim at what is commanded us by the ideals which are forced upon us by the deepened will-to-live! No longer to be in a state of unrest when by lessening our efforts we can have rest! . . . Gently comes the appeal from knowledge to our will to tune itself down to the facts. . . .

That is the fatal state of complete rest in which men, and civilized mankind as a whole, grow numb and die.

And when we think that the riddles by which we are surrounded can no longer harm us, there once more rises up before us somewhere or other the most terrifying of them all, the fact that the will-to-live can be shattered in suffering or in spiritual night. This enigma, too, before which our will-to-live shudders as before the most inexplicable of all inexplicable things, we must learn to leave unsolved.

Thus does pessimistic knowledge pursue us closely right on to our last breath. That is why it is so profoundly important that the will-to-live should rouse itself at last, and once for all insist on its freedom from having to understand the world, and that it should show itself capable of letting itself be determined solely by that which is given within itself. Then with humility and courage it can make its way through the endless chaos of enigmas, fulfilling its mysterious destiny by making a reality of its union with the infinite Will-to-live.

Chapter 24

THE PROBLEMS OF ETHICS, STARTING FROM

THE HISTORY OF ETHICS

An ethic of self-devotion, or an ethic of self-perfecting?

Ethics and a theory of knowledge. Ethics and natural happenings. The enthusiastic element in ethics.

The ethic of ethical personality, and the ethic of society.

The problem of a complete ethic.

PROFOUND THOUGHT, THEN, ARRIVES AT UNSHAKEABLE WORLD- AND life-affirmation. Let it now try whether it can lead us to ethics. But that we may not wander, as so often happens, merely at random, we must gather from the thought which has hitherto been devoted to ethics all the guidance which is there to be found.

What does the history of ethics teach?

In general we learn from it, that the object of ethical enquiry is the discovery of the universal basic principle of the moral.

The basic principle of the moral must be recognized as a necessity of thought, and must bring man to an unceasing, living, and practical conflict and understanding with reality.

The principles of the moral which have hitherto been offered us are absolutely unsatisfying. This is clear from the fact that they cannot be thought out to a conclusion without either leading to paradoxes, or losing in ethical content.

Classical thought tried to conceive of the ethical as that which brings rational pleasure. It did not succeed, however, from that starting-point in arriving at an ethic of active devotion. Confined to the egoistic-utilitarian, it ended in an ethically-coloured resignation.

The ethical thought of modern times is from the outset social-utilitarian. It is to it a matter of course that the individual must devote himself in every respect to his fellow-individuals, and to society. But when it tries to give a firm foundation to the ethic of altruism which seems to it so much a matter of course, and to think that matter out to a conclusion, it is driven to the most remarkable consequences, consequences inconsistent with each other in the most varied directions. At one time it explains altruism as a refined egoism; at another as something which society forcibly imposes on individuals; at another as something which it develops in him by education; next, as in Bentham, as something which he adopts as one of his convictions on the ground of the urgent representations of society; or again, as an instinct which he obeys. The first assumption cannot be maintained; the second, third, and, fourth are unsatisfying because they make ethics reach men from the outside; the last leads to a *cul-de-sac*. If, for example, self-devotion is an instinct, it must, of course, be made conceivable how thought can influence it, and raise it to the level of a considered, widely inclusive, voluntary activity, at which level it first becomes ethical. This, which is its peculiar problem, utilitarianism does not recognize, much less solve. It is always in too much of a hurry to reach practical results. At last it sells its soul to biology and social science, which lead it to conceive itself as herd-mentality, wonderfully developed and capable of still further development. And with this it finally sinks far below the level of real ethics.

Strange to say, therefore, although starting from what is most elementary and essential in ethics, the ethics of altruism fail to take shape in a way which satisfies thought. It is as if the true basic principle of ethics were within their reach, yet these ethics of altruism always grasped to right or left of it.

Along with these two attempts to understand ethics either as effort to procure rational pleasure, or as devotion to one's neighbour and to society, there is a third method, which tries to explain ethics as effort for self-perfecting. This enterprise has in it something abstract and venturesome. It disdains to start from a universally acknowledged content of the ethical, as utilitarianism does, and in contrast to that sets before thought the task of deriving the whole content of ethics from the effort for self-perfecting.

Plato, the first representative in the West of the ethics of self-perfecting, and Schopenhauer try to solve the problem by setting up, as do the Indians, world- and life-negation as the basic principle of the ethical. That, however, is no solution. World- and life-negation, if consistently thought out and developed does not produce ethics but reduces ethics to impotence.

Kant, the modern restorer of the ethics of self-perfecting, sets up the conception of absolute duty, but without giving it any content. He thereby admits his inability to derive the content of ethics from the effort for self-perfecting.

If the ethic of self-perfecting tries really to acquire a content, it must allow that ethics consist either in world- and life-negation or in higher world- and life-affirmation. The first need not be considered; there remains, therefore, only the other.

Spinoza conceives the higher world- and life-affirmation as contemplative absorption in the universe. He does not, however, arrive thereby at real ethics, but only at an ethically-coloured resignation. Schleiermacher uses much art to lend this ethical colouring a more brilliant tone. Nietzsche avoids the paths of resignation, but reaches thereby a world- and life-affirmation which is ethical only in so far as it feels itself to be an effort for self-perfecting.

The only thinker who succeeds to some extent in giving to self-perfecting within world- and life-affirmation an ethical content is J. G. Fichte. The result, however, is valueless, because it presupposes an optimistic-ethical view of the nature of the universe and the position of man within it, which is based upon inadmissible speculation.

The ethic of self-perfecting is therefore not capable of so establishing the basic principle of the moral, that it has a content which is ethically satisfying; the ethic of altruism, on the other hand, starting from a pre-supposed content, cannot reach a basic principle of ethics which is founded on thought.

The attempt made by antiquity to conceive ethics as that which brings rational pleasure we need no longer consider. It is only too clear that it does not sufficiently take into account the enigma of self-sacrifice, and can never solve it. So there remain for consideration only the two undertakings, so strangely opposed to one another, one of which starts from altruism as a generally accepted content of the ethical in order to conceive it as belonging to the self-perfecting of man, while the other starts from self-perfecting and seeks to conceive altruism as an item in its content which is a necessity of thought.

Is there a synthesis of these two? In other words, do altruism and the perfecting of the self belong together in such a way that the one is contained in the other?

If this inward unity has not been visible hitherto, may not the cause be that reflection, whether upon devotion or upon self-perfecting, did not go deep enough and was not sufficiently comprehensive?

*   *   *

Before thought attempts to investigate more profoundly and completely the essential nature of altruism and of self-perfecting, it must proceed further to visualize what is offered in the way of different kinds of knowledge and other considerations on its journey through the Western search for ethics.

It may be accepted as fully recognized that ethics have nothing to expect from any theory of knowledge. Depreciation of the reality of the material world brings merely apparent profit. Thought believes it can draw from the possibility of a spiritual-izing of the world some advantage for the optimistic-ethical interpretation of it. It has, however, been established by this time that ethics can no more be derived from an ethical inter-pretation of the world than world- and life-affirmation can be referred back to an optimistic interpretation of it, but that they must rather find their foundation in themselves in a world which is known to be absolutely mysterious. At once and for ever, then, all attempts to bring ethical and epistemological idealism into connection with one another must be recognized as useless for ethics. Ethics can let space and time go to the devil.

In epistemological investigations into the nature of space and time ethics feel a satisfaction which is strong but uninterested. They view them as efforts after knowledge which must be made, but know that the results can never touch what is essential in any conception of the world or of life. It suffices to know that the whole world of the senses is a manifestation of forces, that is to say of mysteriously manifold will-to-live. In this their thought is spiritualistic. It is materialistic, however, so far as it presupposes manifestation and force to be connected in such a way that any effect produced upon the former influences the force which lies behind it. Ethics feel that if it were not thus possible for one will-to-live to produce through its manifestations effects on another will-to-live, they would have no reason for existing. But to investigate how this relation between force and its manifestation is to be explained from the standpoint of epistemology, and whether it can be explained at all, ethics can leave undecided as being none of their business; they claim for themselves, just as does natural science, the right to remain free from preconceptions.

In this connection it is an interesting fact that it is among the representatives of scientific materialism that enthusiastic ethical idealism is often to be met with, while the adherents of spiritualistic philosophy are usually moralists with an unemotional temperament.

With renunciation of all help from epistemological idealism, it follows that ethics ask for nothing and expect nothing from speculative philosophy. They declare they have nothing to do with any kind of ethical interpretation of the world.

Thought gathers, further, from the history of ethics that ethics cannot be conceived as being merely a natural happening which continues itself in man. In the ethical man natural happenings come into contradiction with themselves. Nature knows only a blind affirmation of life. The will-to-live which animates natural forces and living beings is concerned to work itself out unhindered. But in man this natural effort is in a state of tension with a mysterious effort of a different kind. Life-affirmation exerts itself to take up life-negation into itself in order to serve other living beings by self-devotion, and to protect them, even, it may be, by self-sacrifice, from injury or destruction.

It is true that self-devotion plays a certain *rôle* in non-human living beings. As a sporadic instinct it rules in sexual love and in parental love; as a permanent instinct it is found in certain individual members of animal species (*e.g.*, ants, bees) which, because sexless, are incomplete individualities. These manifestations are in a certain way a prelude to the interplay of life-affirmation and life-negation which is at work in the ethical man. But they do not explain it. That which is active elsewhere only as a sporadic instinct, or as an instinct in incomplete individualities and that, too, always within special relations of solidarity with others, becomes now, in man, a steady, voluntary, unlimited form of action, a result of thought, in which individuals endeavour to realize the higher life-affirmation. How does this come about?

Here one is faced once more by the problem of the *rôle* which thought plays in the origin of ethics. It seizes on something of which a preliminary form is seen in an instinct, in order to extend it and bring it to perfection. It apprehends the content of an instinct, and tries to give it practical application in new and consistent action.

In some way or other the *rôle* of thought lies in the fulfilment of life-affirmation. It rouses the will-to-live, in analogy with the life-affirmation which shows itself in the manifold life which is everywhere around it, and to join in its experiences. On the foundation of this world-affirmation, life-negation takes its place as a means of helping forward this affirmation of other life than its own. It is not life-denial in itself that is ethical, but only such as stands in the service of world-affirmation and becomes purposive within it.

Ethics are a mysterious chord in which life-affirmation and world-affirmation are the key-note and the fifth; life-negation is the third.

It is important, further, to know what is to be gathered from ethical inquiry down to the present time about the intensity and the extension of the life-negation which stands in the service of world-affirmation. Again and again the attempt has been made to establish this objectively. In vain. It belongs to the nature of self-devotion that it must live itself out subjectively and without reservations.

In the history of ethics there is downright fear of what cannot be subjected to rules and regulations. Again and again thinkers have undertaken to define altruism in such a way that it remains rational. This, however, is never done except at the cost of the naturalness and living quality of ethics. Life-denial remains an irrational thing, even when it is placed at the service of a purposive aim. A universally applicable balance between life-affirmation and life-negation cannot be established. They remain in a state of continual tension. If any relaxation does take place, it is a sign that ethics are collapsing, for in their real nature they are unbounded enthusiasm. They originate indeed in thought, but they cannot be carried to a logical conclusion. Anyone who undertakes the voyage to true ethics must be prepared to be carried round and round in the whirlpool of the irrational.

*   *   *

Together with the subjectively enthusiastic nature of ethics goes the fact that it is impossible to succeed in developing the ethic of ethical personality into a serviceable ethic of society. It seems so obvious, that from right individual ethics right social ethics should result, the one system continuing itself into the other like a town into its suburbs. In reality, however, they cannot be so built that the streets of the one continue into those of the other. The plans of each are drawn on principles which take no account of that.

The ethic of ethical personality is personal, incapable of regulation, and absolute; the system established by society for its prosperous existence is supra-personal, regulated, and relative. Hence the ethical personality cannot surrender to it, but lives always in continuous conflict with it, obliged again and again to oppose it because it finds its focus too short.

In the last analysis, the antagonism between the two arises from their differing valuations of humaneness. Humaneness consists in never sacrificing a human being to a purpose. The ethic of ethical personality aims at preserving humaneness. The system established by society is impotent in that respect.

When the individual is faced with the alternative of having to sacrifice in some way or other the happiness or the existence of another, or else to bear the loss himself, he is in a position to obey the demands of ethics and to choose the latter. But

society, thinking impersonally and pursuing its aims impersonally, does not allow the same weight to consideration for the
happiness or existence of an individual. In principle humaneness is not an item in its ethics. But individuals come continually into the position of being in one way or another executive
organs of society, and then the conflict between the two points
of view becomes active. That this may always be decided in its
own favour, society exerts itself as much as possible to limit the
authority of the ethic of personality, although inwardly it has
to acknowledge its superiority. It wants to have servants who
will never oppose it.

Even a society whose ethical standard is relatively high, is
dangerous to the ethics of its members. If those things which
form precisely the defects of a social code of ethics develop
strongly, and if society exercises, further, an excessively strong
spiritual influence on individuals, then the ethic of ethical personality is ruined. This happens in present-day society, whose
ethical conscience is becoming fatally stunted by a biologico-
sociological ethic and this, moreover, finally corrupted by
nationalism.

The great mistake of ethical thought down to the present
time is that it fails to admit the essential difference between the
morality of ethical personality and that which is established from
the standpoint of society, and always thinks that it ought, and
is able, to cast them in one piece. The result is that the ethic
of personality is sacrificed to the ethic of society. An end must
be put to this. What matters is to recognize that the two are
engaged in a conflict which cannot be made less intense. Either
the moral standard of personality raises the moral standard of
society, so far as is possible, to its own level, or it is dragged
down by it.

But to prevent such harm as has been caused up to the present, it is not enough to bring individuals to a consciousness that
if they are not to suffer spiritual injury they must be in a state
of continual conflict with the ethics of society. What matters
is to establish a basic principle of the moral, which will put
the ethic of personality in a position to try conclusions with
the ethic of society with consistency and success. Hitherto there
has been no possibility of putting this weapon into its hands.

Ethics have, as we know, always been regarded as the most thorough-going possible self-devotion to society.

The morality of ethical personality, then, and the morality which is established from the standpoint of society cannot be traced back the one to the other, and they are not of equal value. The first only is a real ethic; the other is improperly so called. Thought must aim at finding the basic principle of absolute ethics, if it is to reach ethics at all, and it was because it was not clear on this point that so little progress has been made. Ethical progress consists in making up our minds to think pessimistically of the ethics of society.

The system of ethics established from the standpoint of society consists in its essential nature in society appealing to the moral disposition of the individual in order to secure from him what cannot be forced upon him by compulsion and law. It only comes nearer to real ethics when it enters into discussion with the ethics of personality and tries to bring its own demands on the individual into harmony as far as possible with those of personal morality. In proportion as society takes on the character of an ethical personality, its code of morals becomes the code of ethical society.

*   *   *

In general, thought ought to have busied itself with the question of what is included in the whole field of ethics, and how the different elements within it are connected with each other.

In ethics are included the ethics of passive self-perfecting, effected by inward self-liberation from the world (resignation); the ethics of active self-perfecting, effected by means of the mutual relations between man and man; and the ethics of ethical society. Ethics thus form an extensive gamut of notes. It starts from the not yet ethical where the vibrations of resignation begin to be perceptible as notes of ethical resignation. With increasingly rapid vibrations it passes from the ethics of resignation into the ethics of active self-perfecting. Rising still higher it arrives at the notes of the ethics of society which are already becoming more or less harsh and noisy, and it dies away finally into the legal commands of society which are never more than conditionally ethical.

Up to now all ethical systems have been thoroughly fragmentary. They confine themselves to this or that octave of the gamut. The Indians and, following in their train, Schopenhauer, are, on the whole, concerned only with the ethic of passive self-perfecting; Zarathustra, the Jewish prophets, and the great moralists of China only with that of active self-perfecting. The interest of modern Western philosophy is fixed almost exclusively on the ethic of society. In consequence of the starting-point which they chose, the thinkers of antiquity in the West cannot get any further than an ethic of resignation. The deeper thinkers among our moderns—Kant, J. G. Fichte, Nietzsche, and others—have inklings of an ethic of active self-perfecting.

European thought is characterized by almost always playing in the upper octaves, and not in the lower ones. Its ethic has no bass because the ethic of resignation plays no part in it. An ethic of duty, that is to say, an activist ethic, appears to it to be complete. It is because he is a representative of the ethic of resignation that Spinoza remains such a stranger to his own age.

Inability to understand resignation and the relations prevailing between ethics and resignation, is the fatal weakness of modern European thought.

In what, then, does a complete code of ethics consist? In ethics of passive self-perfecting, combined with ethics of active self-perfecting. The ethics established from the standpoint of of society are supplementary and have to be corrected by the ethics of active self-perfecting.

In view of that fact, a complete system of ethics must be put forward in a shape which compels it to seek to come to terms with the ethics of society.

Chapter 25

THE ETHICS OF SELF-DEVOTION AND THE

ETHICS OF SELF-PERFECTING

The widening of the ethic of self-devotion into a cosmic ethic.

The ethic of self-perfecting and mysticism.

Abstract mysticism and the mysticism of reality.

Supra-ethical and ethical mysticism.

BEING SUFFICIENTLY INFORMED ABOUT THE QUESTIONS WHICH have called for solution and the results attained in the search for ethics down to the present time, the ethics of altruism and the ethics of self-perfecting can now try to combine their ideas, with a view to establishing together the true basic principle of the moral.

Why do they not succeed in mutual interpenetration of thought?

On the side of the ethic of self-devotion the fault must somehow lie in the fact that it is too narrow. As a matter of principle, social utilitarianism is concerned only with the self-devotion of man to man and to human society. The ethic of self-perfecting on the other hand is universal. It has to do with the relation of man to the world. If the ethic of self-devotion, therefore, is to agree with the ethic of self-perfecting, it too must become universal, and let its devotion be directed not only towards man and society but somehow or other towards all life whatever in the world.

But ethics hitherto have been unwilling to take even the first step in this universalizing of altruism.

Just as the housewife who has scrubbed out the parlour takes care that the door is kept shut so that the dog may not get in and spoil the work she has done by the marks of his paws, so do European thinkers watch carefully that no animals run about in the fields of their ethics. The stupidities they are guilty of in trying to maintain the traditional narrow-mindedness and raise it to a principle border on the incredible. Either they leave out altogether all sympathy for animals, or they take care that it shrinks to a mere afterthought which means nothing. If they admit anything more than that, they think themselves obliged to produce elaborate justifications, or even excuses, for so doing.

It seems as if Descartes with his dictum that animals are mere machines had bewitched the whole of European philosophy.

So important a thinker as Wilhelm Wundt mars his ethics with the following sentences: "The only object for sympathy is man. . . . The animals are for us fellow-creatures, an expression by which language already hints at the fact that we acknowledge here a kind of co-ordination with ourselves only with reference to the ultimate ground of everything that happens, namely, creation. Towards animals also, then, there can arise within us stirrings which are to a certain extent related to sympathy, but as to true sympathy with them there is always wanting the fundamental condition of the inner unity of our will with theirs." To crown this wisdom he ends with the assertion that of rejoicing with animals there can at any rate be no question, as if he had never seen a thirsty ox enjoying a drink.

Kant emphasizes especially that ethics have to do only with duties of man towards men. The "human" treatment of animals he thinks himself obliged to justify by putting it forward as a practising of sensibility which helps to improve our sympathetic relations with other human beings.

Bentham, too, defends kindness to animals chiefly as a means of preventing the growth of heartless relations with other men, even though he here and there recognizes it as obviously right.

Darwin in his *Descent of Man* notices that the feeling of sympathy which is dominant in the social impulse, becomes at last so strong that it comes to include all men, and indeed even animals. But he does not pursue the problem and the significance of this fact any further, and contents himself with establishing the ethics of the human herd.

Thus it ranks with European thought as a dogma that ethics properly concerns only a man's relations to his fellows and to society. The motives which emanate from Schopenhauer, Stern, and others, for throwing down the antiquated ring-fence, are not understood.

This backward attitude is the more unintelligible seeing that Indian and Chinese thought, even when they have only scarcely begun to develop, make ethics consist in a kindly relation to all creatures. Moreover, they have come to this view quite independently of each other. The beautiful and far-reaching commands concerning regard for animals in the popular Chinese ethics of the book *Kan Yin Pien (Concerning Rewards and Punishments)* cannot be referred back, as is commonly supposed, to Buddhist influences.[1] They have no connection with metaphysical discussions about the mutual relationship of all beings, such as became effective as the ethical horizon widened in Indian thought, but originate in a living, ethical feeling which dares to draw the consequences which seem to it to be natural.

When European thought refuses to make self-devotion universal, the reason is that its efforts are directed to reaching a rational morality which deals with universally valid judgments, and it sees a prospect of that only when it can keep its feet upon the solid ground of discussion of the interests of human society. But ethics concerned with the relations of man to the whole creation quit that solid ground, being driven into discussions about existence as such. Willing or unwilling, ethics have to

1 This book dates from about the eleventh century A.D. It has been translated into English by James Legge (*Sacred Books of the East,* 1891) and by T. Susuki and P. Carus (Chicago, 1906); into French by M. A. Rémusat (*Le livre des récompenses et des peines,* 1816), and by Stanislas Julien (1835); into German by W. Schuler (*Zeitschrift für Missionskunde,* 1909).

"Be humane with animals, and do no harm to insects, plants, and trees," is the command of one saying in this book. The following acts are condemned: "Hunting men or animals to death; shooting with bow and arrow at birds; hunting quadrupeds; driving insects out of their holes; frightening birds which are asleep in the trees; blocking up the holes of insects, and destroying birds-nests." To delight in hunting is described as a serious moral perversion.

plunge into the adventure of trying to come to terms with nature-philosophy, and the outcome cannot be foreseen.

This is a correct conclusion. But it has already been shown that the objective, standard morality of society, supposing it can be drawn up in this way at all, is never a true code of ethics, but merely an appendix to ethics. It is certain further that true ethics are always subjective, that they have an irrational enthusiasm as the very breath of their life, and that they must be in conflict with nature-philosophy. The ethic of altruism has, therefore, no reason for shrinking from this in any case unavoidable adventure. Its house has been burnt down. It can go out into the world to seek its fortune.

Let ethics, then, venture to accept the thought that self-devotion has to be practised not only towards men but towards all living creatures, yes, towards all life whatever that exists in the world and is within the reach of man. Let them rise to the conception that the relation of men to each other is only an expression of that in which they all stand to Being and to the world in general. Having thus become cosmic, the ethic of self-devotion can hope to meet the ethic of self-perfecting, which is fundamentally cosmic, and unite with it.

* * *

But in order that the ethic of self-perfecting may combine with the ethic of self-devotion, it must first become cosmic in the right way.

It is indeed fundamentally cosmic, because self-perfecting can consist of nothing but man coming into his true relationship to the Being that is in him and outside him. His natural, outward connection with Being he strives to change into a spiritual, inward devotion, letting his passive and active relation to things be determined by this devotion.

In this effort, however, he has never yet advanced further than to a passive self-dedication to Being. He is always driven past active self-devotion to it. It is this one-sidedness which makes it impossible for the ethics of self-perfecting and of self-devotion to inter-penetrate each other, and produce together the complete ethics of passive and active self-perfecting.

But what is the reason that the ethic of self-perfecting, in spite of all efforts, cannot get out of the circle of the passive? It is that it allows the spiritual inward devotion to Being to be directed to an abstract totality of Being instead of to real Being. So nature-philosophy is approached in a wrong way.

Whence this error? It is a result of the difficulties which the ethic of self-perfecting meets when it attempts to be comprehended in nature-philosophy.

In a way which to us seems strange, but is really profound, Chinese thought undertakes to attempt to arrive at this agreement. It thinks that it is somehow or other in the "impersonal" element of the world's activity that the secret of the truly ethical lies. It accordingly makes spiritual devotion to Being consist in our looking away from the subjective stirrings within ourselves, and regulating our behaviour by the laws of objectivity which we discover in the course of nature.

It is with this deep "becoming like the world" that the thought of Lao-tse and that of Chwang-tse are concerned. The motifs of such an ethic ring out in a wonderful fashion in Lao-tse's *Taoteking;* but they cannot be made to produce a complete symphony. The meaning of what happens in the world is a thing we cannot investigate. What we do understand of it is only that all life tries to live itself out. The true ethics of life, therefore, "in the spirit of what happens" would seem to be that of Yang-tse and Friedrich Nietzsche. On the other hand the assumption of an objectivity, dominant in the course of nature, which can be a pattern for our activity is nothing but an attempt, undertaken with the palest of colours, to paint the world as ethical. Correspondingly, this existence in the spirit of the world means with Lao-tse and Chwang-tse an inward liberation from the rule of passion and from outward occurrences, which is accompanied by marked depreciation of all tendencies to activity. Whenever life in the spirit of the world leads to really activist ethics as with Kungtse (Confucius), Mitse (Mo-Di), and others, there has been a corresponding interpretation of the meaning of the world. Whenever, in general, human thinking raises being-like-the-world to the status of ethics, the ethical willing of mankind has somehow or other read into the world-spirit an ethical character in order to be able to find itself in it again.

Since no motives to ethical activity are to be discovered in the course of nature, the ethic of self-perfecting must allow both active and passive ethics to originate side by side in the bare fact of spiritual inward self-dedication to Being. Both must be derived from action as such, without any presupposition of any sort of moral quality in Being. Then only will thought have reached a complete system of ethics without having been guilty of any sort of naïve or tricky proceedings.

That is the problem at which the ethical searching of all peoples and all ages vainly toils, so far as it ventures to think in the spirit of true nature-philosophy. With the Chinese and the Indians, in Stoicism, with Spinoza, Schleiermacher, Fichte, and Hegel, and in all mysticism of union with the Absolute, it reaches only the ethics of resignation, consisting of inward liberation from the world, never at the same time the ethics of working in the world and upon the world.

It is true that it but seldom ventures honestly to admit to itself the unsatisfactory result. As a rule it seeks to widen it, and to maintain in some measure an activist morality in spite of it, letting this morality be combined in some form or other with the ethics of resignation. The more consistent the thinkers, the more modest is the space occupied by this appendage.

With Lao-tse and Chwang-tse, with the Brahmans and the Buddha, with the Stoics of antiquity, with Spinoza, Schleiermacher, and Hegel, and with the great monistic mystics, activist ethics is reduced to little more than nothing. With Confucius and Meng-tse (Mong Dei), with the Hindoo thinkers, with the representatives of the Later Stoicism, and with J. G. Fichte, ethics of this nature make strenuous efforts to stand their ground, but can do so only in so far as the help of either naïve or sophisticated thought is employed.

Every world-and-life-view which is to satisfy thought is mysticism. It must seek to give to the existence of man such a meaning as will prevent him from being satisfied with being a part of the infinite existence in merely natural fashion, but will make him determine to belong to it in soul and spirit also, through an act of his consciousness.

The ethic of self-perfecting is in inmost connection with mysticism. Its own destiny is decided in that of mysticism.

Thinking out the ethic of self-perfecting means nothing else than seeking to found ethics on mysticism. Mysticism, on its side, is a valuable world-and-life-view only in proportion as it is ethical.

And yet it finds it cannot succeed in being ethical. Experience of becoming one with the Absolute, of existence within the world-spirit, of absorption into God, or whatever one may choose to call the process, is not in itself ethical, but spiritual. Of this deep distinction Indian thought has become conscious. With the most varied phrasing it repeats the proposition: "Spirituality is not ethics." We Europeans have remained naïve in matters of mysticism. What appears among us as mysticism is usually mysticism with a more or less Christian, that is to say ethical, colouring. Hence we are inclined to deceive ourselves about the ethical content of mysticism.

If one analyses the mysticism of all peoples and all ages to find out its ethical content, we find that this is extraordinarily small. Even the ethic of resignation, which seems after all to belong naturally to mysticism, is in mysticism more or less afflicted with impotence. Through the absence of the activist ethic with which it should normally be bound up, it to a certain extent loses its hold, and pushes itself more and more into the region of resignation which is no longer ethical. There then arises a mysticism that ceases to help the effort for self-perfecting, which is the profound task to which it is called, but makes absorption into the Absolute become an aim in itself. The purer the mysticism, the further has this evolution developed. Mysticism becomes then a world- and life-view of the merging of the finite existence in the infinite, if indeed it does not get reversed, as with the Brahmans, into the lofty mysticism of the existence of infinite existence within the finite. The ethic of self-perfecting, which should arise out of mysticism, is always therefore in danger of perishing in mysticism.

The tendency of mysticism to become supra-ethical is quite natural. As a matter of fact its connection with an Absolute which has neither qualities nor needs has nothing more to do with self-perfecting. It becomes a pure act of consciousness, and leads to a spirituality which is just as bare of content as the hypothetical Absolute. Feeling its weakness, mysticism does all it can to be more ethical than it is, or at any rate to appear so. Even the Indian form of it makes efforts in this direction, although again on the other hand it has courage to be veracious enough to rank the spiritual above the ethical.

In order to judge what mysticism is worth ethically, one must reckon only with what it contains in itself in the way of ethics, not what it does or says beyond that. Then, however, the ethical content of even Christian mysticism is alarmingly small. Mysticism is not a friend of ethics but a foe. It devours ethics. And yet the ethic which is to satisfy thought must be born of mysticism. All profound philosophy, all deep religion, are ultimately a struggle for ethical mysticism and mystical ethics.

Dominated by efforts to secure an activist ethical conception of the world and of life, we Westerners do not allow mysticism to come into its own. It leads among us a furtive, intermittent existence. We feel instinctively that it stands in antagonism to activist ethics, and we have therefore no inward relationship to it.

Our great mistake, however, is thinking that without mysticism we can reach an ethical world- and life-view, which shall satisfy thought. Up to now we have done nothing but compose world- and life-views. They are good because they keep men up to activist ethics, but they are not true, and therefore they are always collapsing. Moreover they are shallow. Hence European thought makes men ethical indeed, but superficial, and the European, because he is surfeited with philosophy which has been fabricated with a view to activist ethics, has no equanimity and no inward personality, nor indeed any longer a feeling of need for these qualities.

It is indeed time for us to abandon this error. Depth and stability in thinking come to the world- and life-view of activist ethics only when this outlook springs from mysticism. The question of what we are to make of our life is not solved by our being driven out into the world with an impulse to activity, and never being allowed to come to our right senses. It can be really answered only by a philosophy which brings man into a spiritual inward relation to Being, from which there result of natural necessity ethics both passive and active.

The hitherto accepted mysticism cannot effect this because

it is supra-ethical. The struggle of thought must therefore be directed upon ethical mysticism. We must rise to a spirituality which is ethical, and to an ethic which includes all spirituality. Then only do we become profoundly qualified for life.

Ethics must originate in mysticism. Mysticism, for its part, must never be thought to exist for its own sake. It is not a flower, but only the calyx of a flower. Ethics are the flower. Mysticism which exists for itself alone is the salt which last lost its savour.

The hitherto accepted mysticism leads into the supra-ethical because it is abstract. Abstraction is the death of ethics, for ethics are a living relationship to living life. We must therefore abandon abstract mysticism, and turn to the mysticism which is alive.

*　*　*

The Essence of Being, the Absolute, the Spirit of the Universe, and all similar expressions denote nothing actual, but something conceived in abstractions which for that reason is also absolutely unimaginable. The only reality is the Being which manifests itself in phenomena.

How does thought come to such a meaningless proceeding as making man enter into a spiritual relation with an unreal creation of thought? By yielding to temptation in two ways, one general, one particular.

Thrown back upon the necessity of expressing itself in words, thought adopts as its own the abstractions and symbols which have been coined by language. But this coinage should have no more currency than allows it to represent things in an abbreviated way, instead of putting them forward with all the detail in which they are given. But in time it comes about that thought works with these abstractions and symbols as if they represented something which really exists. That is the general temptation.

The particular temptation lies in this case in this, that man's devotion to infinite Being with the help of abstractions and symbols is given expression in an enticingly simple way. It is taken to consist of entrance into relation with the totality of Being, that is to say, with its spiritual essence.

That looks very well in words and in thoughts. But reality

knows nothing about the individual being able to enter into connection with the totality of Being. As it knows of no Being except that which manifests itself in the existence of individual beings, so also it knows of no relations except these of one individual being to another. If mysticism, then, intends to be honest, there is nothing for it to do but to cast from it the usual abstractions, and to admit that it can do nothing rational with this imaginary essence of Being. The Absolute may be as meaningless to it as his fetish is to a converted Negro. It must in all seriousness go through the process of conversion to the mysticism of reality. Abandoning all stage decorations and declamation, let it try to get its experience in living nature.

There is no Essence of Being, but only infinite Being in infinite manifestations. It is only through the manifestations of Being, and only through those with which I enter into relations, that my being has any intercourse with infinite Being. The devotion of my being to infinite Being means devotion of my being to all the manifestations of Being which need my devotion, and to which I am able to devote myself.

Only an infinitely small part of infinite Being comes within my range. The rest of it passes me by, like distant ships to which I make signals they do not understand. But by devoting myself to that which comes within my sphere of influence and needs me, I make spiritual, inward devotion to infinite Being a reality and thereby give my own poor existence meaning and richness. The river has found its sea.

From self-devotion to the Absolute there comes only a dead spirituality. It is a purely intellectual act. No motives to activity are given in it. Even the ethics of resignation can only eke out a miserable existence on the soil of such an intellectualism. But in the mysticism of reality self-devotion is no longer a purely intellectual act, but one in which everything that is alive in man has its share. There is therefore dominant in it a spirituality which carries in itself in elemental form the impulse to action. The gruesome truth that spirituality and ethics are two different things no longer holds good. Here the two are one and the same.

Now, too, the ethics of self-perfecting and the ethics of altruism can interpenetrate each other. They now become cosmic in nature-philosophy, which leaves the world as it is. Hence they cannot but meet each other in a thought, which satisfies in every direction the laws of thinking, of living devotion to Being which lives. In this thought lie passive and active self-perfecting in mutual agreement and perfect union. They comprehend each other as the working out of one and the same inner compulsion. Having become one, they no longer need first of all to exert themselves to establish by joint efforts the completed ethics of influencing the world on the basis of liberation from the world. The completeness is now automatically attained. Now there ring out in wonderful harmonies all the notes in the gamut of ethics, from the vibrations in which resignation begins to be audible as ethics, up to the higher notes in which morality passes over into the harsh noises of the commands which are proclaimed by society to be ethical.

Subjective responsibility for all life which comes within his reach, responsibility which widens out extensively and intensively to the limitless, and which the man who has become inwardly free from the world experiences and tries to make a reality, that is ethics. It originates in world- and life-affirmation. It becomes a reality in life-negation. It is completely bound up with optimistic willing. Never again can the belief-in-progress get separated from ethics, like a badly-fastened wheel from a cart. The two turn inseparably on the same axle.

The basic principle of ethics, that principle which is a necessity of thought, which has a definite content, which is engaged in constant, living, and practical dispute with reality, is: Devotion to life resulting from reverence for life.

Chapter 26

THE ETHICS OF REVERENCE FOR LIFE

The basic principle of the moral.

The ethic of resignation. An ethic of veracity towards oneself, and an activist ethic.

Ethics and thoughtlessness. Ethics and self-assertion.

Man and other living creatures. The ethic of the relation of man to man.

Personal and supra-personal responsibility. Ethics and humanity.

COMPLICATED AND LABORIOUS ARE THE ROADS ALONG WHICH ethical thought, which has mistaken its way and taken too high a flight, must be brought back. Its course, however, maps itself out quite simply if, instead of taking apparently convenient short cuts, it keeps to its right direction from the very beginning. For this three things are necessary: It must have nothing to do with an ethical interpretation of the world; it must become cosmic and mystical, that is to say, it must seek to conceive all the self-devotion which rules in ethics as a manifestation of an inward, spiritual relation to the world; it must not lapse into abstract thinking, but must remain elemental, understanding self-devotion to the world to be self-devotion of human life to every form of living being with which it can come into relation.

The origin of ethics is that I think out the full meaning of the world-affirmation which, together with the life-affirmation in my will-to-live, is given by nature, and try to make it a reality.

To become ethical means to begin to think sincerely.

Thinking is the argument between willing and knowing which goes on within me. Its course is a naïve one, if the will demands of knowledge to be shown a world which corresponds to the impulses which it carries within itself, and if knowledge attempts to satisfy this requirement. This dialogue, which is doomed to produce no result, must give place to a debate of the right kind, in which the will demands from knowledge only what it really knows.

If knowledge answers solely with what it knows, it is always teaching the will one and the same fact, namely, that in and behind all phenomena there is will-to-live. Knowledge, though ever becoming deeper and more comprehensive, can do nothing except take us ever deeper and ever further into the mystery that all that is, is will-to-live. Progress in science consists only in increasingly accurate description of the phenomena in which life in its innumerable forms appears and passes, letting us discover life where we did not previously expect it, and putting us in a position to turn to our own use in this or that way what we have learnt of the course of the will-to-live in nature. But what life is, no science can tell us.

For our conception of the universe and of life, then, the gain derived from knowledge is only that it makes it harder for us to be thoughtless, because it ever more forcibly compels our attention to the mystery of the will-to-live which we see stirring everywhere. Hence the difference between learned and unlearned is entirely relative. The unlearned man who, at the sight of a tree in flower, is overpowered by the mystery of the will-to-live which is stirring all round him, knows more than the scientist who studies under the microscope or in physical and chemical activity a thousand forms of the will-to-live, but, with all his knowledge of the life-course of these manifestations of the will-to-live, is unmoved by the mystery that everything which exists is will-to-live, while he is puffed up with vanity at being able to describe exactly a fragment of the course of life.

All true knowledge passes on into experience. The nature of the manifestations I do not know, but I form a conception of it in analogy to the will-to-live which is within myself. Thus my knowledge of the world becomes experience of the world. The knowledge which is becoming experience does not allow me to remain in face of the world a man who merely knows, but forces upon me an inward relation to the world, and fills me with reverence for the mysterious will-to-live which is in all things. By making me think and wonder, it leads me ever upwards to the heights of reverence for life. There it lets my hand go. It cannot accompany me further. My will-to-live must now find its way about the world by itself.

It is not by informing me what this or that manifestation of life means in the sum-total of the world that knowledge brings me into connection with the world. It goes about with me not in outer circles, but in the inner ones. From within outwards it puts me in relation to the world by making my will-to-live feel everything around it as also will-to-live.

With Descartes, philosophy starts from the dogma: "I think, therefore I exist." With this paltry, arbitrarily chosen beginning, it is landed irretrievably on the road to the abstract. It never finds the right approach to ethics, and remains entangled in a dead world- and life-view. True philosophy must start from the most immediate and comprehensive fact of consciousness, which says: "I am life which wills to live, in the midst of life which wills to live." This is not an ingenious dogmatic formula. Day by day, hour by hour, I live and move in it. At every moment of reflection it stands fresh before me. There bursts forth from it again and again as from roots that can never dry up, a living world- and life-view which can deal with all the facts of Being. A mysticism of ethical union with Being grows out of it.

As in my own will-to-live there is a longing for wider life and for the mysterious exaltation of the will-to-live which we call pleasure, with dread of annihilation and of the mysterious depreciation of the will-to-live which we call pain; so is it also in the will-to-live all around me, whether it can express itself before me, or remains dumb.

Ethics consist, therefore, in my experiencing the compulsion to show to all will-to-live the same reverence as I do to my own. There we have given us that basic principle of the moral which is a necessity of thought. It is good to maintain and to encourage life; it is bad to destroy life or to obstruct it.

As a matter of fact, everything which in the ordinary ethical valuation of the relations of men to each other ranks as good can be brought under the description of material and spiritual maintenance or promotion of human life, and of effort to bring it to its highest value. Conversely, everything which ranks as bad in human relations is in the last analysis material or spiritual destruction or obstruction of human life, and negligence in the endeavour to bring it to its highest value. Separate individual categories of good and evil which lie far apart and have apparently no connection at all with one another fit together like the pieces of a jig-saw puzzle, as soon as they are comprehended and deepened in this the most universal definition of good and evil.

The basic principle of the moral which is a necessity of thought means, however, not only an ordering and deepening, but also a widening of the current views of good and evil. A man is truly ethical only when he obeys the compulsion to help all life which he is able to assist, and shrinks from injuring anything that lives. He does not ask how far this or that life deserves one's sympathy as being valuable, nor, beyond that, whether and to what degree it is capable of feeling. Life as such is sacred to him. He tears no leaf from a tree, plucks no flower, and takes care to crush no insect. If in summer he is working by lamplight, he prefers to keep the window shut and breathe a stuffy atmosphere rather than see one insect after another fall with singed wings upon his table.

If he walks on the road after a shower and sees an earthworm which has strayed on to it, he bethinks himself that it must get dried up in the sun, if it does not return soon enough to ground into which it can burrow, so he lifts it from the deadly stone surface, and puts it on the grass. If he comes across an insect which has fallen into a puddle, he stops a moment in order to hold out a leaf or a stalk on which it can save itself.

He is not afraid of being laughed at as sentimental. It is the fate of every truth to be a subject for laughter until it is generally recognized. Once it was considered folly to assume that men of colour were really men and ought to be treated as such, but the folly has become an accepted truth. To-day it is thought to be going too far to declare that constant regard for everything that lives, down to the lowest manifestations of life, is a demand made by rational ethics. The time is coming, however, when people will be astonished that mankind needed so long a time to learn to regard thoughtless injury to life as incompatible with ethics.

Ethics are responsibility without limit towards all that lives.

As a general proposition the definition of ethics as a relationship within a disposition to reverence for life, does not make a very moving impression. But it is the only complete one. Compassion is too narrow to rank as the total essence of the ethical. It denotes, of course, only interest in the suffering will-to-live. But ethics include also feeling as one's own all the circumstances and all the aspirations of the will-to-live, its pleasure, too, and its longing to live itself out to the full, as well as its urge to self-perfecting.

Love means more, since it includes fellowship in suffering, in joy, and in effort, but it shows the ethical only in a simile, although in a simile that is natural and profound. It makes the solidarity produced by ethics analogous to that which nature calls forth on the physical side, for more or less temporary purposes between two beings which complete each other sexually, or between them and their offspring.

Thought must strive to bring to expression the nature of the ethical in itself. To effect this it arrives at defining ethics as devotion to life inspired by reverence for life. Even if the phrase reverence for life sounds so general as to seem somewhat lifeless, what is meant by it is nevertheless something which never lets go of the man into whose thought it has made its way. Sympathy, and love, and every kind of valuable enthusiasm are given within it. With restless living force reverence for life works upon the mind into which it has entered, and throws it into the unrest of a feeling of responsibility which at no place and at no time ceases to affect it. Just as the screw which churns its way through the water drives the ship along, so does reverence for life drive the man.

Arising, as it does, from an inner compulsion, the ethic of reverence for life is not dependent on the extent to which it can be thought out to a satisfying conception of life. It need give no answer to the question of what significance the ethical man's work for the maintenance, promotion, and enhancement of life can be in the total happenings of the course of nature. It does not let itself be misled by the calculation that the maintaining and completing of life which it practises is hardly worth consideration beside the tremendous, unceasing destruction of life which goes on every moment through natural forces. Having the will to action, it can leave on one side all problems regarding the success of its work. The fact in itself that in the ethically developed man there has made its appearance in the world a will-to-live which is filled with reverence for life and devotion to life is full of importance for the world.

In my will-to-live the universal will-to-live experiences itself otherwise than in its other manifestations. In them it shows itself in a process of individualizing which, so far as I can see from the outside, is bent merely on living itself out to the full, and in no way on union with any other will-to-live. The world is a ghastly drama of will-to-live divided against itself. One existence makes its way at the cost of another; one destroys the other. One will-to-live merely exerts its will against the other, and has no knowledge of it. But in me the will-to-live has come to know about other wills-to-live. There is in it a yearning to arrive at unity with itself, to become universal.

Why does the will-to-live experience itself in this way in me alone? Is it because I have acquired the capacity of reflecting on the totality of Being? What is the goal of this evolution which has begun in me?

To these questions there is no answer. It remains a painful enigma for me that I must live with reverence for life in a world which is dominated by creative will which is also destructive will, and destructive will which is also creative.

I can do nothing but hold to the fact that the will-to-live in me manifests itself as will-to-live which desires to become one with other will-to-live. That is for me the light that shines in the darkness. The ignorance in which the world is wrapped has no existence for me; I have been saved from the world. I am thrown, indeed, by reverence for life into an unrest such as the world does not know, but I obtain from it a blessedness which the world cannot give. If in the tenderheartedness produced by being different from the world another person and I help each other in understanding and pardoning, when otherwise will would torment will, the division of the will-to-live is at an end. If I save an insect from a puddle, life has devoted itself to life, and the division of life against itself is ended. Whenever my life devotes itself in any way to life, my finite will-to-live experiences union with the infinite will in which all life is one, and I enjoy a feeling of refreshment which prevents me from pining away in the desert of life.

I therefore recognize it as the destiny of my existence to be obedient to this higher revelation of the will-to-live in me. I choose for my activity the removal of this division of the will-to-live against itself, so far as the influence of my existence can reach. Knowing now the one thing needful, I leave on one side the enigma of the universe and of my existence in it.

The surmisings and the longings of all deep religiousness are contained in the ethics of reverence for life. This religiousness, however, does not build up for itself a complete philosophy, but resigns itself to the necessity of leaving its cathedral unfinished. It finishes the chancel only, but in this chancel piety celebrates a living and never-ceasing divine service.

* * *

The ethic of reverence for life shows its truth also in that it includes in itself the different elements of ethics in their natural connection. Hitherto no system of ethics has been able to present in their parallelism and their interaction the effort after self-perfecting, in which man acts upon himself without outward deeds, and activist ethics. The ethics of reverence for life can do this, and indeed in such a way that they not only answer academic questions, but also produce a deepening of ethical insight.

Ethics are reverence for the will-to-live within me and without me. From the former comes first the profound life-affirmation of resignation. I apprehend my will-to-live as not only something which can live itself out in happy occurrences, but also something which has experience of itself. If I refuse to let this self-experience disappear in thoughtlessness, and persist in feeling it to be valuable, I begin to learn the secret of spiritual self-realization. I win an unsuspected freedom from the various destinies of life. At moments when I had expected to find myself shattered, I find myself exalted in an inexpressible and surprising happiness of freedom from the world, and I experience therein a clarification of my life-view. Resignation is the vestibule through which we enter ethics. Only he who in deepened devotion to his own will-to-live experiences inward freedom from outward occurrences, is capable of devoting himself in profound and steady fashion to the life of others.

Just as in reverence for my own will-to-live I struggle for freedom from the destinies of life, so I struggle too for freedom from myself. Not only in face of what happens to me, but also with regard to the way in which I concern myself with the world, I practise the higher self-maintenance. Out of reverence for my own existence I place myself under the compulsion of veracity towards myself. Everything I might acquire would be purchased too dearly by action in defiance of my convictions. I fear that if I were untrue to myself, I should be wounding my will-to-live with a poisoned spear.

The fact that Kant makes, as he does, sincerity towards oneself the central point of his ethics, testifies to the depth of his ethical feeling. But because in his search for the essential nature of the ethical he fails to find his way through to reverence for life, he cannot comprehend the connection between veracity towards oneself and activist ethics.

As a matter of fact, the ethics of sincerity towards oneself passes imperceptibly into that of devotion to others. Such sincerity compels me to actions which manifest themselves as self-devotion in such a way that ordinary ethics derive them from devotion.

Why do I forgive anyone? Ordinary ethics say, because I feel sympathy with him. They allow men, when they pardon others, to seem to themselves wonderfully good, and allow them to practise a style of pardoning which is not free from humiliation of the other. They thus make forgiveness a sweetened triumph of self-devotion.

The ethics of reverence for life do away with this crude point of view. All acts of forbearance and of pardon are for them acts forced from one by sincerity towards oneself. I must practise unlimited forgiveness because, if I did not, I should be wanting in sincerity to myself, for it would be acting as if I myself were not guilty in the same way as the other has been guilty towards me. Because my life is so liberally spotted with falsehood, I must forgive falsehood which has been practised upon me; because I myself have been in so many cases wanting in love, and guilty of hatred, slander, deceit, or arrogance, I must pardon any want of love, and all hatred, slander, deceit or arrogance which have been directed against myself. I must forgive quietly and unostentatiously; in fact I do not really pardon at all, for I do not let things develop to any such act of judgment. Nor is this any eccentric proceeding; it is only a necessary widening and refining of ordinary ethics.

We have to carry on the struggle against the evil that is in mankind, not by judging others, but by judging ourselves. Struggle with oneself and veracity towards oneself are the means by which we influence others. We quietly draw them into our efforts to attain the deep spiritual self-realization which springs from reverence for one's own life. Power makes no noise. It is there, and works. True ethics begin where the use of language ceases.

The innermost element then, in activist ethics, even if it appears as self-devotion, comes from the compulsion to sincerity towards oneself, and obtains therein its true value. The whole ethics of being other than the world flow pure only when they come from this source. It is not from kindness to others that I am gentle, peaceable, forbearing, and friendly, but because by such behaviour I prove my own profoundest self-realization to be true. Reverence for life which I apply to my own existence, and reverence for life which keeps me in a temper of devotion to other existence than my own, interpenetrate each other.

*   *   *

Because ordinary ethics possess no basic principle of the ethical, they must engage at once in the discussion of conflicting duties. The ethics of reverence for life have no such need for hurry. They take their own time to think out in all directions their own principle of the moral. Knowing themselves to be firmly established, they then settle their position with regard to these conflicts.

They have to try conclusions with three adversaries: these are thoughtlessness, egoistic self-assertion, and society.

To the first of these they usually pay insufficient attention, because no open conflicts arise between them. This adversary does, nevertheless, obstruct them imperceptibly.

There is, however, a wide field of which our ethics can take possession without any collision with the troops of egoism. Man can accomplish much that is good, without having to require of himself any sacrifice. And if there really goes with it a bit of his life, it is so insignificant that he feels it no more than if he were losing a hair or a flake of dead skin.

Over wide stretches of conduct the inward liberation from the world, the being true to oneself, the being different from the world, yes, and even self-devotion to other life, is only a matter of giving attention to this particular relationship. We fall short so much, because we do not keep ourselves up to it. We do not stand sufficiently under the pressure of any inward compulsion to be ethical. At all points the steam hisses out of the boiler that is not tightly closed. In ordinary ethics the resulting losses of energy are as high as they are because such ethics have at their disposal no single basic principle of the moral which acts upon thought. They cannot tighten the lid of the boiler, indeed, they do not ever even examine it. But reverence for life being something which is ever present to thought, penetrates unceasingly and in all directions a man's observation, reflection, and resolutions. He can keep himself clear of it as little as the water can prevent itself from being coloured by the dye-stuff which is dropped into it. The struggle with thoughtlessness is started, and is always going on.

But what is the position of the ethics of reverence for life in the conflicts which arise between inward compulsion to self-sacrifice, and the necessary upholding of the ego?

I too am subject to division of my will-to-live against itself. In a thousand ways my existence stands in conflict with that of others. The necessity to destroy and to injure life is imposed upon me. If I walk along an unfrequented path, my foot brings destruction and pain upon the tiny creatures which populate it. In order to preserve my own existence, I must defend myself against the existence which injures it. I become a persecutor of the little mouse which inhabits my house, a murderer of the insect which wants to have its nest there, a mass-murderer of the bacteria which may endanger my life. I get my food by destroying plants and animals. My happiness is built upon injury done to my fellow-men.

How can ethics be maintained in face of the horrible necessity to which I am subjected through the division of my will-to-live against itself?

Ordinary ethics seek compromises. They try to dictate how much of my existence and of my happiness I must sacrifice, and how much I may preserve at the cost of the existence and happiness of other lives. With these decisions they produce experimental, relative ethics. They offer as ethical what is in reality not ethical but a mixture of non-ethical necessity and ethics. They thereby bring about a huge confusion, and allow the starting of an ever-increasing obscuration of the conception of the ethical.

The ethics of reverence for life know nothing of a relative ethic. They make only the maintenance and promotion of life rank as good. All destruction of and injury to life, under whatever circumstances they take place, they condemn as evil. They do not keep in store adjustments between ethics and necessity all ready for use. Again and again and in ways that are always original they are trying to come to terms in man with reality. They do not abolish for him all ethical conflicts, but compel him to decide for himself in each case how far he can remain ethical and how far he must submit himself to the necessity for destruction of and injury to life, and therewith incur guilt. It is not by receiving instruction about agreement between ethical and necessary, that a man makes progress in ethics, but only by coming to hear more and more plainly the voice of the ethical, by becoming ruled more and more by the longing to preserve and promote life, and by becoming more and more obstinate in resistance to the necessity for destroying or injuring life.

In ethical conflicts man can arrive only at subjective decisions. No one can decide for him at what point, on each occasion, lies the extreme limit of possibility for his persistence in the preservation and furtherance of life. He alone has to judge this issue, by letting himself be guided by a feeling of the highest possible responsibility towards other life.

We must never let ourselves become blunted. We are living in truth, when we experience these conflicts more profoundly. The good conscience is an invention of the devil.

*   *   *

What does reverence for life say about the relations between man and the animal world?

Whenever I injure life of any sort, I must be quite clear whether it is necessary. Beyond the unavoidable, I must never go, not even with what seems insignificant. The farmer, who has mown down a thousand flowers in his meadow as fodder for his cows, must be careful on his way home not to strike off in wanton pastime the head of a single flower by the road side, for he thereby commits a wrong against life without being under the pressure of necessity.

Those who experiment with operations or the use of drugs upon animals, or inoculate them with diseases, so as to be able to bring help to mankind with the results gained, must never quiet any misgivings they feel with the general reflection that their cruel proceedings aim at a valuable result. They must first have considered in each individual case whether there is a real necessity to force upon any animal this sacrifice for the sake of mankind. And they must take the most anxious care to mitigate as much as possible the pain inflicted. How much wrong is committed in scientific institutions through neglect of anæsthetics, which to save time or trouble are not administered! How much, too, through animals being subjected to torture merely to demonstrate to students generally known phenomena! By the very fact that animals have been subjected to experiments, and have by their pain won such valuable results for suffering humanity, a new and special relation of solidarity has been established between them and us. From that springs for each one of us a compulsion to do to every animal all the good we possibly can. By helping an insect when it is in difficulties, I am only attempting to cancel part of man's ever new debt to the animal world. Whenever an animal is in any way forced into the service of man, every one of us must be concerned with the sufferings which for that reason it has to undergo. None of us must allow to take place any suffering for which he himself is not responsible, if he can hinder it in any way. He must not soothe his conscience with the reflection that he would be mixing himself up in something which does not concern him. No one must shut his eyes and regard as non-existent the sufferings of which he spares himself the sight. Let no one regard as light the burden of his responsibility. While so much ill-treatment of animals goes on, while the moans of thirsty animals in railway trucks sound unheard, while so much brutality prevails in our slaughter-houses, while animals have to suffer in our kitchens painful death from unskilled hands, while animals have to endure intolerable treatment from heartless men, or are left to the cruel play of children, we all share the guilt.

We are afraid of making ourselves conspicuous if we let it be noticed how we feel for the sufferings which man brings upon the animals. At the same time we think that others have become more "rational" than we are, and regard what we are excited about as usual and a matter of course. Yet suddenly they will let slip a word which shows us that they too have not yet learnt to acquiesce. And now, though they were strangers, they are quite near us. The mask in which we deceived each other falls off. We know now, from one another, that we feel alike about being unable to escape from the gruesome proceedings that are taking place unceasingly around us. What a making of a new acquaintance!

The ethics of reverence for life guard us from letting each other believe through our silence that we no longer experience what, as thinking men, we must experience. They prompt us to keep each other sensitive to what distresses us, and to talk and act together, just as the responsibility we feel moves us, and without any feeling of shyness. They make us join in keeping on the look-out for opportunities of bringing some sort of help to animals, to make up for the great misery which men inflict on them, and thus to step for a moment out of the incomprehensible horror of existence.

In the matter also of our relation to other men, the ethics of reverence for life throw upon us a responsibility so unlimited as to be terrifying.

Here again they offer us no rules about the extent of the self-maintenance which is allowable; again, they bid us in each case to thrash the question out with the absolute ethics of self-devotion. I have to decide in accordance with the responsibility of which I am conscious, how much of my life, my possessions, my rights, my happiness, my time, and my rest I must devote to others, and how much I may keep for myself.

In the question of possessions, the ethics of reverence for life are outspokenly individualist in the sense that wealth acquired or inherited should be placed at the service of the community, not through any measures taken by society, but through the absolutely free decision of the individual. They expect everything from a general increase in the feeling of responsibility. Wealth they regard as the property of society left in the sovereign control of the individual. One man serves society by carrying on a business in which a number of employees earn their living; another by giving away his wealth in order to help his fellows. Between these two extreme kinds of service, let each decide according to the responsibility which he finds determined for him by the circumstances of his life. Let no man judge his neighbour. The one thing that matters is that each shall value what he possesses as means to action. Whether this is accomplished by his keeping and increasing his wealth, or by surrender of it, matters little. Wealth must reach the community in the most varied ways, if it is to be of the greatest benefit to all.

Those who possess little to call their own are most in danger of holding what they have in a purely selfish spirit. There is profound truth in the parable of Jesus which makes the servant who had received least the least loyal to his duty.

My rights too the ethics of reverence for life do not allow to belong to me. They forbid me to still my conscience with the reflection that, as the more efficient man, by quite legitimate means I am advancing myself at the cost of one who is less efficient than I. In what the law and public opinion allow me, they set a problem before me. They bid me think of others, and make me ponder whether I can allow myself the inward right to pluck all the fruit that my hand can reach. Thus it may happen that, in obedience to consideration for the existence of others, I do what seems to ordinary opinion to be folly. Yes, it may even show itself to be folly by the fact that my renunciation has not been any use to him for whom it was made. And yet I was right. Reverence for life is the highest court of appeal. What it commands has its own significance, even if it seems foolish or useless. We all look, of course, in one another, for the folly which indicates that we have higher responsibilities making themselves felt in our hearts. Yet it is only in proportion as we all become less rational, in the meaning given it by ordinary calculation, that the ethical disposition develops in us, and allows problems to become soluble which have hitherto been insoluble.

Nor will reverence for life grant me my happiness as my own. At the moments when I should like to enjoy myself without restraint, it wakes in me reflection about misery that I see or suspect, and it does not allow me to drive away the uneasiness I feel. Just as the wave cannot exist for itself, but is ever a part of the heaving surface of the ocean, so must I never live my life for itself, but always in the experience which is going on around me. It is an uncomfortable doctrine which the true ethics whisper into my ear. You are happy, they say; therefore you are called upon to give much. Whatever more than others you have received in health, natural gifts, working capacity, success, a beautiful childhood, harmonious family circumstances, you must not accept as being a matter of course. You must pay a price for them. You must show more than average devotion of life to life.

To the happy the voice of the true ethics is dangerous, if they venture to listen to it. When it calls to them, it never damps down the irrational which glows within it. It assails them to see whether it can get them off their smooth track and turn them into adventurers of self-devotion, people of whom the world has too few. . . .

Reverence for life is an inexorable creditor! If it finds anyone with nothing to pledge but a little time and a little leisure, it lays an attachment on these. But its hard-heartedness is good, and sees clearly. The many modern men who as industrial machines are engaged in callings in which they can in no way be active as men among men, are exposed to the danger of merely vegetating in an egoistic life. Many of them feel this danger, and suffer under the fact that their daily work has so little to do with spiritual and ideal aims and does not allow them to put into it anything of their human nature. Others acquiesce; the thought of having no duties outside their daily work suits them very well.

But that men should be so condemned or so favoured as to be released from responsibility for self-devotion as men to men, the ethics of reverence for life will not allow to be legitimate. They demand that every one of us in some way and with some object shall be a human being for human beings. To those who have no opportunity in their daily work of giving themselves in this way, and have nothing else that they can give, it suggests their sacrificing something of their time and leisure, even if of these they have but a scanty allowance. It says to them, find for yourselves some secondary activity, inconspicuous, perhaps secret. Open your eyes and look for a human being, or some work devoted to human welfare, which needs from someone a little time or friendliness, a little sympathy, or sociability, or labour. There may be a solitary or an embittered fellow-man, an invalid or an inefficient person to whom you can be something. Perhaps it is an old person or a child. Or some good work needs volunteers who can offer a free evening, or run errands. Who can enumerate the many ways in which that costly piece of working capital, a human being, can be employed? More of him is wanted everywhere! Search, then, for some investment for your humanity, and do not be frightened away if you have to wait, or to be taken on trial. And be prepared for disappointments. But in any case, do not be without some secondary work in which you give yourself as a man to men. It is marked out for you, if you only truly will to have it. . . .

Thus do the true ethics speak to those who have only a little time and a little human nature to give. Well will it be with them if they listen, and are preserved from becoming stunted natures because they have neglected this devotion of self to others.

But to everyone, in whatever state of life he finds himself, the ethics of reverence for life do this: they force him without cessation to be concerned at heart with all the human destinies and all the other life-destinies which are going through their life-course around him, and to give himself, as man, to the man who needs a fellow-man. They will not allow the scholar to live only for his learning, even if his learning makes him very useful, nor the artist to live only for his art, even if by means of it he gives something to many. They do not allow the very busy man to think that with his professional activities he has fulfilled every demand upon him. They demand from all that they devote a portion of their life to their fellows. In what way and to what extent this is prescribed for him, the individual must gather from the thoughts which arise in him, and from the destinies among which his life moves. One man's sacrifice is outwardly insignificant. He can accomplish it while continuing to live a normal life. Another is called to some conspicuous act of self-sacrifice, and must therefore put aside regard for his own progress. But let neither judge the other. The destinies of men have to be decided in a thousand ways in order that the good may become actual. What he has to bring as an offering is the secret of each individual. But one with another we have all to recognize that our existence reaches its true value only when we experience in ourselves something of the truth of the saying: "He that loseth his life shall find it."

* * *

The ethical conflicts between society and the individual arise out of the fact that the latter has to bear not only a personal, but also a supra-personal responsibility. When my own person only is concerned, I can always be patient, always forgive, always exercise forbearance, always be merciful. But each of us comes into a situation where he is responsible not for himself only, but also for a cause, and then is forced into decisions which conflict with personal morality.

The craftsman who manages a business, however small, and the musician who conducts public performances, cannot be men in the way they would like to be. The one has to dismiss a worker who is incapable or given to drink, in spite of any sympathy he has for him and his family; the other cannot let a singer whose voice is the worse for wear appear any longer, although he knows what distress he thus causes.

The more extensive a man's activities, the oftener he finds himself in the position of having to sacrifice something of his humanity to his supra-personal responsibility. From this conflict customary consideration leads to the decision that the general responsibility does, as a matter of principle, annul the personal. It is in this sense that society addresses the individual. For the soothing of consciences for which this decision is too categorical, it perhaps lays down a few principles which undertake to determine in a way that is valid for everybody, how far in any case personal morality can have a say in the matter.

No course remains open to current ethics but to sign this capitulation. They have no means of defending the fortress of personal morality, because it has not at its disposal any absolute notions of good and evil. Not so the ethics of reverence for life. These possess, as we can see, what the other lacks. They therefore never surrender the fortress, even if it is permanently invested. They feel themselves in a position to persevere in holding it, and by continual sorties to keep the besiegers on the *qui vive*.

Only the most universal and absolute purposiveness in the maintenance and furtherance of life, which is the objective aimed at by reverence for life, is ethical. All other necessity or expediency is not ethical, but only a more or less necessary necessity, or a more or less expedient expediency. In the conflict between the maintenance of my own existence and the destruction of, or injury to, that of another, I can never unite the ethical and the necessary to form a relative ethical; I must choose between ethical and necessary, and, if I choose the latter, must take it upon myself to incur guilt by an act of injury to life. Similarly I am not at liberty to think, that in the conflict between personal and supra-personal responsibility I can balance the ethical and the expedient to make a relative ethical, or even annul the ethical with the purposive; I must choose between the two. If, under the pressure of the supra-personal responsibility, I yield to the expedient, I become guilty in some way or other through failure in reverence for life.

The temptation to combine with the ethical into a relative

ethical the expedient which is commanded me by the supra-personal responsibility is especially strong, because it can be shown, in defence of it, that the person who complies with the demand of this supra-personal responsibility, acts unegoistically. It is not to his individual existence or his individual welfare that he sacrifices another existence or welfare, but he sacrifices an individual existence and welfare to what forces itself upon him as expedient in view of the existence or the welfare of a majority. But ethical is more than unegoistic. Only the reverence felt by my will-to-live for every other will-to-live is ethical. Whenever I in any way sacrifice or injure life, I am not within the sphere of the ethical, but I become guilty, whether it be egoistically guilty for the sake of maintaining my own existence or welfare, or unegoistically guilty for the sake of maintaining a greater number of other existences or their welfare.

This so easily made mistake of accepting as ethical a violation of reverence for life, if it is based upon unegoistic considerations, is the bridge by crossing which ethics enter unawares the territory of the non-ethical. The bridge must be broken down.

Ethics go only so far as does humanity, humanity meaning consideration for the existence and the happiness of individual human beings. Where humanity ends, pseudo-ethics begin. The day on which this boundary is once for all universally recognized, and marked out so as to be visible to everyone, will be one of the most important in the history of mankind. Thenceforward it can no longer happen that ethics which are not ethics at all are accepted as real ethics, and deceive and ruin individuals and peoples.

The system of ethics hitherto current has hindered us from becoming as earnest as we ought to be by the fact that it has `utterly deceived us as to the many ways in which each one of us, whether through self-assertion, or by actions justified by supra-personal responsibility, becomes guilty again and again. True knowledge consists in being gripped by the secret that everything around us is will-to-live and in seeing clearly how again and again we incur guilt against life.

Fooled by pseudo-ethics, man stumbles about in his guilt like a drunkard. If he gains knowledge and becomes serious, he seeks the road which least leads him into guilt.

We are all exposed to the temptation of lessening the guilt of inhumanity, which comes from our working under supra-personal responsibility, by withdrawing as far as possible into ourselves. But such freedom from guilt is not honestly obtained. Because ethics start with world- and life-affirmation, they do not allow us this flight into negation. They forbid us to be like the housewife who leaves the killing of the eel to her cook, and compel us to undertake all duties involving supra-personal responsibility which fall to us, even if we should be in a position to decline them for reasons more or less satisfactory.

Each one of us, then, has to engage, in so far as he is brought to it by the circumstances of his life, in work which involves supra-personal responsibility. But we must do this not in the spirit of the collective body, but in that of the man who wishes to be ethical. In every individual case, therefore, we struggle to preserve as much humanity as is possible, and in doubtful cases we venture to make a mistake on the side of humanity rather than on that of the object in view. When we have become aware and earnest, we think of what is usually forgotten: that all public activity has to do not only with the facts which are to be made actual in the interests of the collective body, but also with the creation of the state of mind which promotes the welfare of that body. The creation of such a spirit and temper is more important than anything directly attained in the facts. Public activity in which the utmost possible effort is not made to preserve humanity ruins the character. He who under the influence of supra-personal responsibility simply sacrifices men and human happiness when it seems right, accomplishes something. But he has not reached the highest level. He has only outward, not spiritual influence. We have spiritual influence only when others notice that we do not decide coldly in accordance with principles laid down once and for all, but in each individual case fight for our sense of humanity. There is too little among us of this kind of struggle. From the most insignificant man who is engaged in the smallest business, right up to the political ruler who holds in his hands the decision for peace or war, we act too much as men who in any given case can prepare without effort to be no longer men, but merely the executive of general interests. Hence there is no longer among us any trust in a righteousness lighted up with human feeling. Nor have we any longer any real respect for one another. We all feel ourselves in the power of a mentality of cold, impersonal, and usually unintelligent opportunism, which stiffens itself with appeals to principle, and in order to realize the smallest interests is capable of the greatest inhumanity and the greatest folly. We therefore see among us one temper of impersonal opportunism confronting another, and all problems are resolved in a purposeless conflict of force against force because there is nowhere at hand such a spirit as will make them soluble.

It is only through our struggles for humanity that forces which work in the direction of the truly rational and expedient can become powerful while the present way of thinking prevails. Hence the man who works with supra-personal responsibilities has to feel himself answerable not only for the successful result which is to be realized through him, but for the general disposition which has to be created.

Thus we serve society without abandoning ourselves to it. We do not allow it to be our guardian in the matter of ethics. That would be as if the solo violinist allowed his bowing to be regulated by that of the double-bass player. Never for a moment do we lay aside our mistrust of the ideals established by society, and of the convictions which are kept by it in circulation. We always know that society is full of folly and will deceive us in the matter of humanity. It is an unreliable horse, and blind into the bargain. Woe to the driver, if he falls asleep!

All this sounds too hard. Society serves ethics by giving legal sanction to its most elementary principles, and handing on the ethical principles of one generation to the next. That is much, and it claims our gratitude. But society is also something which checks the progress of ethics again and again, by arrogating to itself the dignity of an ethical teacher. To this, however, it has no right. The only ethical teacher is the man who thinks ethically, and struggles for ethics. The conceptions of good and evil which are put in circulation by society are paper-money, the value of which is to be calculated not by the figures printed upon it, but by its relation to its exchange value in the gold of the ethics of reverence for life. But so measured, the rate of exchange is revealed as that of the paper-money of a half-bankrupt state.

The collapse of civilization has come about through ethics being left to society. A renewal of it is possible only if ethics become once more the concern of thinking human beings, and if individuals seek to assert themselves in society as ethical personalities. In proportion as we secure this, society will become an ethical, instead of the purely natural, entity, which it is by origin. Previous generations have made the terrible mistake of idealizing society as ethical. We do our duty to it by judging it critically, and trying to make it, so far as is possible, more ethical. Being in possession of an absolute standard of the ethical, we no longer allow ourselves to make acceptable as ethics principles of expediency or of the vulgarest opportunism. Nor do we remain any longer at the low level of allowing to be current, as in any way ethical, meaningless ideals of power, of passion or of nationalism, which are set up by miserable politicians and maintained in some degree of respect by bewildering propaganda. All the principles, dispositions, and ideals which make their appearance among us we measure, in their showy pedantry, with a rule on which the measures are given by the absolute ethics of reverence for life. We allow currency only to what is consistent with the claims of humanity. We bring into honour again regard for life and for the happiness of the individual. Sacred human rights we again hold high; not those which political rulers exalt at banquets and tread underfoot in their actions, but the true rights. We call once more for justice, not that which imbecile authorities have elaborated in a legal scholasticism, nor that about which demagogues of all shades of colour shout themselves hoarse, but that which is filled to the full with the value of each single human existence. The foundation of law and right is humanity.

Thus we confront the principles, dispositions, and ideals of the collective body with humanity. At the same time we shape them in accordance with reason, for only what is ethical is truly rational. Only so far as the current disposition of men is animated by ethical convictions and ideals is it capable of truly purposive activity.

The ethics of reverence for life put in our hands weapons for fighting false ethics and false ideals, but we have strength to use them only so far as we—each one in his own life—preserve our humanity. Only when those men are numerous who in thought and in action bring humanity to terms with reality, will humanity cease to be current as a mere sentimental idea and become what it ought to be, a leaven in the minds of individuals and in the spirit of society.

Chapter 27

THE CIVILIZING POWER OF THE ETHICS OF

REVERENCE FOR LIFE

Civilization as a product of reverence for life.

The four ideals of civilization. The struggle for a civilized mankind in the machine age.

Church and State as historical entities, and as ideals of civilization.

The moralizing of the religious and political community.

THE REVERENCE FOR LIFE WHICH HAS GROWN UP IN THE WILL-TO-live which has become reflective, contains world- and life-affirmation and ethics side by side and interpenetrating each other. It therefore cannot but continually think out and will all the ideals of ethical civilization, and strive to bring them into agreement with reality.

Reverence for life will not allow the validity of the purely individualistic and inward conception of civilization as it rules in Indian thought and in mysticism. That man should make efforts for self-perfecting by withdrawing into himself is to it a deep, but an incomplete, ideal of civilization.

In no way does reverence for life allow the individual to give up interest in the world. It is unceasingly compelling him to be concerned about all the life that is round about him, and to feel himself responsible for it. Whenever life whose development we can influence is in question, our concern with it, and our responsibility for it, are not satisfied by our maintaining and furthering its existence as such; they demand that we shall try to raise it to its highest value in every respect.

The being that can be influenced in its development by us is man. So reverence for life compels us to imagine and to will every kind of progress of which man and humanity are capable. It throws us into a restless condition of ever imagining and willing civilization, but as ethical men.

Even a not yet deepened world- and life-affirmation produces this imagining and willing of civilization, but it leaves a man to exert himself more or less without guidance. In reverence for life, however, and the will, which accompanies it, to raise men and humanity to their highest value in every respect, he possesses the guidance which leads him to complete and purified ideals of civilization which with full consciousness of their goal struggle to come to terms with reality.

Defined from outside and quite empirically, complete civilization consists in realizing all possible progress in discovery and invention and in the arrangements of human society, and seeing that they work together for the spiritual perfecting of individuals which is the real and final object of civilization. Reverence for life is in a position to complete this conception of civilization and to build its foundations on what lies at the core of our being. This it does by defining what is meant by the spiritual perfecting of man, and making it consist in reaching the spirituality of an ever deepening reverence for life.

In order to give a meaning to the material and spiritual progress which is to be made actual by the individual man and mankind, the ordinary representation of civilization has to assume an evolution of the world, in which such progress has a meaning. But to do so, it puts itself in dependence on a play of phantasy which reaches no result. It is impossible to depict an evolution of the world in which the civilization produced by the individual man and mankind has any meaning.

In reverence for life, on the contrary, civilization recognizes that it has nothing at all to do with the evolution of the world, but carries its meaning in itself. The essence of civilization consists in this, that the reverence for life which in my will-to-live is struggling for recognition does get stronger and stronger in individuals and in mankind. Civilization, then, is not a phenomenon of any world-evolution, but an experience of the will-to-live within us, which it is neither possible nor necessary to bring into relation with the course of nature as we know it from outside. As a perfecting of our will-to-live it is sufficient for itself. What the development that takes place in us means in the totality of the development in the world we leave on one side as inscrutable. That, as a result of all the progress which men and mankind can make, there shall exist in the world as much as possible of will-to-live, putting reverence for life into practice on all life which comes within the sphere of its influence, and seeking perfection in the spiritual atmosphere of reverence for life: this and nothing else is civilization. So completely does it carry its value in itself, that even the certainty of the human race ceasing to exist within a calculable period would not be able to disconcert us in our efforts to attain to civilization.

As a development in which the highest experience of the will-to-live lives itself out, civilization has a meaning for the world without needing any explanation of the world.

*   *   *

The will-to-live which is filled with reverence for life is interested in the most lively and persevering way that can be imagined in all kinds of progress. Moreover, it possesses a standard by which to assess their value correctly, and can create a state of mind which allows them all to work in with one another in the most effective way.

Three kinds of progress come within the purview of civilization: progress in knowledge and power; progress in the social organization of mankind; progress in spirituality.

Civilization is made up of four ideals: the ideal of the individual; the ideal of social and political organization; the ideal of spiritual and religious social organization; the ideal of humanity as a whole. On the basis of these four ideals thought tries conclusions with progress.

Progress in knowledge has a directly spiritual significance when it is moulded by thought. It makes us recognize, ever more completely, that everything which exists is power, that is to say, will-to-live; it is ever making larger the circle of the will-to-live of which we can form conceptions by analogy with our own.

What importance it has for our meditation on the world that we have discovered in the cell an individual existence, in whose faculties, active and passive, we see repeated the elements of our own vitality! By our ever-widening knowledge, we are roused to ever greater astonishment at the mystery of life which surrounds us on every hand. From naïve simplicity we arrive at a more profound simplicity.

From our knowledge comes also power over the forces of nature. Our powers of movement and of action are increased in an extraordinary way. There comes about a far-reaching change in the circumstances of our life.

The progress which accompanies it, however, is not to the same extent an advantage for the development of man. By the power we obtain over the forces of nature we do indeed free ourselves from nature, and make her serviceable to us, but at the same time we thereby also cut ourselves loose from her, and slip into conditions of life whose unnatural character brings with it manifold dangers.

We press the forces of nature into our service by means of machines. There is a story in the writings of Chwang-tse of how a pupil of Confucius saw a gardener who, to get water for his flower-beds, repeatedly went down to the spring with his bucket. So he asked him whether he would not like to lessen his labour. "How can I?" replied the other. "You take a long piece of wood for a lever," said Confucius' pupil, "weighted behind, but light in front; with this you dip for the water and it comes up without the least trouble. They call this device a draw-well." But the gardener, who was something of a philosopher, answered: "I have heard my teacher say: 'If a man uses machines, he carries on all the affairs of life like a machine; whoever carries on his affairs like a machine gets a machine-like heart; and when anyone has a machine-like heart in his breast, he loses true simplicity.' "

The dangers that were suspected by that gardener in the fifth century B.C. are active among us in full force. Purely mechanical labour has become the lot of numbers among us to-day. Without houses of their own or any ground of their own which might feed them, they live in a depressing, materialist state of serfdom. As a result of the revolution which machines have brought about, we are almost all subjected to an existence of labour which is far too much governed by rule, too limited in its nature, and too strenuous. Reflection and concentration are made difficult for us. Family life and the upbringing of our children suffer. We are all more or less in danger of becoming human things instead of personalities. Many kinds of material and spiritual injury to human existence form therefore the dark side of the achievements of discovery and invention.

Even our capacity for civilization can be questioned. Claimed entirely by so severe a struggle for existence, many among us are no longer in a position to think about ideals which make for civilization. They cannot reach the objective mood which is necessary for it. All their attention is directed to the improvement of their own existence. The ideals which they set up for this object they proclaim to be ideals of civilization, thus causing confusion in the general conception of what civilization is.

In order to be a match for the state of things produced by the results of these achievements of discovery and invention which are at the same time beneficial and injurious, we must think out an ideal of humanity and wrestle with circumstances to make them hinder as little, and help as much, as possible the development of man up to this ideal.

The ideal of civilized man is none other than that of a man who in every relation of life preserves true human nature. To be civilized men means for us approximately this: that in spite of the conditions of modern civilization we remain human. It is only taking thought for everything which belongs to true human nature that can preserve us, amid the conditions of the most advanced external civilization, from going astray from civilization itself. It is only if the longing to become again truly man is kindled in the man of to-day, that he will be able to find his way out of the confusion in which, blinded by conceit at his knowledge and pride in his powers, he is at present wandering. Only then, too, will he be in a position to strive against the pressure of those relations of life which threaten his human nature.

Reverence for life demands, therefore, as the ideal of the material and spiritual being of man, that with the completest possible development of all his faculties and in the widest possible freedom, both material and spiritual, he should struggle to be honest with himself and to take a sympathetic and helpful interest in all the life that is around him. In earnest concern about himself, he must ever keep in mind all the responsibilities which are his lot, and so, whether active or passive, preserve in his relation to himself and to the world a living spirituality. There should ever be before him as true human nature the duty of being ethical in the profound world- and life-affirmation of reverence for life.

If it is recognized as the aim of civilization that every man shall attain to true human nature in an existence which is as fully as possible worthy of him, then the uncritical overvaluing of the external elements of civilization which we have taken over from the end of the nineteenth century can no longer prevail among us. We are forced more and more into reflection which compels us to distinguish between the essentials and the unessentials of civilization. Senseless pride in civilization loses its power over us. We dare to face the truth that with the progress of knowledge and power civilization has become not easier, but more difficult. We become conscious of the problem of the mutual relations between the material and the spiritual. We know that we all have to wrestle with circumstances on behalf of our human nature, and make it our concern to transform the almost hopeless struggle which many have to carry on to preserve their human nature, into a contest which offers some hope.

As spiritual aid in this struggle we offer them the way of thinking which will allow no man ever to be sacrificed to circumstances, as if he were a mere human thing. Formulated by so-called thinkers and popularized in all possible forms, the conviction is general that civilization is the privilege of an *élite*, and that man in the mass is only a means for realizing it. At the same time the spiritual help to which they are entitled is denied to these men who have a hard struggle to preserve their human nature. That is the effect of the sense of reality to which we have surrendered ourselves. But reverence for life rebels against it, and creates a way of thinking in which there is offered to every man in the thoughts of others the human value and the human dignity which the circumstances of life would deny him. The struggle has thus lost its extreme bitterness. Man has now to assert himself only against his circumstances, and no longer against his fellowmen as well.

Further, the spirit of reverence for life helps those who have to struggle hardest on behalf of their humanity by keeping alive the conception of human nature as the value which must be preserved at any price. It keeps them from going astray with one-sided aims in their struggle for the diminishing of their material bondage, and bids them bethink themselves that much more of humanity and freedom of soul can be combined with their actual life-circumstances than they actually secure. It leads them to preserve equanimity and spirituality when they have hitherto given them up.

There must come about a spiritualizing of the masses. The mass of individuals must begin to reflect about their lives, about what they want to secure for their lives in the struggle for existence, about what makes their circumstances difficult, and about what they deny themselves. They are wanting in spirituality because they have only a confused conception of what spirituality is. They forget to think, because elementary thought about themselves has become unfamiliar. In what is in our day cultivated as spirituality and practised as thought, there is absolutely nothing that comes directly home to them as necessary for themselves. But if it comes about that the thoughts suggested by reverence for life become common among us, there will be a mode of thought which will affect us all, and spirituality will become general and active. Even those who are engaged in the hardest struggle on behalf of their human nature will then be led to reflection and inwardness, and will thereby obtain powers which they did not before possess.

Though all of us are alike aware that the maintenance of civilization is dependent first and foremost on the gushing forth of the fountains of spiritual life which are in us, we shall nevertheless zealously take in hand our economic and social problems. The highest possible material freedom for the greatest possible number is a requirement of civilization.

The recognition that we evidently have so little power over economic relations does not discourage us. We know this to be to a considerable extent a result of the fact that hitherto facts were contending with facts, and passions with passions. Our impotence comes from our feeling for reality. We shall be able to deal with things much more effectively, if we resolve to try to solve our problems by a change in our way of thinking. And we are at length ready for the recognition of this. The efforts for control which were made on the strength of economic theories and Utopias were in every respect inexpedient, and have brought us to a terrible state of affairs. There remains nothing for us to do but to try a radical change of policy, that is to say, the solution of our problems in an appropriate way by means of helpful understanding and confidence. It is reverence for life alone which can create the disposition needed for this. The understanding and confidence which we mutually accord to each other with a view to what is most purposive, and by means of which we obtain the utmost power that is possible over circumstances, can be enjoyed only if everyone can assume in everyone else reverence for the existence of the other and regard for his material and spiritual welfare as a disposition which influences them to the depths of their being. Only through reverence for life can we attain the standards of economic justice, about which we have to come to an understanding with each other.

Will it be possible to bring about this development? We must, if we are not all to be ruined together, materially and spiritually. All progress in discovery and invention evolves at last to a fatal result, if we do not maintain control over it through a corresponding progress in our spirituality. Through the power which we gain over the forces of nature, in sinister fashion we get control as human beings over other human beings. With the possession of a hundred machines a single man or a company is given a supremacy over all who work the machines. Some new invention may make it possible for one man by a single movement to kill not merely a hundred, but ten thousand of his fellow-men. In no sort of struggle is it possible to avoid becoming ruinous to one another by economic or physical power. At best the result is that the oppressor and the oppressed exchange rôles. The only thing that can help is that we renounce the power which is given us over one another. But that is an act of spirituality.

Intoxicated by the progress in discovery and invention with

which our age has been flooded, we forgot to trouble ourselves about men's progress in immaterial matters. In the absence of all thought we slid unawares into the pessimism of believing in all sorts of progress, but no longer in the spiritual progress of the individual and of mankind.

Facts call us now to bethink ourselves, just as movements of their capsizing vessel drive the crew up on to the deck and into the rigging. Belief in the spiritual progress of the individual and of mankind has already become almost impossible for us, but with the courage of despair we must force ourselves to that belief. That we shall all unanimously again will this spiritual progress and again hope for it: that is the reversal of the helm which we must succeed in making, if our vessel is at the last moment to be brought once more before the wind.

Only through thoughtful reverence for life shall we become capable of this achievement. If that reverence begins anywhere to work in our minds, then the miracle is possible. The power of the elementary and living spirituality that is to be found in it is beyond calculation.

*   *   *

State and Church are only modalities of the organization of men towards humanity. The ideals of social-political and religious organization are therefore determined by the necessity of these entities being made effective aids to the ethical spiritualizing of men, and to their organization towards humanity.

The fact that the ideals of State and Church among us are not in power in their true form is due to our historical sense. The men of the "Aufklärung" assumed that State and Church had come into existence by reason of estimates made of their usefulness. They sought to comprehend the nature of these two entities by means of theories about their origins, but in this proceeding they did nothing but read back their own view into history. Not feeling the least reverence for any natural historical entity, they found it easy to approach them with demands suggested by a rational ideal. We, on the contrary, have such a measure of this reverence that we feel shy of wishing to transform in accordance with theoretical ideas what had a quite different origin.

But State and Church are not merely natural historical entities; they are also necessary entities. The only way in which reflection can deal with them is to be always at work, transforming them from what they are as received, into organisms which are in accordance with reason and effective in every respect. Only in this capacity for development is their existence fully apprehended and justified.

The natural historical entity presents us always only with initial facts which lead on to corresponding further happenings, but never with facts in which the nature of society, that is to say the way in which we are to behave towards it and to belong to it, can be determined. If one allows that in the conception of the natural entity there is also given one of a self-determined purpose, there arises a fundamental confusion in people's notion of the organization of society. The individual and humanity as a whole, which are just as truly natural entities as the two historical ones, are robbed of their rights and sacrificed to the latter. The increased understanding with which we now study the natural policy of societies with historical origin can therefore not alter at all our demand that State and Church shall direct their course more and more with reference to the ideals of man and of humanity as their natural poles, and be obliged to find in them their higher effectiveness.

Civilization demands, then, that State and Church become capable of development. This presupposes that the relations of influence between the collective body and its individual members will become different from what they have been. In the last generations the individual confronted with State and Church has surrendered more and more of his spiritual independence. He received his way of thinking from them, instead of the attitude of mind that was growing within him working as a formative influence upon State and Church.

This abnormal relation was unavoidable. The individual had, of course, nothing in which he could be spiritually independent. He had, therefore, no spirit and temper in which he could come to terms with the entities of real life. Nor was he in a position to think out ideals which could affect reality. There was no course left for him but to adopt as an ideal an idealized reality.

But in the world- and life-view of reverence for life he obtains the means to a firm and valuable self-determination. It is with a will and a hope which he carries ready shaped within himself that he faces reality. It is to him self-evident that every society that is formed among men must serve towards the maintenance, the advancement, and the higher development of life, and the growth of true spirituality.

That which is decisive for the commencement of a development of State and Church which has civilization for its object, is that the mass of men belong to these two entities in the attitude of mind of reverence for life and the ideals which grow from it: when that is the case there arises in States and Churches a spirit which works for their transformation into ethical and spiritual values.

A forecast of the course this process will take cannot be made, nor is one needed. The mental attitude of reverence for life is a force which works effectively in every respect. The important thing is that it shall be present with a strength and constancy which will suffice to bring about the transformation.

*   *   *

If the Church is to accomplish its task, it must unite men in elementary, thoughtful, ethical religiousness. This it has hitherto done very imperfectly. How far it is from being what it ought to be was revealed by its absolute failure in the war. There devolved on it the duty of summoning men out of the struggle of national passions to reflection, and of keeping them in the spirit and temper of the highest ideals. It was not able to do this, and indeed did not seriously make the attempt. Only too completely historical, and too well organized, and too little a directly religious association, it succumbed to the spirit of the time and mixed up with religion the dogmas of nationalism and pragmatism. There was only one tiny church, the community of the Quakers, which attempted to defend the unconditional validity of reverence for life, as it is contained in the religion of Jesus.

The spirit of reverence for life is able to work for the transformation of the Church to the ideal of a religious association, because it is itself deeply religious. In all historically formulated belief it seeks to bring into general acceptance as the elemental and essential constituent of piety the ethical mysticism of oneness with the infinite Will, which experiences itself in us as the will to love. By putting in the very centre of things the most living and universal element of piety, it leads the different re-religious associations out of the narrowness of their historical past, and paves the way for understanding and union between them.

But this attitude of mind does even more than that. Besides bringing the existing historical religious associations out of their historical existence into a development towards the ideal of religious association, it operates also where they can do nothing, namely in the sphere of non-religion. There are many non-religious people among us. They have become so partly through thoughtlessness and absence of any world-view, and partly because as a result of honest thinking they could no longer be content with a traditional religious conception of the universe. The world- and life-view of reverence for life enables these non-religious minds to learn that every philosophy of life which is based on sincere thought necessarily becomes religious. Ethical mysticism reveals to them the necessity to thought of the religion of love, and thus leads them back to paths which they believed they had abandoned forever.

Just as the transformation of the religious association must be the result primarily of a change of heart, so also must be that of the social and political community.

It is true, indeed, that to believe in the possibility of transforming the modern state into the civilized state is a piece of heroism. The modern state finds itself to-day in an unprecedented condition of material and spiritual penury. Collapsing under the weight of debts, torn by economic and political conflicts, stripped of all moral authority, and scarcely able any longer to maintain its authority in practical matters, it has to struggle for its existence in a succession of fresh troubles. In the face of all these things whence is it to get power to develop into a truly civilized state?

What crises and catastrophes the modern state is still destined to go through cannot be foreseen. Its position is further endangered especially by the fact that it has far overstepped the limits of its natural sphere of operation. It is an extraordinarily

complicated organism which intervenes in all social relationships, which tries to regulate everything, and therefore in every
respect functions ineffectively; it tries to dominate economic life
as it dominates spiritual life; and for its activities over this
extensive field it works with machinery which in itself at once
constitutes a danger.

At some time and in some way or other the modern state
must emerge from its financial trouble, and reduce its activity
to a normal standard, but by what methods it can ever again
get back to a natural and healthy condition remains still a riddle.

The tragic thing is, then, that we have to belong to the
unsympathetic and unhealthy modern state while cherishing the
will to transform it into a civilized state. There is demanded
from us an all but impossible achievement of faith in the power
of the spirit. But the ethical outlook on the world and on life
gives us strength for the task.

Living in the modern state and thinking the ideal of the
civilized state, we first of all put an end to the illusions which
the former cherishes about itself. Only by the majority of its
members taking up a critical attitude towards it can it come to
itself again in reflection about itself. The absolute impossibility
of the continuance of the state in its present condition must
become the universal conviction before things can become in
any way better.

But at the same time, through meditation on the civilized
state, the perception must become common property that all
merely external measures for raising and making healthy the
modern state, however expedient they may be in themselves, will
have only a quite imperfect result unless the spirit of the state
becomes quite different. Let us, then, undertake to drive the
modern state, so far as the power of our thought reaches, into the
spirituality and the morality of the civilized state as it is to be,
according to the idea contained in reverence for life. We demand
from it that it shall become more spiritual and more ethical
than any state has hitherto been expected to become. Only with
efforts to reach the true ideal do we get progress.

The objection is raised that, according to all experience, the
state cannot exist by relying merely on truth, justice, and ethical
considerations, but in the last resort has to take refuge in oppor-

tunism. We smile at this experience. It is refuted by the dreary results. We have, therefore, the right to declare the opposite course to be true wisdom, and to say that true power for the state as for the individual is to be found in spirituality and ethical conduct. The state lives by the confidence of those who belong to it; it lives by the confidence felt in it by other states. Opportunist policy may have temporary successes to record, but in the long run it assuredly ends in failure.

Thus ethical world- and life-affirmation demands of the modern state that it shall aspire to making itself an ethical and spiritual personality. It presses this obstinately upon the state, and does not let itself be deterred by the smiles of superior persons. The wisdom of to-morrow has a different tone from that of yesterday.

Only by a new attitude of mind ruling within it can the state attain to peace within its borders; only by a new attitude of mind arising between them can different states come to understand each other, and cease to bring destruction upon each other; only by treating the overseas world in a different spirit from that of the past and of to-day can modern states cease to load themselves in that connection with guilt.

Such moral talk about the civilized state has often been heard in the past. Certainly it has. But it acquires a special tone at a time when the modern state is perishing in misery, because it refused in the past to continue to be in any way spiritually ethical. It possesses a new authority, too, to-day because in the world- and life-view of reverence for life there is revealed the significance of the ethical in its full extent and its full profundity.

We are therefore freed from any duty of forming a conception of the civilized state which accords with the specifications of nationalism and national civilization, and we are at liberty to turn back to the profound *naïveté* of thinking it to be a state which allows itself to be guided by an ethical spirit of civilization. With confidence in the strength of the civilized attitude of mind which springs from reverence for life we undertake the task of making this civilized state an actuality.

Feeling ourselves responsible to the civilized way of thinking we look beyond peoples and states to humanity as a whole. To anyone who has devoted himself to ethical world- and life-affirmation, the future of men and of mankind is a subject of anxiety and of hope. To become free from this anxiety and hope is poverty; to be wholly surrendered to it is riches. Thus it is our consolation that in a time of difficulty and without knowing how much we may still experience of a better future, we are paving the way, solely by our confidence in the power of the spirit, for a civilized mankind which is to come.

Kant published, with the title *Towards Perpetual Peace*, a work containing rules which were to be observed with a view to lasting peace whenever treaties of peace were concluded. It was a mistake. Rules for treaties of peace, however well intentioned and however ably drawn up, can accomplish nothing. Only such thinking as establishes the sway of the mental attitude of reverence for life can bring to mankind perpetual peace.

INDEX TO PART II